The Rainbow Serpent

World Anthropology

General Editor

SOL TAX

Patrons

CLAUDE LEVI-STRAUSS
MARGARET MEAD
LAILA SHUKRY EL HAMAMSY
M. N. SRINIVAS

MOUTON PUBLISHERS · THE HAGUE · PARIS
DISTRIBUTED IN THE USA AND CANADA BY ALDINE, CHICAGO

The Rainbow Serpent

A Chromatic Piece

Editors

IRA R. BUCHLER
KENNETH MADDOCK

MOUTON PUBLISHERS · THE HAGUE · PARIS
DISTRIBUTED IN THE USA AND CANADA BY ALDINE, CHICAGO

Distributed in the United States of America and Canada
by Aldine Publishing Company, Chicago, Illinois
ISBN 90–279–7680–5 (Mouton)
0–202–90090–8 (Aldine)
Jacket photo by Charles P. Mountford
Cover and jacket design by Jurriaan Schrofer
Indexes by Society of Indexers, Great Britain
Printed in Great Britain

General Editor's Preface

This remarkable book owes its origin to Charles P. Mountford, who submitted to the Congress his essay on the rainbow-serpent myths of Australia. It was clearly an important contribution by a senior field-worker. The paper was reproduced by the Congress and sent to registrants all over the world who wished to read it in preparation for its discussion in Chicago. Illness prevented Dr. Mountford himself from making the long journey from South Australia to the Congress; but the paper was discussed by others in his absence.

All agreed that the paper should be published in the series to emerge from the Congress. But there was a problem. The paper was of a length (167 pages of typescript and photographs) between a monograph and an article. We were publishing William Bascom's *African dilemma tales* as a separate book in the series, but it was twice this length. It happened that no other papers submitted to the Congress were of an appropriate subject matter to be paired with Mountford's. Then came a most timely coincidence. On June 1, 1974 came word from Alan Dundes, who was editing a book of short Congress papers, *Varia folklorica*, that he had recently been sent a stimulating, monograph-length exegesis of this very rainbow-serpent myth, prepared by Ira Buchler for a seminar only two months earlier! He suggested that if it and the Mountford piece were published together they would make "a rather neat package which could well become a classic source/reference in the mythology literature." I wrote to Buchler at once, sending him a copy of the Mountford paper and receiving in turn his own. We quickly agreed; I wrote to Mountford who agreed happily (under date of August 19, 1974) adding that "Dr. Buchler's worldwide approach to the Rainbow Serpent Myth, coupled with my local approach to the subject should make a considerable contribution."

The problem of finding a perfect Editor for the volume was solved when Buchler suggested Dr. Kenneth Maddock, Macquarie University in

Australia, who eventually agreed to include his own paper, to write the Introduction, and to help to edit the book.

Unfortunately Charles Mountford did not live to see this book in print. His widow wrote that "Monty . . . had put so much of himself into the preparation of his paper on the 'Rainbow Serpent Myth' and his dreams of attending the Congress at Chicago that the world had become a wonderful dream place" (February 27, 1978). Indeed, "Monty" would have enjoyed a unique Congress which made a lasting impression on those who came.

Like most contemporary sciences, anthropology is a product of the European tradition. Some argue that it is a product of colonialism, with one small and self-interested part of the species dominating the study of the whole. If we are to understand the species, our science needs substantial input from scholars who represent a variety of the world's cultures. It was a deliberate purpose of the IXth International Congress of Anthropological and Ethnological Sciences to provide impetus in this direction. The *World Anthropology* volumes, therefore, offer a first glimpse of a human science in which members from all societies have played an active role. Each of the books is designed to be self-contained; each is an attempt to update its particular sector of scientific knowledge and is written by specialists from all parts of the world. Each volume should be read and reviewed individually as a separate volume on its own given subject. The set as a whole will indicate what changes are in store for anthropology as scholars from the developing countries join in studying the species of which we are all a part.

The IXth Congress was planned from the beginning not only to include as many of the scholars from every part of the world as possible, but also with a view toward the eventual publication of the papers in high-quality volumes. At previous Congresses scholars were invited to bring papers which were then read out loud. They were necessarily limited in length; many were only summarized; there was little time for discussion; and the sparse discussion could only be in one language. The IXth Congress was an experiment aimed at changing this. Papers were written with the intention of exchanging them before the Congress, particularly in extensive pre-Congress sessions; they were not intended to be read aloud at the Congress, that time being devoted to discussions—discussions which were simultaneously and professionally translated into five languages. The method for eliciting the papers was structured to make as representative a sample as was allowable when scholarly creativity—hence self-selection—was critically important. Scholars were asked both to propose papers of their own and to suggest topics for sessions of the Congress which they might edit into volumes. All were then informed of the suggestions and encouraged to re-think their own papers and the topics. The process, therefore, was a continuous one of feedback and exchange and it has continued to be so even after the Congress. The some two thousand papers comprising *World Anthropology* certainly then offer a substantial sample of world anthropology. It has been said that anthropology is at a turning point; if this is so, these volumes will be the historical direction-markers.

As might have been foreseen in the first post-colonial generation, the large majority of the Congress papers (82 percent) are the work of scholars identified with the industrialized world which fathered our traditional discipline and the institution of the Congress itself: Eastern Europe (15 percent); Western Europe (16 percent); North America (47 percent); Japan, South Africa, Australia, and New Zealand (4 percent). Only 18 percent of the papers are from developing areas: Africa (4 percent); Asia-Oceania (9 percent); Latin America (5 percent). Aside from the substantial representation from the U.S.S.R and the nations of Eastern Europe, a significant difference between this corpus of written material and that of other Congresses is the addition of the large proportion of contributions from Africa, Asia, and Latin America. "Only 18 percent" is two to four times as great a proportion as that of other Congresses; moreover, 18 percent of 2,000 papers is 360 papers, 10 times the number of "Third World" papers presented at previous Congresses. In fact, these 360 papers are more than the total of *all* papers published after the last International Congress of Anthropological and Ethnological Sciences which was held in the United States (Philadelphia, 1956).

The significance of the increase is not simply quantitative. The input of scholars from areas which have until recently been no more than subject matter for anthropology represents both feedback and also long-awaited theoretical contributions from the perspectives of very different cultural, social, and historical traditions. Many who attended the IXth Congress were convinced that anthropology would not be the same in the future. The fact that the next Congress (India, 1978) will be our first in the "Third World" may be symbolic of the change. Meanwhile, sober consideration of the present set of books will show how much, and just where and how, our discipline is being revolutionized.

In addition to the two books casually mentioned (*African dilemma tales* and *Varia folklorica*), there are many others in this series which describe and analyze the works of the mind and of the spirit, from the earliest beginnings and in every part of the world.

Chicago, Illinois   SOL TAX
June 20, 1978

Preface

The book has as its central theme a chromatic image: a mythical being known in aboriginal Australia as the Rainbow Serpent. In the introductory piece to this volume, Kenneth Maddock outlines the history of anthropological concern with this conception, and its relationships to other aspects of Australian art, ritual and mythology.

My concern is limited to the ontogeny of this volume. Many have served who are not mentioned elsewhere, and the contribution that they made needs to be noted. Like the terms that define a riddle, some of the pieces that have been brought within a common frame were initially intended to stand apart. Other essays, in the manner of an arranged marriage, were written with a volume in mind. The design of the volume as a whole is the artifact of a bit of history, described in detail in the General Editor's Preface.

I would like to express my thanks to Karen Tkach, Mouton's World Anthropology Editor, for helping to expedite matters and to Elizabeth Krijgsman whose copy editing helped us sort out a variety of tangles that might have otherwise gone unnoticed. Barbara Buchler has given intellectual and personal support from the first faltering steps in Paris, from the dreaming to the present. More than thanks, this is a confession of gratitude and affection.

The initial conception for the Mountford-Buchler volume was worked out very nearly four years ago. As a novice in matters of Australian mythology, I was honored to participate in a duet with a distinguished Australian naturalist and ethnographer. In the interlude between conception and production, death has taken Charles Mountford from us. I hope that this book serves as a modest token of our respect and admiration for his contributions to anthropology.

A final thought must be offered to the Australian aborigines. Seduced by the power and harmony, the emotional depth and ecological fidelity of their mythical thought, we have attempted to offer a bit more in return than program notes. Being in this world of mythology and its logics, at least for a moment it belonged to both of us: where there was no longer anything to either give or to take.

IRA BUCHLER

Table of Contents

Introduction

KENNETH MADDOCK

The papers here published are concerned with the beautiful image of the rainbow serpent which recurs in aboriginal Australian art, myth, and ritual. That belief in such a being is widespread among aborigines and important to them was maintained more than forty years ago by Radcliffe-Brown. I do not know that anyone has disagreed; yet, as the articles in this book show, the nature of the belief remains an open question. Because the papers to follow are diverse in character—Mountford's an illustrated survey, Buchler's a structural analysis after the manner of Lévi-Strauss, mine a local study—it may be useful first to consider conclusions reached by others. These can be reduced essentially to two positions.

There is, on the one hand, the opinion that the rainbow serpent is a clearly delineated figure filling what is normally an important place among the other figures with which aboriginal mythology has populated the world. His properties enable him to be easily distinguished from them. It is characteristic of this position that its exponents speak of rainbow serpents in the singular and with the definite article. There is, on the other hand, the view that what are called rainbow serpents belong amid a host of fleeting forms in and through which a fundamental conception of the world is expressed.

Should it be objected that these approaches differ only as the two sides of a coin, then it can be answered that they take inquiry in different directions. The first leads the student of a society to look for a discrete personage comparable with seemingly similar figures from other

This introduction was written during a sabbatical year spent in Nijmegen. I am indebted to Macquarie University for its grant of leave, to the Instituut voor Culturele en Sociale Antropologie at Nijmegen for the use of its library and other facilities, and to Professors S. Tax and I. R. Buchler for suggesting that I write an introductory piece.

societies. He brings them into relation because they share one or more features: rainbows, but also snakes; in the water, but also in the sky; responsible for female fecundity, but responsible also for destructive forces. It follows from this approach that a figure will be left out of account if it lacks most or all of the features taken to be critical. The second view leads the student to look for complex configurations of thought and imagery in which the different figures are drawn with shifting outlines so that they seem often to merge with one another.

Radcliffe-Brown is undoubtedly in the leading position among defenders of the first view, and many writers on the subject have followed in his footsteps. Even when there was information pointing in other directions, they failed to reassess the orientation he had given.[1] Attempts to show the "deeper" significance of rainbow serpents have admittedly introduced considerations unmentioned by Radcliffe-Brown, but this has not stopped these beings from continuing to be conceived of just as he did.

Thus, for Ronald Berndt (1951: 12–13, 31), the rainbow serpent symbolizes "the Penis" and is the male counterpart of the All-Mother, who symbolizes "the Uterus" (see also Berndt and Berndt 1951: 128–129). For Elkin (1951: 9), commenting on the Berndts' data, "no deep analysis is needed to show that the mythical Snake is a sexual symbol"; and for Schmidt (1953: 909), discussing the same data, the rainbow serpent represents "the male element (membrum virile)" or, which is perhaps not quite the same, "the male idea of the penis." For Triebels (1958: 129–130), in his unjustly neglected comparative study, the rainbow serpent symbolizes, in its snake aspect, the spirally formed cosmic power that lay in the world's virgin waters (*het oerwater*), and it is, in its rainbow aspect, an emanation of the snake; in the course of time the rainbow serpent, depicted more or less anthropomorphically, gained in prominence over the spirally formed cosmic power. For Eliade (1973: 115–116), the rainbow serpent is no more a rainbow than it is a snake; it is a "religious structure" that unites opposites in a totality. For Hiatt (1975: 158), writing on male rainbow serpents, the rainbow serpent is "an appropriate symbol for intimidating neophytes and for representing cosmic power because real fathers, especially in their phallic aspects, may seem intimidating and powerful to their small sons."

Differences are evident among these and other explanations, and this, allowing that some writers have had regional or otherwise specific rather than continental or universal phenomena in mind, shows how interesting their subject is. It is striking, however, that a wide measure of agreement exists on the exterior of the beast to be explained. The differences are about the significance of rainbow serpents, and the main dividing line is between those who favor a psychosexual and those who favor a metaphys-

---

[1]   Radcliffe-Brown's influence on rainbow-serpent studies has thus been analogous to his effect on studies of kinship (see Rose 1976) and local organization (see Hiatt 1962; 1966).

ical meaning. But what is said in the ethnographic reports shows that identity, too, poses difficult questions, and it is open to doubt that there can be a satisfactory general explanation, as distinct from plausible partial explanations, while the identity problem is left neglected. Let us, then, turn from explanation back to identification. This, of course, means turning back to Radcliffe-Brown, with whom it all began.

According to Radcliffe-Brown's first paper on the subject, "the rainbow-serpent is not confined in Australia to any particular ethnological province, but is very widespread and may very possibly be practically universal. In other words it is characteristic of Australian culture as a whole and not of any one part or stratum of it" (1926: 24). His second paper attaches still greater importance to this being: "The rainbow-serpent as it appears in Australian belief may with some justification be described as occupying the position of a deity" (1930: 342). Radcliffe-Brown used to speak as if there were one rainbow serpent, despite contrary indications in some of the reports on which he relied.[2] This tendency was less pronounced in his first paper, where one may read, for example, that "In the tribes around Perth it is called *wogal*, and certain water-holes are pointed out as being each the abode of a *wogal*" (1926: 22), and "the rainbow-serpent, whether regarded as a rainbow or as a serpent, or species of serpent . . ." (1926: 24). One notices that Radcliffe-Brown vacillated between singular and plural in referring to *wogal*.

The treatment Radcliffe-Brown's second paper gave to some southeast Australian data shows his fondness for reducing many to one. Thus he identified *kurrea*, a Euahlayi word reported by Mrs. Parker and translated as "crocodile" by her, as "really the rainbow-serpent" (1930: 343). From Mrs. Parker's observations it appears that a medicine man keeps a tiny *kurrea* within himself, that crocodiles (rainbow serpents in Radcliffe-Brown's interpretation) swallowed Baiame's wife, and that *kurrea* who swallow their victims whole live in some waterholes. There are, in short, many rainbow serpents (assuming the crocodile=rainbow serpent identification to be correct) and they are of different sorts. Radcliffe-Brown thought that the *kurrea* Mrs. Parker reported from the Euahlayi and Mathews from the Kamilaroi "is identical with the *wawi* of the Weilwan and other tribes" (1930: 343). If these beings are indeed many in number and sort, is it likely that there should be identity, as distinct from some broad resemblances, among the *kurrea* and *wawi* of a number of different peoples? Of a being called Myndie or Mindii in his sources and reported there to be controlled by the men of a certain group,

[2] Goudsblom (1974: 104–111) has commented critically on the common preference for the singular above the plural in sociological writings. One speaks, for example, of "the family today" rather than of "families today." Of those who would dismiss this distinction as pedantry, Goudsblom observes that they would never allow themselves a like nonchalance in the use of statistics.

Radcliffe-Brown stated, "This was evidently the horde to whose territory the chief home of the rainbow-serpent belonged, and therefore the men of the horde had power over it" (1930: 347). It is typical that he did not speak of "the home of the chief rainbow-serpent" or of "the (chief) home of a rainbow-serpent."

The 1930 paper introduced a small symposium to which Elkin, Piddington, and McConnel were the other contributors. Elkin and Piddington covered some of the same ground, and it is instructive to compare their accounts. According to Elkin (1930b: 351), the Karadjeri call their rainbow serpent Maiangara and identify him with a mythical water snake named Pulang. According to Piddington (1930: 354), the Karadjeri explain rainbows by a myth about *maiangara* [rainbow, death adder] and deny that he is in any way connected with *bulaing*. Although *bulaing* (presumably Elkin's Pulang) "apparently corresponds to the rainbow-serpent elsewhere in Australia (he) is in no way connected with the rainbow" (1930: 352). McConnel (1930: 348) thanked Radcliffe-Brown for pointing out a connection between a northern Queensland being called *yero* and the rainbows that appear in the spray of waterfalls. Is the implication that the connection was so little obvious to her that she had to be prompted to make it?

A clear lesson of the 1930 symposium is that large differences exist among the beings identified as rainbow serpents and that a certain freedom enters into their identification. The same conclusion can be drawn from Mountford's paper in the present volume. One might try to get out of these difficulties by appealing to Wittgenstein's concept of family resemblances, which he used to explicate games; but that would only create another problem, for one speaks of family resemblances only in cases in which the persons who resemble one another are related to one another. Otherwise one speaks simply of resemblances. Is it right to assume that rainbow-serpent beliefs have an ancestral belief in common?

It is curious that rainbow serpents, in spite of the auspicious start they had in Australian anthropology, are usually referred to perfunctorily and rarely receive the attention due an important deity.[3] The comparative study by Triebels (1958) has been ignored by Australianists, and the field studies by Lommel (1952) and Petri (1954) have fared little better. In 1961, at a Canberra conference foreshadowing the foundation of the Australian Institute of Aboriginal Studies, Marie Reay suggested that it

[3]   Compare the fate of rainbow serpents with that of the All-Fathers reported from southeast Australia. Debates flourished around the latter late in the last century and early in this. The first round of controversy was followed by a substantial review of the earlier theories and an original reassessment of the data by Schmidt (1926: 134–487). Fahrenfort (1927: 169–241, 289–306) replied lengthily and polemically, only to be criticized in his turn by Bellon (1948: 233–304). More recently still, the issues have once again been canvassed by Eliade (1973: 2–41). Rainbow serpents have never had such analysis and interpretation devoted to them.

was time to restudy the distribution of the rainbow-snake theme as part of a wider study of current themes in mythology (Shiels 1963: 279), but who has responded?

This lack of interest in really searching studies results, I think, from a combination of two factors. The field data cannot be accommodated within Radcliffe-Brown's terms of reference, and there is a reluctance to break decisively with his terms. They may once have stimulated inquiry, but now they stultify it. Any modern inquiry must traverse three problem areas, and it is accordingly to them that the remainder of this introduction will be devoted: first, ambiguities in aboriginal depictions of rainbow serpents; second, likenesses between rainbow serpents and other mythical beings; and third, rainbow serpents as forms picturing fundamentals of existence.

AMBIGUITIES IN ABORIGINAL DEPICTIONS OF RAINBOW SERPENTS

A paper by Stanner on the Murinbata of the northern Northern Territory shows how hard it is to do justice to aboriginal imagery if working within Radcliffe-Brown's conception of the rainbow serpent. Stanner found that Radcliffe-Brown's "more essential" features[4] are secondary with the Murinbata and useful mainly for taxonomic purposes (1961: 235), but he weakened this concession, if not withdrawing it altogether, by observing that the Murinbata rainbow serpent is obscured and loses its unity when account is taken of contextual information to enlarge upon myth narratives (1961: 247). In what, then, can the usefulness of the criteria of classification consist?

A bare outline of the long and brilliant myth reported by Stanner (1961: 240–246) is that the bat forced himself sexually upon his two sisters, daughters of the rainbow serpent. The girls had their revenge when they made him fall down a cliff, but he recovered from his injuries and speared his father, the rainbow serpent, who then entered the water. Although the rainbow serpent is one of the two main characters in this myth, the Murinbata are uncertain of his name, number, gender, outward appearance, and family relationships, and Stanner had to conclude that there is a throng of visionary shapes of unknown age of which each telling of the myth is a partial attempt at systematization (1961: 247–251).

As to the rainbow serpent's name, Kunmanggur and Kanamgek are used interchangeably. Sometimes he is called Kulaitj, ordinarily an adjective meaning "older" or "eldest" (hence he can be thought of as The

---

[4] The features are that the rainbow snake is a huge serpent, associated with rain and the making of rain and with quartz crystals and mother-of-pearl, who lives in deep, permanent waters (Radcliffe-Brown 1926: 24–25).

Oldest One). As to number, sometimes it is said that there were two brothers Kunmanggur, and that Kanamgek was Kunmanggur's son. As to gender, the name Kulaitj sometimes seems to refer instead to a female or, if referring to Kunmanggur, to mean that "he" was bisexual. Even those Murinbata who affirm Kunmanggur's maleness say that he had woman's breasts. Different versions make him look like a huge snake with a hooked tail, a scorpion, a huge person, and a figure reminiscent of the northwest-Australian *wondjina* images. There is no unanimity about his relation to rainbows: thus the darkest band is variously identified as Kunmanggur, Kulaitj, Kirindilyin, and Ngamur; and sometimes the top and bottom bands are distinguished as Kunmanggur and Kanamgek. As to family relationships, Kulaitj, Kirindilyin, Ngamur, and Walumuma are given as names of Kunmanggur's wives, but there is no agreement on how many he had or what all their names were; Walumuma, furthermore, is given sometimes as his daughter (compare the ambiguous Kanamgek).

It is evident from this that Murinbata data alone will not convey much that is certain about the rainbow serpent. To take but one doubtful point, is Kulaitj Kunmanggur or Kunmanggur's wife or Kunmanggur's female other self? And, above all, what significance is to be accorded to the fact that a character who is apparently the same has differing identities? It is therefore fortunate that Stanner was able to collect fragmentary rainbow-serpent myths among the neighbors of the Murinbata (1961: 238–240), since they, in spite of their incomplete state, are sufficient to demonstrate some invariant relational properties of rainbow-serpent ideology in the region.

In a Marithiel myth, the rainbow serpent, who had no wife, stole one from the flying fox, who had two. The flying fox speared him and he went down into the water while the flying fox flew up into the sky. A Wagaman myth is similar, except that the rainbow serpent stole both wives from the flying fox. A Nangiomeri myth tells that two women whom the rainbow serpent had given to the flying fox ran back to him, which is why the flying fox speared him. The Nangiomeri, like the Murinbata, impute bisexuality to the rainbow serpent. In the Wagaman and Nangiomeri myths, the rainbow serpent and the flying fox are in the wife's–brother/sister's–husband relationship, whereas with the Murinbata they are father and son ("flying fox" is, according to Stanner, used incorrectly by aborigines for creatures that are bats, but I shall use "flying fox" because of its widespread acceptance in aboriginal English in the northern areas of the Northern Territory).

These comparative considerations establish that the rainbow serpent stands in opposition to the flying fox. The incidents of their antagonism are such that the additional oppositions of sky and water, above and below, upward movement and downward movement may also be accepted as invariant. Sexual trouble having to do with a pair of women is always the basis of antagonism. When the relation between the opponents is one of alliance, the rainbow serpent is sexually at fault, since he takes or receives another's wives; when their relation is one of descent, it is the flying fox who is at fault. (Their relation is not given in the Marithiel myth, but one may hazard the conjecture that it is an alliance relation.) How widespread these associations are has yet to be established, but they are not confined to the four peoples whose rainbow-serpent myths are reported by Stanner.

For example, in the *Gunabibi*, further to the east in Arnhem Land, rainbow-serpent imagery is predominant and flying foxes appear to women at a moment when bull-roarers (rainbow-serpent symbols) are sounding in concealment (hence unseen by women) nearby. There are rock paintings in which rainbow serpent and flying fox are associated (Maddock 1970: 447, 452). The blue-tongue lizard has an important part to play in the *Gunabibi*: Walumuma, Kunmanggur's wife or daughter, is said to have been a blue-tongue lizard (Stanner 1961: 248)![5]

In Stanner's myths the rainbow serpent and the flying fox become polarized in relation to each other. The terms "water," "below," and "downward movement" form a cluster around one opponent and the terms "sky," "above," and "upward movement" a cluster around the other. The middle ground, on which human life is played out and which the opponents shared until trouble over women led them to separate vertically, is abandoned. The myths thus sketch a tripartite cosmos. It needs no special acumen to see that rainbow serpents are at home in a world so divided, for a being who lives below in the water but shows above as a rainbow embodies the polarities between which the middle ground is framed.

The polarization theme common to Stanner's myths is presented inversely in a myth from the northwest-Australian Garad'are (Worms 1940: 239–244), in which a rainbow serpent separates other characters instead of being one of the characters who becomes separated. Two sisters went out to gather food, but the elder left behind a snake she used to carry about with her. The younger sister returned to fetch the snake but could not find it, for in their absence it "had crawled as deeply into the earth as the rainbow stands above the earth"! When the younger sister tried to rejoin the elder she found that there was water lying about the bush that before had been dry. Everywhere there was water, to her right and to her left, until at last she arrived at a river, not present earlier, that was too wide to cross. The elder sister was standing on the other bank. A rainbow bridged the water, but the elder knew it to be the snake and called out to her younger sister to stay where she was. The snake can be seen in the sky before sunrise with a sister to each side. The Bād, a little to the north, have a cognate myth (see Worms 1940: 244).

[5] For additional data on flying foxes and blue-tongue lizards, rainbow serpents and rainbow-serpent-like water snakes, see Berndt (1951) and Warner (1937).

A basic contrast between Stanner's myths and Worms's is that, whereas the former group displays definitive polarization vertically (rainbow serpent down in the water, flying fox up in the sky), the latter group displays it horizontally (a sister to each side of the river or snake). A tripartite division is thus common to the two groups, but they work it out complementarily. Another basic contrast is that whereas the former group shows the rainbow serpent as polarized in relation to the flying fox, the latter group shows him polarizing the sisters. The pair of women in Stanner's myths are therefore functionally equivalent to the serpent in Worms's myths, for they remain in the middle and separate others; the pair of women in Worms's myths are functionally equivalent to the rainbow serpent and the flying fox in Stanner's myth, for they become separated.

That the serpent has no male opponent in the northwest-Australian myths can be seen as compression rather than impoverishment. A flying fox who goes up into the sky is the other self of a serpent who goes down into the water: a rainbow serpent is in essence a split representation, since it shows in the sky above but lives in the water below. The snake in the Garad'are myth "crawled as deeply into the earth as the rainbow stands above the earth"; later he appeared to the sisters as a rainbow over a river. The Garad'are myth knows how to convey a split representation in the person of one character;[6] the myths of the Murinbata and their neighbors divide the representation along its line of cleavage into two characters.

The conclusion to be drawn from these data is, accordingly, that a unity is conveyed in rainbow-serpent ideologies. The ambiguities and inconsistencies in the Murinbata depiction of Kunmanggur do not stand in the way of acceptance of this conclusion, for the unity is one of opposites held together in a split representation. If anything, the ambiguities and inconsistencies (is Kunmanggur one or more than one? male or female? anthropomorphic or zoomorphic?) are confirmations of unity.

This conclusion bears some resemblance to interpretations to be found in other writers. Van der Leeden, for example, remarked of the Nunggubuyu of eastern Arnhem Land that

Rainbow Serpent strikes one as the logical extension of all other symbols relating to contacts between males and females; to be both male and female . . .; to be associated with both fire and water; . . . to combine an "inner truth" (men's secret) with an outer (natural) appearance; . . . to be both benignant and malicious (1975: 92).

The volume in which Van der Leeden published his observations contains an article by Hiatt (1975: 143–162), in which he discusses the common

---

[6]   The snake in the Bād myth is not expressly mentioned as a rainbow serpent, but his role in relation to the two sisters is virtually the same as that of the snake in the Garad'are myth.

Australian association of swallowing and regurgitation by (rainbow) snakes with initiatory rituals that withdraw youths from the company of women and introduce them to an exclusively masculine circle. Rainbow-serpent ideology thus functions in ritual episodes organized around such pairs of opposites as entry and exit, separation and aggregation, death and rebirth; as in the myths reported by Worms, a snake polarizes other characters. According to Eliade, the Ungarinyin rainbow serpent described by Elkin "represents the mythological expression of the effort to unite the opposites, to articulate the polarities in a single paradoxical unity" (1973: 79).

It is evident, however, that the conception of a unity of opposites, of a split representation, can be conveyed in contrasting ways. This came out in the comparison of myths reported by Stanner and Worms and may be enlarged upon by referring briefly to papers by De Josselin de Jong and Radcliffe-Brown. In his classic contribution to the subject of the divine trickster (*goddelijke bedrieger*), De Josselin de Jong (1929) argued in response to Kristensen (1928) that it is the essence of this figure to be a divided unity (*twee-eenheid*). He combines contraries—masculinity and femininity, beneficence and maleficence, life and death, and so on—as aspects of his total character and not as chance results of syncretism or degeneration in religious thought. The fruits of this way of thinking are clearly to be seen in Van der Leeden's 1975 paper.

Radcliffe-Brown (1951) speaks of the unity of opposites, but he has another possibility in mind. For him, this relation exists between clearly delineated characters, as in Australian myths about social dualism in which white cockatoo and black, or eaglehawk and crow, are opponents. There is at once a similarity and a contrariety between the members of such pairs, just as there is between the moieties in a dual social organization. It is interesting to notice that De Josselin de Jong's commemorative article (1956) on Radcliffe-Brown drew attention to the latter's principle of the unity of opposites, but not to the difference that exists in the ways in which it may be conceived, even though the alternative conception had long before been set out by De Josselin de Jong himself.

That the principle of unity of opposites should be worked out in contrasting ways sheds a clarifying light on Stanner's data. The rainbow serpent in the myths of the Murinbata and their neighbors is a member of a pair of opposites of which the flying fox is the other member; he is one half and the flying fox the other half of a split representation. This is the unity of opposites as conceived by Radcliffe-Brown. But in the discursive thought of the Murinbata, Kunmanggur is a pair of opposites, he is the totality of a split representation, for he is no longer defined in opposition to another. He can keep the properties ascribed to him in each telling of a myth and add to them their opposites. This is the unity of opposites as conceived by De Josselin de Jong.

These alternative portraits of ostensibly the same person result, or so it may be conjectured, from contrasting imperatives to which aborigines are subject. He who tells a myth subjects himself to what may be termed a narrative imperative. He must depict characters in relation to one another, which may most economically be achieved by putting them at opposed poles. A complicated criss-cross emerges in which, for example, rainbow serpent and flying fox are opposed as water and sky, below and above, downward movement and upward, but in which they are united against a pair of women as male to female.

He who thinks discursively about the world subjects himself to what may be termed a metaphysical imperative. In trying to grasp the essence of things he may unite contraries, for he need not portray character concretely. Combinations of qualities take the place of casts of characters, and he may unite the poles; for, in the world he is trying to depict, an endless number of oppositions are present. Thus a parade of beings passes before us who are male but have a womb or female breasts, who are down in the water but up in the sky, who are one but father and son or brothers, who, to borrow examples from the Berndts, look like a snake but also like a woman (1951: 113) or are the "good Mother" but also the "bad Mother" (1970: 229).

It is a distinctive feature of aboriginal thought that the same words can function as names of characters in narrative and as metaphysical terms. The one word is twice a focus of attention. This difference correlates with the contrast between the narrative and metaphysical modes and accounts for the apparent confusion that results from attempts to explore the character of such a rainbow serpent as Kunmanggur. He is both a person in a story and a symbol in a system of thought.

Yet, if this conjecture about the state in which rainbow-serpent materials come to us were to be confirmed by further inquiry, there would remain a serious difficulty.

LIKENESSES BETWEEN RAINBOW SERPENTS AND OTHER MYTHICAL BEINGS

There exist striking resemblances between rainbow serpents and beings which are not called rainbow serpents or which are stated not to be rainbow serpents. Piddington denied that the Karadjeri *bulaing* was associated with rainbows in spite of its other resemblances to the rainbow serpents described in the 1930 symposium. Warner (1937: 248–259) gave a myth in which a huge water snake plays a decisive role, but he did not mention rainbows in connection with it. Berndt (1951: 16) and Hiatt (1975: 147) have identified Warner's snake as a rainbow serpent, but their opinion rests on later or circumstantial evidence. The snake in

Worms's Bād myth plays a part similar to that of the snake in his Garad'are myth, but there is no mention of any rainbow associations. An even more noteworthy practice is to identify as rainbow serpents beings that are not snakes. Examples are to be found in Mountford's paper in the present volume: for example, lizards in Groote Eylandt mythology (the 1975 paper by Van der Leeden, who worked on the mainland opposite Groote Eylandt, may be consulted with reference to this part of Mountford's survey).

If the equation of snake and rainbow is taken as the criterion for selection of material, then many myths telling of characters and actions like those in rainbow-serpent myths will have to be left out of account. Why treat an association with rainbows as critical? That it can be arbitrary to limit study to cases in which a snake is identified or otherwise associated with rainbows may be shown by comparing a myth reported by Stanner (1960: 260–262) with other Arnhem Land materials.

Mutjingga, the Old Woman, swallowed children left in her care. She fled along a river but was overtaken and killed. The children were taken alive from her belly and painted as initiated novices are. Characters named Left Hand and Right Hand played a prominent part in these events.

According to Stanner (1960: 260), the Mutjingga myth is central to a ceremony called *Punj* or *Karwadi*. The ceremony initiates youths to manly status, and its rites include a putative swallowing by the Old Woman, whose material symbol is the bull-roarer (1959: 112–115). A bird made the first bull-roarer after Mutjingga's death and its sound is her voice (1960: 263, n. 22). She is an All-Mother and can be conceived of as like a snake (1959: 110, 112; 1960: 259, n. 17). Although her ceremony is a cognate of the *Gunabibi*, in which water or rainbow snakes are important (see Warner 1937; Berndt 1951), the Old Woman appears not to be connected with rainbows; and Stanner did not mention her name in his 1961 paper on the rainbow serpent except to show structural congruences between her myth and that of Kunmanggur and to state that a pristine female named Kulaitj Mutjingga [literally, "the oldest woman"] is associated with sea-mist. Kulaitj, we have seen, is used sometimes as a name for Kunmanggur himself or one of his wives or the darkest band of the rainbow, but Stanner did not suggest an identity of this being with the Mutjingga of the swallowing myth.

If an association with rainbows is critical, then the Mutjingga myth will have to be omitted from consideration, despite its likeness to myths to the east in which rainbow serpents play parts strongly reminiscent of Mutjingga's. I have collected a Dalabon myth in which Jingana, a snakelike All-Mother, had all life within her but would not let it out. She had to be speared by a left-hander before the beings within her could come forth. Jingana is a rainbow serpent. Another Dalabon myth has it that

Lumaluma, a snakelike All-Mother who is Jingana or a version of her, used to swallow *Gunabibi* actors until at last a father–son pair decided that thenceforth they would celebrate the ceremony without her. A bull-roarer was made by a bird to substitute for Lumaluma and its sound is her voice. During *Gunabibi* performances the novices are putatively swallowed by her (see Maddock 1976: 166–167).

The Mutjingga, Jingana, and Lumaluma myths group together like incidents. Mutjingga and Lumaluma play cognate ritual roles, but some of the mythical events associated with Mutjingga are to be found in the Jingana instead of the Lumaluma myth: for example, a spearing, a left-hander, a freeing of life. It would be contrived to treat the Dalabon myths as belonging to the rainbow-serpent corpus and the Murinbata myth not, merely because Mutjingga, unlike Jingana and Lumaluma, is not expressly said to be associated with rainbows.

The suspicion that there must be close historical connections between these myths is strengthened by information published by the Berndts. According to Ronald Berndt (1951: 12–13, 24–25, 31), Kunapipi in northeast Arnhem Land expresses the dual concept of fertility mother(s) and rainbow serpent(s). It was from the former that life came forth, but she was acting together with the latter. Here mother and rainbow serpent are separate figures expressing the opposition of female and male, uterus and penis; but, as there are female as well as male rainbow serpents, the way stands open for the conception of a snake-like All-Mother. The Mutjingga, Jingana, and Lumaluma myths may accordingly be thought to coalesce notions that Berndt's informants separated. Information published jointly by Ronald and Catherine Berndt (1970: 20, 117, 229) is even more to the point: Maung predominantly view the rainbow serpent as masculine, but their Gunwinggu neighbors use the feminine suffix for the rainbow serpent and their creation myth has her giving birth to the first people. The *Ubar*, *Maraian*, and *Gunabibi* ceremonies are dominated by "the Mother," known also as "the Old Woman," who appears sometimes as Ngaljod, the rainbow serpent. Comparable data were reported in an earlier work (see Berndt and Berndt 1951: 113, 127–128, 131–132, 136–137).

There is, then, a set of permutations stretching across Arnhem Land eastward from the Murinbata, in which the primary configurations result from a play with a few equations and their negations:

snake = rainbow	snake ≠ rainbow
rainbow = female	rainbow ≠ female
female = snake	female ≠ snake

The proper subject of study, at least in this part of Australia, must surely be the set and not an arbitrary rainbow-serpent isolate.

Despite its expansion, the material looks manageable, but unluckily there are more myths pressing for consideration. I have collected a Dalabon myth in which a tortoise swallowed a child left in her care to whom she was related as mother's mother. A fight broke out when the child's mother, a porcupine, discovered what had happened. The porcupine struck the tortoise with a stone—hence her shell; and the tortoise speared the porcupine—hence her quills. The tortoise then took to the water. An outcome of these incidents was that a goanna lizard founded the *Jabuduruwa*, a Jiridja-moiety ceremony complementary to the Dua moiety's *Gunabibi*.

Swallowing, spearing, maternal relationships, entry into the water, a ceremony—it is precisely these motifs that recur in the rainbow-serpent myths thus far considered in this section. The tortoise myth can hardly be treated apart from them.

A Walbiri myth from central Australia may also be cited (see Meggitt 1966: 55–60; and for discussion, Hiatt 1975; Maddock 1976). A pair of men set out on a journey after circumcising their sons. While they were away the boys were swallowed by their mothers. The men returned, killed the two women, and revived their sons with a bird ritual. This myth is associated with the *Gadjari*, a *Gunabibi*-type ceremony, in which novices are said to be swallowed by a pair of old women (Meggitt 1966: 54). The Walbiri myth calls for consideration together with more northern mother and rainbow-serpent myths. It is not exactly like them, but then they are not exactly like one another. It is related to them as they are related to one another, namely as a variant.

Part of the interest of Buchler's paper in the present volume is that it suggests a solution to the problem that arises when one takes account of the likenesses between rainbow serpents and other mythical beings. The problem is that it is arbitrary to restrict one's attention to myths expressly about rainbow serpents (for example, the Kunmanggur, Jingana, and Lumaluma stories and the Garad'are myth) and ignore myths with different characters (for example, the Mutjingga and tortoise stories and the Bād and Walbiri myths), but that by widening the field of study to include such obviously related material, one seems to set oneself on a path that leads to comparing all Australian myths. Surely the material to be studied is impossibly proliferant. Buchler has applied methods worked out by Lévi-Strauss and sought to isolate relational and permutational properties within the profusion of narrative details. The hope that inspires such a structural approach is that it is possible to construct a grammar or logic of which all myths are expressions. If the approach works, then it will eventually enable us to give an account of mythology that is more economical than the myths for which it accounts.

There remains, however, yet another side to rainbow-serpent materials. It is documented in some remarkable reports from northwest

Australia and suggests that the likenesses discussed in this section may be more than apparent.

RAINBOW SERPENTS AS FORMS PICTURING FUNDAMENTALS OF EXISTENCE

A description of the Ungarinyin word *ungud*, published by Elkin in the same year and journal as the 1930 symposium, put rainbow serpents in a new perspective:

The name *Ungud* is sometimes used as though it referred to a person, sometimes as though it referred to a far-off time, and sometimes, too, for the rainbow-serpent water spirit. It is also given as the ultimate explanation of such significant things as the obvious artificial arrangement of stones. To the question "What is that?" the answer given is simply *"Ungud"* (1930a: 263).

Elkin's paper was devoted to rock paintings. The most striking figures he discusses show mythical beings called *wondjina*,[7] which he found to be intimately linked with *ungud*: "Wondjina is the rain, or the rain-power" (1930a: 263); some Ungarinyin refer to paintings of *wondjina* as *ungud* (1930a: 269, n. 8, 275); and fertility functions are ascribed to them both, for rain comes when the paintings are retouched, child-spirits are sent by *ungud*, and other species, too, are sustained by rites held at the *wondjina* galleries (1930a: 263–264, 270, 275–277).

Elkin concluded that

It is perhaps permissible to regard wondjina as the regenerative and reproductive power in nature and man—a power which is especially associated with rain. I am not sure whether wondjina is really thought of in terms of sex. Some of the paintings are said to be women while other references to wondjina seem to make him male. Then again, he is also the rainbow-serpent, and one of his functions as such is to "make" spirit-children. He is apparently a generalised power who can be thought of in different ways according to his different functions, in the same way as the natives talk of different wondjina at different *banja*, and yet admit that these different beings are "all one," "all the same" (1930a: 279).

The neglect suffered by Elkin's paper is perhaps the fault of its title, which refers to rock paintings, not to rainbow serpents or forms of thought. Some issues are obscure, for example the precise nature of the connection between the zoomorphic rainbow serpent and the anthropomorphic *wondjina*, but there is a clear suggestion that *ungud* is not only the name of a thing or being (or class of things or beings) but also in effect the name of the distinctive property or quality of such things or

---

[7]   A good impression of the *wondjina* art and the country in which it is found is to be had in Crawford (1968).

beings. *Ungud* is singular, yet plural; exists specifically, yet is the explanation of much else. Although Elkin did not reformulate Radcliffe-Brown's conception of the rainbow serpent, it is evident that his Ungarinyin materials call for a more complicated conception.

Lévy-Bruhl is one of the few to have paid attention to Elkin's findings. He was familiar with the then-latest reports from Australia—apart from Elkin's work, he referred also to work published in *Oceania* by Piddington and Radcliffe-Brown (*Oceania* began publication in 1930)—but what captured his interest was the evidence for a form of thought, not the evidence for a zoomorphically conceived deity or spirit of water. He did not refer to Radcliffe-Brown's 1926 and 1930 papers on the rainbow serpent.

Lévy-Bruhl (1935: xxxvii–xl) interpreted *ungud* and *wondjina* as terms designating a diffuse reality as well as individual beings. They are comprehensive representations lacking in logical generality and cannot be analyzed with our habitual intellectual procedures. Indeed, he criticized Elkin for conveying the impression that we understand their significance. Although the beneficent natural effects aimed at by the rock paintings are apparent enough, the mental complexes or representations are impenetrable for our minds. To speak of *ungud* and *wondjina* as concepts, notions, or ideas is to distort what one pretends to explain, it is to assimilate Ungarinyin mental modes to our own.

The data on which Lévy-Bruhl relied were exiguous and were certainly too few to establish a theory of aboriginal thought or affectivity. His great merit is to have seen a form of thought where others saw individualized mythic beings. Since then publications by Lommel and Petri, who took part in the 1938–1939 Frobenius expedition to northwest Australia, have made us better able than Lévy-Bruhl was to appreciate the structure of the ideology to which Elkin was the first to draw attention. Lommel worked with the Unambal, northern neighbors of the Ungarinyin, and Petri with the Ungarinyin themselves and their southern neighbors, the Nyigina.[8]

The key to Unambal ideology is, on Lommel's account of it (1952: 7–37), the proper name "Ungud." Ungud, a huge snake who lived in the earth at the beginning of time, controls rain and shows himself as a rainbow. He cooperated to create the world with Wallanganda, the Milky Way. The *wondjina*, too, acted creatively to help give the earth the appearance it now has. They left rock paintings of themselves at the spots where they died on earth and live on in pools of water, whence they emanate child-spirits. Each Unambal local group has its own *wondjina* and *wondjina* place. Two birds named Kuranguli and Banar, after whom the moieties are called, were especially important in forming Unambal cultural institutions.

[8] I have for convenience ignored certain peculiarities of spelling used by Lommel and Petri.

There are persistent suggestions that all these beings are in some sense the same. Ungud found the *wondjina* in a dream as men today find child-spirits. The child-spirits which the *wondjina* emanate are also said to come from Ungud and are described as Ungud-parts. The sky dweller, Wallanganda, is a *wondjina*, and the culture heroes Kuranguli and Banar were Ungud snakes and showed themselves as Ungud, *wondjina*, men, and animals. When Ungud made the different creatures in his dreams he would change himself (or herself, for Ungud is male, female and bisexual) into the being he was creating. If child-spirits are Ungud-parts, then it looks as though Ungud is part of everyman; if *wondjina* were found by him in a dream, it looks as though he was finding himself in finding them; and if all the other creative beings were *wondjina* or Ungud snakes, it looks as though Ungud is the soul of all beings who can act creatively (or who acted creatively in the beginning) as well as being himself.

The data reported by Petri (1954) are even more comprehensive and have the added merit of enabling us to see more clearly the relationships between the different beings the ideology depicts.

The Ungarinyin distinguish *ungud*, *wondjina*, and *ungur* (Petri 1954: 104). *Ungud* is primarily to be understood as the rainbow serpent and *wondjina* as anthropomorphic beings, but secondarily they are all personifications of fertility, increase, and rain. *Ungur* may be understood narrowly to mean "sacred place" and broadly to mean the creative epoch. The Ungarinyin say that these three terms are all the same, but Petri, who presumably had Lévy-Bruhl in mind, insisted that this does not come from any inability to draw conceptual distinctions. It was during the *ungur* period that *ungud* and *wondjina* arose and did their work. The *wondjina* then changed themselves into *ungud* (compare Lommel's culture heroes, who were Ungud snakes as well as *wondjina*). Since then they have emanated child-spirits from the *ungur* places.

It is clear that *ungud* is more than a singular term. There is the fact that the numerous *wondjina* turned into rainbow serpents after their work on earth was done. But even before that transformation occurred, there was more than one *ungud*. It is said that there were masculine as well as feminine *ungud* snakes (Petri 1954: 103), and that transformed *wondjina* are not meant can be seen on the same page, for it is added that the female counterparts of the *wondjina* were *mulu-mulu*. Furthermore, a myth tells that its hero Ngunyari met an *ungud* snake and a *wondjina* while traveling (1954: 118).

Ungud is, however, spoken of in the singular as well as in the plural. Thus she had neither mouth nor ears when she came from the sea (1954: 108), she closed the mouths of the *wondjina* (1954: 107), and, after making land rise from the sea, she traveled across it laying eggs that hatched into *wondjina* (1954: 101). The last detail was one man's story, but it tallies with the common opinion that, although *ungur, ungud,* and *wondjina* were the same, *ungud* was "more Boss" than the *wondjina* (1954: 102). It is from her that men's souls come (1954: 157). They have the appearance of small snakes (*ungud* are snakes!), are found in dreams, and, after death, return, in the opinion of some, to the *ungur* places in which they had lived before incarnation as rainbow-serpent emanations.

Finally, the dual significance of *ungud* may be noted (1954: 111–116). A sky dweller named Walanganda, who threw child-spirits down to earth and appears as the Milky Way, turned into an *ungud* snake, in which form he lies coiled in the heavens. The duality of the *ungud*–Walanganda relation is remarkable, for apart from the association of *ungud*—or at least of the original *ungud*—with the lower spheres and of Walanganda with the higher, of one with rainbows and the other with the Milky Way, of one with a zoomorphic and the other with an anthropomorphic form, there is the crediting of nature to the one and culture to the other. The underlying unity, or even identity, of these polarized beings is shown by the transformation of the one into the other (or the type of the other).

Nyigina beliefs show differences with those of the Ungarinyin (Petri 1954: 323–326). Ingurug, the name of the All-Mother, a rainbow serpent, denotes also a class of rainbow serpents. Some of them are male, others female. The Nyigina draw a distinction between natural and cultural creativity and associate rainbow serpents only with the former. The culturally creative powers did not turn into rainbow serpents after their work was done, and child-spirits are not thought to come from Ingurug (or *ingurug*). Keeping in mind especially the materials considered in the section on "Likenesses between rainbow serpents and other mythical beings," it is reasonable to see the culturally creative counterparts of the naturally creative Ingurug (or *ingurug*) as close variants on the Ungarinyin *wondjina* and Walanganda. The main difference between the Nyigina to the south and the Ungarinyin and Unambal to the north is, then, that the latter, unlike the former, have expressly conceptualized an essential identity among all world-creative powers.

It is useful in thinking about these beings to distinguish different applications of the same word. Thus the renderings Ungud and Ingurug might be used to refer to the apical power, an All-Mother and rainbow serpent, of the Ungarinyin and Nyigina (the Unambal Ungud is a rainbow serpent, too, but is sexually ambiguous, and it is not clear that one would be justified in speaking of it as an All-Mother). The renderings *ungud* and *ingurug* would then be used to refer to all the other rainbow serpents. These are associated with local groups and are thus dispersed across the countryside, but they can also have a strongly dual significance. That is the case, for example, with the Unambal culture heroes Kuranguli and Banar, and it comes forward in the opposition of Ungud and Wallanganda (or Walanganda) that is so important with the Unambal and Ungarinyin. An even more fragmented appearance of Ungud (or *ungud*) is to be seen in the child-spirits, the incarnation of which is necessary if there are to be people.

In addition to their substantival use, *ungud* and *ingurug* might be understood to function adjectivally to show properties or qualities of beings who are Ungud or Ingurug, *ungud* or *ingurug*. To belong to such a class, a being must exhibit a certain character, namely the character that can be expressed adjectivally as *ungud* or *ingurug*.

That this mystical power, or essence of mystical power, can be divided and classified as suggested does not entail disunity. It can be located with human individuals, with local groups, with the moieties, and, in the person of its apical manifestation, Ungud or Ingurug, with the whole world or at least the whole of nature. But the use of the same name for beings at different levels and the occurrence of transformations between levels, for example the Ungarinyin *wondjina* turning into *ungud*, or the Unambal Ungud dreaming the first *wondjina* and other creatures, or the return of the souls of men, their Ungud-parts or *wondjina* emanations, to the power whence they originated as child-spirits, show that the dividing lines are contextual. It is for this reason that specific shapes assumed by the world-creative powers are evanescent or, at any rate, contextually bound. Walanganda is now the Milky Way and now a coiled rainbow serpent. A being is now a *wondjina* and later a rainbow serpent and later still a generator of human souls.[9]

Conceptions such as these are far removed from the rainbow serpent as classically conceived by Radcliffe-Brown. It is true that neither Lommel nor Petri entered as deeply as he might have into the implications of the data he collected. Transformation of one form into another, generation of one form from another, and coalescence of separate forms are evidently among the defining processes in Unambal–Ungarinyin metaphysics, yet they are discussed interstitially in the northwest Australian reports. Nevertheless, the data they contain are more than sufficient to vindicate the alternative conception of rainbow serpents that Elkin formulated without, perhaps, being aware of the significance of his words. It is to be hoped that further inquiries will not limit themselves to natural histories of mythic beings but will try to take the further step of outlining and elucidating the systems of thought expressed in and through these mythic beings and their deeds.

CONCLUSIONS

Three species of difficulty to which any survey of rainbow-serpent

---

[9]   The interpretation here advanced follows in large lines that which I put forward of the Dalabon *bolung* conception (compare Karadjeri *bulaing*) in two earlier publications (Maddock 1970, 1972). I was ignorant at the time of the work of Lommel and Petri.

ideologies would be subject have now been reviewed. Thanks especially to data published by Stanner, Petri, Lommel, Elkin, and the Berndts, it has become clear that taking "the rainbow serpent" as an object of study is likely to be profitless. The aboriginal words thus translated are of complex significance and call for other or additional renderings. Even when "rainbow serpent" is acceptable in context, the entity so styled is hard to comprehend. On the one hand, his character is ambiguous, and initial appearances of simplicity and clarity mislead (my use of the possessive pronoun "his" can illustrate the point, for sexual ambiguities mean that "her" or "its" would often be equally or more apt). On the other hand, many beings that are not rainbow serpents are so like those that are that a study has to extend to include them. There are therefore very great difficulties awaiting anyone who attempts the restudy of the rainbow-serpent theme urged by Marie Reay.

Another direction of study is suggested by the materials considered here. This is that "rainbow serpent" is a partial, concrete, and zoomorphic rendering of what might more abstractly be conveyed in some such expression as "totemic essence," "life principle," "spirit," or "divinity." Rainbow serpents, *wondjina*, the souls of men, and all the other forms contextually assumed by this underlying reality exhibit processes of transformation by which their appearances fluctuate. They frequently separate from or merge into one another. It follows that it is better to address oneself to this thought-complex than to focus on one of the many transitory shapes. The shapes are mainly of interest, first, because comparison of them is needed if transformation processes are to be ascertained; second, because they are fixed in the static representations of art, myth, and ritual; and third, because it is characteristic of aboriginal thought that it imputes tangible qualities, however kaleidoscopic their configuration, to the forms it posits.

REFERENCES

BELLON, K. L.
1948   *Inleiding tot de natuurlijke godsdienstwetenschap*. Antwerp: Standaard Boekhandel.
BERNDT, R. M.
1951   *Kunapipi: a study of an Australian aboriginal religious cult*. Melbourne: Cheshire.
BERNDT, R. M., C. H. BERNDT
1951   *Sexual behaviour in western Arnhem Land*. New York: Viking Fund.
1970   *Man, land and myth in north Australia: the Gunwinggu people*. Sydney: Ure Smith.
CRAWFORD, I. M.
1968   *The art of the wandjina*. Melbourne: Oxford University Press.

DE JOSSELIN DE JONG, J. P. B.
    1929   De oorsprong van den goddelijken bedrieger. *Mededeelingen der Koninklijke Akademie van Wetenschappen*, Afdeeling Letterkunde, 68(B): 1–29.
    1956   Herdenking van Alfred Reginald Radcliffe-Brown (17 januari 1881–24 oktober 1955). *Jaarboek der Koninklijke Nederlandse Akademie van Wetenschappen*: 1–8.

ELIADE, M.
    1973   *Australian religions: an introduction*. Ithaca, N.Y.: Cornell University Press.

ELKIN, A. P.
    1930a   Rock-paintings of north-west Australia. *Oceania* 1: 257–279.
    1930b   The rainbow-serpent myth in north-west Australia. *Oceania* 1: 349–352.
    1951   "Foreword," in *Sexual behaviour in western Arnhem Land*. By R. M. Berndt and C. H. Berndt. New York: Viking Fund.

FAHRENFORT, J. J.
    1927   *Het hoogste wezen der primitieven: studie over het oermonotheisme bij enkele der laagste volken*. Groningen: Wolters.

GOUDSBLOM, J.
    1974   *Balans van de sociologie*. Utrecht: Het Spectrum.

HIATT, L. R.
    1962   Local organization among the Australian aborigines. *Oceania* 32: 267–286.
    1966   The lost horde. *Oceania* 37: 81–92.
    1975   "Swallowing and regurgitation in Australian myth and rite," in *Australian aboriginal mythology*. Edited by L. R. Hiatt. Canberra: Australian Institute of Aboriginal Studies.

KRISTENSEN, W. B.
    1928   De goddelijke bedrieger. *Mededeelingen der Koninklijke Akademie van Wetenschappen*, Afdeeling Letterkunde, 66(B): 1–25.

LÉVY-BRUHL, L.
    1935   *La mythologie primitive: le monde mythique des Australiens et des Papous*. Paris: Presses Universitaires de France.

LOMMEL, A.
    1952   *Die Unambal: ein Stamm in Nordwest-Australien*. Hamburg: Hamburgisches Museum für Völkerkunde.

MADDOCK, K.
    1970   Imagery and social structure at two Dalabon rock art sites. *Anthropological Forum* 2: 444–463.
    1972   *The Australian aborigines: a portrait of their society*. London: Penguin.
    1976   "Communication and change in mythology," in *Tribes and boundaries in Australia*. Edited by N. Peterson. Canberra: Australian Institute of Aboriginal Studies.

McCONNEL, U.
    1930   The rainbow-serpent myth in north Queensland. *Oceania* 1: 347–349.

MEGGITT, M. J.
    1966   *Gadjari* among the Walbiri aborigines of central Australia. *Oceania* 36: 43–75.

PETRI, H.
    1954   *Sterbende Welt in Nordwest-Australien*. Braunschweig: Albert Limbach.

PIDDINGTON, R.
1930   The water-serpent in Karadjeri mythology. *Oceania* 1: 352–354.

RADCLIFFE-BROWN, A. R.
1926   The rainbow-serpent myth of Australia. *Journal of the Anthropological Institute of Great Britain and Ireland* 56: 19–25.
1930   The rainbow-serpent myth in south-eastern Australia. *Oceania* 1: 342–347.
1951   The comparative method in social anthropology. *Journal of the Royal Anthropological Institute* 81: 15–22.

ROSE, F.
1976   "Boundaries and kinship systems in aboriginal Australia," in *Tribes and boundaries in Australia*. Edited by N. Peterson. Canberra: Australian Institute of Aboriginal Studies.

SCHMIDT, W.
1926   *Der Ursprung der Gottesidee: eine historische-kritische und positive Studie*, part 1. Münster: Aschendorffsche Verlagsbuchhandlung.
1953   Sexualismus, Mythologie und Religion in Nord-Australien. *Anthropos* 48: 898–924.

SHIELS, H., *editor*
1963   *Australian aboriginal studies: a symposium of papers presented at the 1961 research conference*. Melbourne: Oxford University Press.

STANNER, W. E. H.
1959   On aboriginal religion, I. The lineaments of sacrifice. *Oceania* 30: 108–127.
1960   On aboriginal religion, II. Sacramentalism, rite and myth. *Oceania* 30: 245–278.
1961   On aboriginal religion, IV. The design-plan of a riteless myth. *Oceania* 31: 233–258.

TRIEBELS, L. F.
1958   *Enige aspecten van de regenboogslang: een vergelijkende studie*. Nijmegen: Gebr. Janssen.

VAN DER LEEDEN, A. C.
1975   "Thundering gecko and emu: mythological structuring of Nunggubuyu patrimoieties," in *Australian aboriginal mythology*. Edited by L. R. Hiatt. Canberra: Australian Institute of Aboriginal Studies.

WARNER, W. L.
1937   *A black civilization: a social study of an Australian tribe*. New York: Harper.

WORMS, E.
1940   Religiöse Vorstellungen und Kultur einiger nordwestaustralisches Stämme in fünfzig Legenden. *Annali Lateranensi* 4: 213–282.

The Rainbow-Serpent Myths of Australia

CHARLES P. MOUNTFORD†

There are widespread beliefs throughout the world in great serpentlike creatures who inhabit water supplies and who are usually associated with the rainbow. These beliefs appear to belong to all peoples, irrespective of time and race.

The aborigines of Australia have a similar belief in creatures, often of immense length and size, which live in their deep waterholes. They are usually highly colored (like a rainbow) and have manes and beards and, often, long projecting teeth with which they destroy their victims.

In general, the aborigines are afraid of these huge creatures and, when drinking at their waterholes, take great care to obey the strict laws and taboos associated with such an act. If they do not, the rainbow serpent[1] will rise into the air and create storms so heavy that the offender will be drowned.

The rainbow serpent is essentially the element of water, and any sign of its opposite element—fire, even fumes of smoke—is sufficient to drive

We wish to acknowledge the help of many people in the preparation of this paper, especially Dr. Grant Inglis, Director of the South Australian Museum, for accommodation and the facilities of his institute and the help of his staff, and Mr. R. Olding, the chief librarian of the State Library of South Australia, for the use of his facilities and the help of his photographic staff.

I wish also to express my special personal thanks to my immediate helpers: to Mrs. Jean Truran, who, during a period of over twenty years, has assisted in the production of all my major works, to Mrs. Olga Hardy, my daughter-in-law Mrs. Peggy Mountford, and my wife Mrs. Bessie Mountford, for their artwork and editorial assistance.

To all these people I offer my heartfelt thanks. It is doubtful that this contribution would ever have been completed without their help.

† The editors and publisher regret that Mr. Mountford died during the preparation of the present volume.

[1] We have used the term "rainbow serpent," which, although not always relevant, is the term generally applied to these mythical creatures.

this mythical creature back to its home under the water. Knowing this, the aborigines usually protect themselves when drinking at a waterhole either by carrying a burning stick, as shown in Plate 1, or by lighting a small fire nearby.

These rainbow serpents are of many different temperaments. Some are so belligerent that even the owners of the country will not approach the waterhole without taking the greatest precautions; other serpents, much more congenial, will allow well-behaved strangers to drink from their waterholes without harm.

This survey has shown that the belief in this giant mythical serpent, which is, and was, universal among the aborigines throughout Australia, is still important in the lives of the aborigines, even though many of them have accepted the white man's way of life.

The myth attracted little attention from the early colonists, except that

Plate 1.   Aboriginal with smoking fire-stick on edge of Uluru rock hole, Ayers Rock

many of them, believing the statements of the aborigines that certain waterholes were the homes of the mythical creatures, would not camp nearby.

A few odd references to rainbow serpents did appear in the records of the early settlers, but Smyth of Victoria (1878) was the first to offer, in literature, any information about these mythical creatures.

Except for occasional descriptions by interested people, we had to wait for about another fifty years before Professor A. R. Radcliffe-Brown

(1926: 24) published a short paper surveying the existing knowledge and beliefs about the rainbow-serpent myths of Australia.

Later, after the same writer had accepted the chair of anthropology at the University of Sydney, he contributed another paper to the subject (1930: 342), at the same time stimulating some of his students to do the same. Before then, however, the Rev. J. R. B. Love had given an address in Perth in 1929 that described, for the first time, the function of the curious *wandjina* figures in the Kimberley Ranges, discovered by Sir George Grey in 1838 on his famous journey along the coasts of north-western Australia. The *wandjina* have functions similar to but not identical with those of the rainbow serpents.

The rainbow-serpent myth can be roughly divided into four geographical areas, the characteristics of each varying from the others:

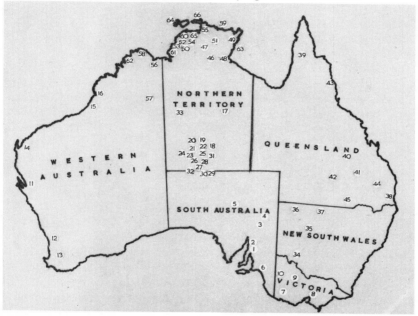

Map 1.   Australia: distribution of rainbow-serpent myths

1. An area including the whole of South Australia from point 6 on Map 1 through central Australia (point 21), etc., to Anna Springs in Western Australia (point 15);

2. The area extending from Victoria (point 8) to Cape York (point 39), the myths of which are unlike those in the above area because of the unusual links between the rainbow serpent, the medicine men, quartz crystals, and a magic rope;

3. The area extending from northeastern Arnhem Land (point 49) to the Murinbata tribe (point 61); and

4. Northwestern Australia (point 62), where the powerful rainbow-serpent beliefs are entirely replaced by the equally powerful *wandjina* cult first described by Love.

A short section of this paper deals with the myths on Groote Eylandt (point 63) and Bathurst Island (point 64), where the rainbow serpents are replaced by lizards, and with the myths in western Arnhem Land (point 65) and on Melville Island (point 66), which link the stone axes of the aborigines with lightning and thunder.

SOUTH AUSTRALIA

My first experiences and knowledge of the rainbow serpent, known in South Australia as the *bunyip*, came early in life.

Our home was on the edge of the pioneering country, and as a small boy I often sat around our fireside listening to the gossip and folklore of the local cattle- and sheepmen who visited us.

The belief in these strange creatures, the *bunyip*, who lived in deep holes in the watercourses, and punished—usually by drowning—all who trespassed on their domain, was firmly established in the minds of these early settlers, and many were the stories I heard of these mythical creatures.

Rocky River

On one occasion when I was about eleven years of age, one of the cattlemen showed me a deep waterhole in the Rocky River (point 1 on the Map) surrounded by a dense growth of reeds, which, he told me, was the home of a *bunyip*. He said that no one would dare to drink at this waterhole or to bathe in it, because of the fear of being pulled under and drowned by the mythical creature. My companion also said that on occasion he had heard the *bunyip* crashing through the reeds and bellowing like a calf. Although he had never seen the *bunyip*, my companion was fully convinced of its existence.

Broughton River

Some seven years later, when we were visiting the place where my father was born, he told me a story current in the district when he himself was a boy, of a *bunyip* which lived in a long narrow waterhole on the Broughton River (point 2 on the Map). At the same time he described how a local youth, wishing to disprove the ancient aboriginal belief, decided to dive into the home of the *bunyip*. After some persuasion, however, he allowed his companions to tie a line around his waist as a precautionary measure.

According to the story, when he had entered the water and did not come to the surface within a reasonable time, his companions, with some difficulty, pulled him to the surface. The venturesome youth claimed that without the rope he would have been drowned because something was holding him under the water.

This incident convinced everyone in the district at the time (considerably over a hundred years ago) that the *bunyip* in the waterhole, annoyed at the youth for his impertinence, had attempted to drown him.

Plate 2. Ayers Rock from the air; *a*, Uluru rock hole

These incidents of my childhood were almost forgotten until, almost thirty years later, the aborigines at Ayers Rock, shown in Plate 2, in the western deserts of central Australia (point 23 on the Map), told me similar stories of the mythical snakes who live in the permanent waters.

Wilpena Pound

The members of the Adnyamatana tribe of the northern Flinders Ranges of South Australia have two myths dealing with rainbow serpents, known to them as the *akaru*.

The first example is incorporated in the myth of the first circumcision ceremony, which was performed at Wilpena Pound (point 3 on the Map) during creation times; the second tells of the travels of an *akaru* in the rugged Gammon Ranges near Mt. McKinley (point 4).

The first myth describes how two *akaru*, husband and wife, knowing that a circumcision ceremony was about to take place at Wilpena Pound, traveled southward to destroy the whole party.

Waiting until the ceremony had been completed, the two *akaru* surrounded the participants in the ceremony and, by creating powerful whirlwinds, swept the whole party into their mouths, with the exception of the wild-turkey-man, Wala, the kingfisher-man, Yulu, and the initiate, all of whom fled in different directions. Figure 1 is an aboriginal drawing of this event. In the drawing, *a* indicates Wala, the wild-turkey-man, *b* Yulu, the kingfisher-man, and *c* the initiate.

After the bodies of the two *akaru*, lying head to head, were transformed into the steep walls that now surround Wilpena Pound, their spirits made a home in a waterhole at the entrance to the pound, where they became huge creatures of many colors with manes and beards "alla same billy goat."

Figure 1.   The *akaru* destroying the initiation party at Wilpena Pound

Later, these *akaru* left the waterhole and traveled eastward, each creating a home for itself, one in the Emu and the other in the Limestone Spring.

Gammon Ranges

The second myth describes how another *akaru* left Lake Frome and traveled along the Akurula Creek, where it first created the spring in its bed and then, moving westward, made another water supply in the rugged Gammon Ranges (point 4 on the Map), under which it now lives. The aborigines say that this *akaru* is not happy in its present home and often turns over to make itself more comfortable. This movement, according to the aborigines, is the cause of the mysterious subterranean rumblings often heard in those parts of the northern Flinders Ranges. The aborigines take special care to warn that *akaru* when they are approaching his waterhole in the Gammon Ranges, otherwise he may attack them.

Coward Springs

Basedow (1925: 269) refers to a large mythical snake who lives in an artesian water adjacent to the Coward Springs railway station on the edge of the Great Artesian Basin of northern South Australia (point 5 on the Map). The aborigines look upon the spring as the mouth of this giant snake and a hill nearby as its head.

Visiting aborigines are forbidden to drink at the waterhole unless accompanied by aborigines belonging to the same totemic country, who are the only ones who can guard them from the attack of the *akaru*.[2] Should any stranger break this law, the rainbow serpent of Coward Springs will so injure his spirit (not his body) that he will die.

Murray River

A fragment of an early myth recorded by Smyth (1878: 456) describes how the Murray River (point 6 on the Map) was created by a giant mythical snake who traveled from the head of the river to its mouth, forming the valley and the bed of the river.

The snake, however, in making this great excavation disturbed a crow who, disliking the alteration of the landscape, attacked the snake and cut him into many pieces.

---

[2]   One might project, from the ubiquitous myth of the rainbow serpent on the Australian mainland, that it could quite possibly have occurred in Tasmania as well. But, regretfully, the nineteenth-century European colonists who destroyed the aborigines as unnecessary vermin prevented us from finding this out.

VICTORIA

The Bunyip

Smyth (1878: 435–456) states that the earliest settlers of Victoria heard, from time to time and from natives far removed from each other, of mythical water-creatures which were so dreadful in aspect and voracious in their appetites for human beings that belief in them did much to keep the natives in their own country (point 7 on the Map). These mythical beings, who had various names but were principally known as *bunyip*, did not resemble any known creatures.[3]

The aborigines sometimes described these monsters as huge snakes of great length with large eyes and long ears. At other times they depicted them as dingolike creatures, as shown in Figure 2, or as birds, particularly emus, as shown in Figure 3. These *bunyip*, according to the aborigines, had various body coverings: scales, fur, or feathers.

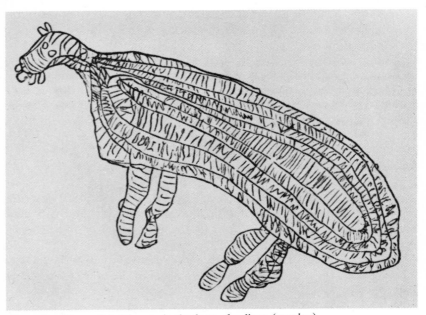

Figure 2.   The mythical *bunyip* in the form of a dingo (*turudun*)

[3]   This is a widespread belief; compare the myths associated with the *myndie* snake of Victoria, the *wanambi* of Piltadi, and the *wollunqua* snake of Warramunga in later sections.

Figure 3.   A drawing of a *bunyip* in the form of an emu (*gourke*)

The Mythical Snake (Myndie)

Smyth (1878:444) states that the aborigines of Melbourne described the mythical snake, the *myndie*, as long and thick and very powerful. But he was not quite like a snake. He had a large head and a triple-pointed tongue, which was only visible when he hissed and ejected poison.

This mythical snake, a rainbow serpent, lived on a mountain, Bukara-bunnal, near Wedderburn (north-northwest of Melbourne, point 8 on the Map), and drank at only one creek, Noelounum. The surface of the ground for some distance around the Bukara-bunnal Creek was covered with a substance like small white hailstones (probably lime-stone nodules); it was so hard that even the heaviest rain would not soften its surface, nor did any trees grow in the area. Also, any strange aborigines who ventured into this place would suffer either sickness or death.

The *myndie* was under the dominance of Pundel, the supreme creator, and when Pundel commanded him, the *myndie* would destroy aborigines both young and old. But he could do nothing by himself, Pundel must first tell him. He was known to all tribes in Victoria, and all tribes were known to him; and if anyone disobeyed his laws—failed to kill aborigines (presumably strangers) who trespassed on his country, or broke the laws of the tribe—Pundel would tell the *myndie* to make him ill or kill him, just as he thought fit.

The *myndie* could extend or contract his size when ordered by Pundel.[4] He could ascend the highest tree and hold onto a branch like a ring-tailed opossum, or he could leave his home and stretch his body across a great forest to reach any tribe, with his tail still in the Bukara-bunnal waterhole, as illustrated in Figure 4, an aboriginal drawing.

Figure 4. The *myndie* traveling by extending his body from his totemic waterhole, Noelounum, over the top of a forest, to a distant locality

The *myndie* was accompanied by many smaller creatures of his own kind, whom he sent out from time to time to carry diseases and afflictions to punish aboriginal tribes who had broken tribal laws. But, although the visits of these little creatures were very troublesome, they were not so dreaded as the visits of the *myndie* himself, who was large and powerful and from whom there could be no escape. All plagues were caused by the *myndie* or his little counterparts.

When the *myndie* was known to be in any district, the aborigines left as fast as they could. They did not stop to pick up their bags, weapons, or rugs, nor even to bury their dead. Some, affected by the *myndie*, lay down and died, but those who were able to run swiftly and escape never suffered from any sickness. These beliefs, of course, were those of the local aborigines.

One aboriginal tribe, however, the Muni-brumbrum, who belonged to the same country as the *myndie*, was in no danger.[5] The aborigines believed that the Muni-brumbrum could control the *myndie* by a wave of their hands or a movement of their fingers.

The Mythical Dingo (Turudun)

In Victoria the aborigines believed in the existence of a huge dingolike

---

[4]   Spencer and Gillen (1904: 399) recorded that the *wollunqua* snake could extend its body from the totemic waterhole in the Murchison Ranges to the place of ceremony, a distance of 150 miles.
[5]   According to other aboriginal groups of Victoria, the Muni-brumbrum are the only people who can set foot in the *myndie*'s country. This belief exists to a greater or lesser degree in many other parts of Australia.

creature, the *turudun*, which lived in the swamps and deep waterholes of the western country (point 9 on the Map) and made the nights hideous with its groanings and bellowings. No aboriginal would go near the waterholes of this mythical creature, knowing that the *turudun* would drown him.

The drawing in Figure 2 of a *turudun* was made in 1848 by an aboriginal, a member of the Murray River tribe. The aboriginal who saw the creature was so afraid that he did not notice either its covering or its habits.

The Mythical Emu (Gourke)

The aborigines were not only afraid of the serpent (*myndie*) who dwelt at Wedderburn (Bukara-bunnal), but also of the various mythical *bunyip* that lived in the swamps and waterholes in the western districts of Victoria.

A swamp on the Western Port plains (point 10 on the Map), which is never dry even in the hottest summer, is the home of a mythical being, the *gourke*, who has the form of an emu (Figure 3). This creature lives both in the deep waters of the swamp and in the mud on the bottom.

No aboriginal would bathe in this swamp, being fearful lest the *gourke* take him under the water and drown him. The drawing of the *gourke* in Figure 3 was made by a local aboriginal.[6]

WESTERN AUSTRALIA

Rainbow Serpent (Wogal)

Radcliffe-Brown writes:

In Western Australia I have been able to trace the belief in Rainbow-Serpents living in deep permanent waterholes throughout all the tribes from the extreme south-west as far north as the Ninety Mile beach and eastward into the desert. In the tribes around Perth [point 11 on the Map], the Rainbow-Serpent is called *wogal* and certain waterholes were pointed out as being the abode of this mythical creature. It is regarded as dangerous for anyone (except a medicine-man) to approach such a waterhole because the Serpent is likely to attack those who venture near its haunts. *Wogal* generally attacks females, and the person it attacks pines away and dies almost imperceptibly. . . . *Wogal* is supposed to have the same shape as that of a winged serpent (1926: 22).

---

[6] This drawing would appear to be incorrect, except that there are five localities in Australia where this mythical creature is depicted as an emu.

INGARDA. Radcliffe-Brown also states (1926: 22) that in the Ingarda tribe (point 12 on the Map) the serpent is called *kajura*. It lives in waterholes and is so feared by the natives that they will only approach the places where it lives with great care. The serpent is under the magical control of the medicine men of the rain totem, and it is only through the power of the serpent that they can make rain. Besides performing the regular rainmaking ceremonies, a member of the rain totem can also produce rain by simply visiting the pool in which the serpent lives.

In the whole of this region, quartz crystals (and in the inland parts, pearl shells) are regarded as possessing magical virtues and are particularly valuable in rainmaking.

SOUTHWESTERN AUSTRALIA. During the closing years of the last century, Mrs. Ethel Hassell kept a series of notes dealing with the aborigines of southwestern Australia (point 13 on the Map).

Many years later, Dr. D. S. Davidson bought those papers from Mrs. Hassell's estate and published them under their joint names. In the last paper (1936: 679) they describe a creature which, although its appearance differs from that of the traditional rainbow serpent, is almost certainly the same creature.

Mrs. Hassell's notes about the aborigines of southwestern Australia before they were destroyed by our white civilization are of particular ethnological value.

UNLOCALIZED. Calvert (1892: 35) includes a reference to a large mythical reptile: "There is also a famous snake called the *bunyip* (somewhat like our Sea-Serpent). It is some fifty feet long, with a snake-like head, and inhabits lagoons, rivers and swamps."

Although this description is limited and unlocalized, it indicates that the *bunyip* (or its equivalent) of western Australia (point 14 on the Map) possessed the same characteristics as the rainbow serpents elsewhere in Australia: it was of great length, it was snakelike in form, and it was associated with freshwater.

ANNA SPRINGS (*bulain*). Piddington (1930: 352) describes an enormous rainbow serpent, the *bulain*, that lives in the waterholes of the Karadjari tribe, whose country is adjacent to Anna Springs (point 15 on the Map). This mythical creature plays an important part in the mythology of the aborigines of the area. As these myths are not relevant to the subject, however, they will not be discussed.

According to the descriptions given by the aborigines, the most striking features of this creature, apart from its huge size, are its large eyes and long ears. According to Piddington, the *bulain* is not associated with the rainbow.

It is believed that serious consequences result from killing and eating a *bulain*. Either violent storms sweep the country, and those associated with the killing become ill; or, according to another version, the *bulain*, when placed on the fire, bursts, and the large quantity of water it contains drowns the offender.[7]

Figure 5.   The rainbow serpent (*unurugu*), Broome

BROOME (*unurugu*). The drawing shown in Figure 5, the work of a highly skilled fullblood aboriginal at Broome (point 16 on the Map), portrays an aboriginal hunter who speared a reptile (which, unknown to him, was the mythical water snake, the *unurugu*), dragged it from the swamp, killed the creature after a long struggle, and was preparing to cook it.

The hunter had just lit a fire and thrown the snake on top in order to remove the scales more easily, when he had a strong presentiment that the snake he had killed was a mythical creature, and that he would be punished for his actions. On looking upward, he saw that the spirit of the mythical snake had already created a heavy rainstorm to drown him.

But the hunter, who had already taken precautions by throwing a magic rope (*murdurgul*) into the sky, escaped by climbing to safety. The storm extinguished the cooking fire; the *unurugu* came to life again and escaped by entering the ground.

As soon as the flood subsided, the hunter, descending from the sky by

[7]   See the subsection, "The cooking of a rainbow serpent," in the next section, "Central Australia."

means of the magic rope, returned to his camp.[8] This story is from my own 1947 field notes.

CENTRAL AUSTRALIA

Rainbow Serpent (Wollunqua)

Spencer and Gillen (1904: 226–256) describe eleven colorful rituals, extending over many weeks, that were associated with an immense mythical snake, the *wollunqua*, of the Warramunga tribe. The home of this creature was in the Thapauerlu waterhole in the Murchison Ranges (point 17 on the Map).

The aborigines described the *wollunqua* as a serpent so huge that if it stood on its tail, its head would reach far into the heavens. The creature could also extend itself so far along the surface of the ground that, although the tail of the creature remained in the Thapauerlu waterhole in the Murchison Ranges, its head could reach the place of the ceremonies witnessed by Spencer and Gillen, about a hundred and fifty miles away.[9]

The aborigines were so afraid of this mythical creature that they used the term "water snake," rather than referring to it as *wollunqua*, fearing that if they did so, the creature would leave its waterhole in anger and swallow everyone. Nevertheless, the Warramunga men, in their ceremonies, have special songs that will—should the need arise—send the mythical snake back to its waterhole.

The *wollunqua* snake, who was created with the other totemic beings during the early days of the world, did not, like them, die and become a natural feature. The *wollunqua* is still looked upon by the natives as a living creature, capable of either befriending or harming them.

Throughout his wanderings during creation times, the *wollunqua* left behind at certain totemic places inexhaustible numbers of spirit-children, who have been, or will be, born as aboriginal infants.[10]

According to Spencer and Gillen (1904: 399), the *wollunqua* ceremonies, extending, as they do, over almost fifty days, were the most elaborate and impressive group of rituals they had ever seen. The two investigators described eleven ceremonies held during that long period, eight of them being ground drawings of considerable beauty.

---

[8]   An examination of the drawing and the myth shows that the beliefs are similar to those associated with the rainbow serpent: the *unurugu* can be killed and come to life again, it still had the power to punish its enemy, and it was associated with rain, thunder, and the magic rope. See also the cooking stories in the previous section.
[9]   See the description and drawing of the mythical *myndie* (Figure 4).
[10]   A number of other rainbow serpents mentioned in the survey left spirit-children behind at certain localities for the women.

It is unfortunate that space does not allow a fuller description of these rituals. Nevertheless, two of the most important of them are illustrated: Plate 3 shows the mound of the *wollunqua* snake, and Plate 4 the last episode in the series of rituals in which the *wollunqua* and a human companion return to their totemic waterhole.

Plate 3. Mound of the mythical *wollunqua* snake, Warramunga tribe (photograph by F. J. Gillen)

Plate 4. Ground drawing of the travel of the mythical *wollunqua* snake, Warramunga tribe (photograph by F. J. Gillen)

But there is a wide difference between the functions of the usual totemic rituals and of those of the *wollunqua* serpent. The totemic rituals were performed to secure the increase of some desirable food, but those associated with the serpent have no other purpose than to so please the mythical snake that it will stay quietly in the Thapauerlu waterhole and not wander about, causing trouble.

Spencer and Gillen also described how their aboriginal companions, when they reached the edge of the totemic waterhole, with bowed heads asked the *wollunqua* to remain quiet and to do them no harm, for they had brought with them two great white men to see where he lived and to tell them all about him. Spencer and Gillen stated that the aborigines believed implicitly that while the white men were being introduced the *wollunqua* was watching them from beneath the surface of the water.[11]

The Myth of the Rain-Man, Atain-tjina

Strehlow (1907–1920: 66), in the myth of "The rain-man, Atain-tjina, and the rainbow," describes the beliefs of the western Aranda tribe of central Australia (point 18 on the Map) concerning rain and its associated manifestations. This account is a slightly modified version:

According to the creation stories, a mythical creator, Atain-tjina, the most important of the rain-men of the Aranda tribe and a member of the *murunta* [water-snake] totem, made his camp on a distant seashore (unidentified). Many young rain-men (*patu-kapi*) also lived in the same camp.

From time to time, Atain-tjina would capture one of these young men and cast him into the sea, where he would be swallowed by an enormous water snake. During that time, the rain and the gleaming white scales (*takula*) with which the body of the water snake was covered entered the body, head, and limbs of the young snake-man. At the end of two days, Atain-tjina, the rain-man, would order the water snake to disgorge the body of the young rain-man into the dense smoke of a large fire.

After having been smoked for some time, the young *patu-kapi* traveled to an open plain where, taking from his body one of the scales which he had acquired while in the body of the snake, he rubbed it on a stone (unidentified). This ritual changed the young snake-man into a cloud that rose into the sky. In this form, the young man turned himself upside down and, letting his hair fall down, allowed the rain to pour from his body to the earth beneath. The young man, still in the form of a cloud, pulled out still more scales from his body and threw them in all directions. These became the lightning flashes. Thunder is the noise made by tadpoles as they run over the clouds before they fall to the ground with the raindrops.

It was then that the spirit of the rain-man, Atain-tjina, leaving his body asleep in his camp by the seashore, appeared in the sky as the rainbow.

[11] I myself had a similar experience when I was introduced to the *wanambi* at Piltadi, central Australia.

The young *patu-kapi*, still in the sky as a cloud, grasped the rainbow (the spirit of his master) and tied it firmly to his head. Together they traveled to the west, and the rain ceased.

There are often great droughts in central Australia which continue for long periods and cause extensive hardships. These droughts continue until the rain-man, Atain-tjina, again throws another young *patu-kapi* into the sea to be swallowed by the giant water snake and thus starts another rain cycle that will provide water for all.

Rainbow Serpent (Kalaia)

My 1942 field notes record a short myth that relates how, during the early days of the world, a small green snake, Kalatita, was transformed into a large *kalaia* [rainbow serpent],[12] which now lives in a waterhole in Standley Chasm (point 19 on the Map), a gorge in the western Macdonnell Ranges of central Australia. Kalatita has a mane and a beard, two characteristics of the desert *wanambi*.

Although the *kalaia* of Standley Chasm does not appear to be associated with rain, the aborigines stated that the small pearl-shell ornaments, *lonka-lonka*, worn by the snake, flash like lightning when he moves.[13]

MOUNT CONWAY. According to my 1942 field notes, some of the Aranda beliefs of central Australia associated with their mythical snakes, the *kalaia*, are similar to those associated with the *wanambi* of the desert people.

A *kalaia* inhabits a waterhole at Mount Conway (point 20 on the Map), which the aborigines will not visit, nor would they do any more than point out its approximate location to us. This *kalaia* kills any aboriginal who approaches too closely to its home by creating a powerful whirlwind that sucks the intruder beneath the waters. The whirlwind is so powerful that it will even break down the mulga trees on the hillsides. There did not appear to be any association, however, between the mythical *kalaia* of Mount Conway and the rainbow; the aborigines, when questioned, claimed that it was the rain that made the rainbow.

They did state, however, that at one time, when hunting near the *kalaia* waterhole at Mount Conway, they had heard loud booming noises which, they believed, were the angry voice of the *kalaia* warning them that they were too close to his home.

[12]	There are numerous references in aboriginal mythology to snakes, usually the brightly colored carpet snakes, being transformed into mythical rainbow serpents.
[13]	Spencer and Gillen (1904: 411) describe the *lonka-lonka* as a fragment of pearl shell traded from northwestern Australia. The flashing of this shell, when it is worn in a ceremony, is supposed to act as a love charm. The same type of pearl-shell ornament is used in the rainmaking ceremonies of the desert aborigines.

Rainbow Serpent (Wangiari)

My 1956 field notes describe a *wanambi*, or rainbow serpent, called Wangiari, who lives in a steep-sided spring, Bulgarin, situated in a short range about six miles east of central Mount Wedge (point 21 on the Map). This mythical creature, black in color and many yards in length, has large eyes, a beard, and a mane similar to that of a horse.

Wangiari, being of friendly disposition toward the aborigines of his own country, will allow them to drink from his water without harm; but, should any strangers endeavor to do so, the mythical serpent will become angry and, calling out with a loud voice (thunder), rise into the air in the form of a rainbow and destroy the intruder. The angry serpent will then create heavy storms of wind which will uproot the trees and, by blowing the water from the Bulgarin Spring into the air, drown everyone.

The calamities are unlikely to happen, however, because the *wanambi*, being afraid of fire, will, at the slightest smell of burning wood, retreat to his subterranean home under the Bulgarin Spring.

Rainbow Serpent (Naba-tjukurupa)

My 1960 field notes describe a permanent waterhole, Watelbring, in the Sidderley Ranges (point 22 on the Map), the home of a mythical serpent, a *naba-tjukurupa*. This mythical creature is many hundreds of yards in length and highly colored, with red, yellow, and blue stripes. The *naba-tjukurupa* has two large projecting teeth with which he bites the *kurunba* [spirit] of all who offend him and long hair but no beard; nor does he appear to be associated with the rainbow.

This serpent is not greatly feared by the aborigines who drink at Watelbring because, should they even throw a stone into the water-hole as they approach, the serpent will quickly retreat into large under-ground caverns beneath the water and allow the visitors to drink in safety.

Should, however, too many people visit Watelbring at one time, par-ticularly if they are boisterous, the *naba-tjukurupa* will create a whirlwind so large that it will gather the intruders together, drag them below the surface, and drown them.

Rainbow Serpent (Wanambi)

ULURU. Plate 5 shows Ayers Rock (point 23 on the Map). In its summit is the steep-sided rock hole, Uluru (indicated by *a* in Plate 2), which is the home of an enormous *wanambi* (Mountford 1965: 134). This mythical creature, who lives in huge caverns under the waters, is regarded as the most dangerous in the country. It is many hundreds of yards long and has an enormous head, long projecting teeth and a beard, and a skin which has the same colors as a rainbow, a form which the Ayers Rock *wanambi* often assumes.

Plate 5.   Ayers Rock, site of Uluru rock hole from the west

An aboriginal who drinks at Uluru without taking the precaution of first lighting a small fire on its rim or carrying a fire stick (as shown in Plate 1) will so offend the *wanambi* that it will rise into the air in the form of a rainbow and kill the intruder. As further punishment, the *wanambi* will take all the water, not only from the Uluru rock hole but also from all the other rock holes around the base of Ayers Rock.

The Ayers Rock *wanambi* is so feared that our old informant, Balinga, would not allow us to go near its rock hole, although he pointed out its position to us. He was sure that, had we disobeyed him, the great serpent would have killed us.

When we last visited Ayers Rock during 1961, all the rock holes were dry, and even Mutitjulda waterhole, on the southern side, considered to be one of the safe waters in the country, was almost exhausted. Munbun, my informant on that occasion, who had never seen this waterhole so low, was convinced that the *wanambi* of Uluru, probably angered by the behavior of some visitors at his rock hole, was taking away all the waters from Uluru as a punishment.

Plate 6.   Mount Olga, Katatjuta, from the west

Plate 7.   Walpa Gorge, Katatjuta

KATATJUTA. Mount Olga (Wanambi-pidi) (point 24 on the Map), rising over 1,800 feet above the surrounding plain, is the highest point in the Katatjuta group, shown in Plate 6.

According to my field notes, this monolith and the adjacent Walpa Gorge, shown in Plate 7, are the permanent home of an immense, highly colored *wanambi* with a flowing mane, a beard, and long projecting teeth. During the rainy season this mythical snake lives in one or another of the rock holes on the summit of Mount Olga, but during the dry season it makes its home in the Katatjuta waterhole on the eastern end of Walpa gorge. Should this waterhole dry up, as it often does at the end of the dry season, the *wanambi* will retire to his camp inside Wanambi-pidi until the rains again fill his waterholes.[14]

Plate 8.   Mount Olga, Katatjuta, from the east; the vertical marks *a* are the hair and beard of the *wanambi*

The vertical black stains on the eastern end of Wanambi-pidi, marked *a* in Plate 8, are looked upon as the transformed beard and hair of the mythical snake, and the many caves on its steep sides are believed to be places where he sometimes camped.

There is always a wind blowing in the Walpa Gorge (*Walpa* means "wind"). Sometimes it is mild, but on other occasions it reaches hurricane force. The aborigines contend that this wind is the breath of the *wanambi*, and should this mythical creature be offended, particularly by someone lighting a fire in the Walpa Gorge or by unauthorized strangers drinking at his waterhole, he will first cause violent storms of wind to issue from the

[14]   It is unusual for a *wanambi* to be dissociated from any form of water supply. It is possible that the aborigines believe that there are waterholes inside Wanambi-pidi.

mouth of the gorge, then kill the intruders by taking their spirits (*kuran*) from them. Therefore the aborigines are most circumspect in their behavior when passing through the Walpa Gorge.

MARATJARA SPRING. A creation story of the desert refers to the time when a number of *wanambi* at Maratjara Spring, western central Australia (point 25 on the Map), would not allow the sandhill snakes (that is, the pythons or *wararunkala*), the venomous saltbush snakes (*kulukudjari*), the brown snakes, and many others to drink from the Maratjara Spring.

First the sandhill snakes decided to kill all the *wanambi* at Maratjara so that they could drink when they wished. But after a short encounter, all but one of the *wanambi* left for another locality. The sandhill snakes and the one remaining *wanambi* at Maratjara made peace with each other and now all use the same water.

Nevertheless, the aborigines of the surrounding country still fear the remaining *wanambi* and always light a number of small fires near the Maratjara Spring before they drink.

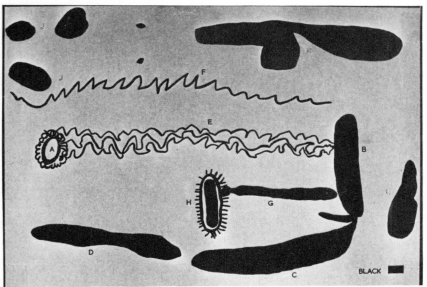

Figure 6.   The *wanambi* and the snakes at Maratjara Spring; see the text for explanation of the key

Figure 6 illustrates the myth. Oval *A* (left) indicates the camp of the *wararunkala* and other sandhill snakes; *B* (right) is Maratjara Spring, the camp of the *wanambi*, and *H*, another spring at Maratjara.

One hot day, when the sandhill reptiles were very thirsty, a *wararunkala* snake from camp *A*, creeping behind sandhills *C* and *D*, threw a boomerang at a *wanambi* in his camp at *B*, injuring him so badly that his urine (*G*), poured out and contaminated the water in Maratjara (*H*).

The other snakes at camp *A*, traveling along meandering lines (*E*), endeavored to capture the wounded *wanambi*, but he escaped and entered the spring (*H*), where he still lives.

The other *wanambi*, who were out hunting at the time, were terrified by the attack of the sandhill snakes on their companion and escaped to another distant waterhole.

Plate 9. Mount Conner, home of *wanambi*

MOUNT CONNER. My field notes record that at one time there were two *wanambi* at Mount Conner (point 26 on the Map), shown in Plates 9, 10, and 11. One, who lived at Atila Spring (marked *a* on Plate 10), was greatly feared, and another, who lived at Aneri Spring (point 27 on the Map, marked *a* on Plate 11), was not dangerous.

ATILA SPRING. There was once a spring halfway up the southern slopes of Atila (*a* in Plate 10) which, until a comparatively short time ago, was the home of a *wanambi*. He was so feared that the aborigines would not drink at the spring until they had warned him of their approach by lighting a number of small fires. These made the snake retreat to his home beneath the water.

This spring had been dry for some time due to the falling water table throughout the whole of the western deserts of central Australia, a result of the draining of water from the Great Artesian Basin. At the time of our visit, the opening of this *wanambi* water could still be seen, a small hole a few inches in diameter from which, at one time, the water used to flow. There was evidence, too, that the water was still there but inaccessible. The grass, although dry, was plentiful, and a small healthy bloodwood tree grew within twenty feet of the opening.

Plate 10.   Mount Conner; *a* was once the home of the stolen *wanambi*

Plate 11.   Mount Conner; *a* marks Aneri Spring, the home of a *wanambi*

The aborigines of Mount Conner believe that the *wanambi* who once lived in their waterhole had been stolen from them by the medicine men of the southern Pitjandjara tribe and placed in the Owellinna Spring of their own country so that they would have more water.

The older aborigines told me that at one time Owellinna was only a waterhole, but that after the Mount Conner *wanambi* had been added to it, the creek became a running stream, shown in Plate 12. Thus, since the water flow had increased in Owellinna Spring and Atila Spring had gone dry, it was reasonable for the aborigines at Mount Conner to assume that the people at Owellinna had stolen their *wanambi*.

Plate 12.   Owellinna Spring, new home of the stolen *wanambi*

The meandering design marked *A* in Figure 7 is the *wanambi* in his spring at Atila, and *B* and *D* are his mane and whiskers. The outer design *C, C* represents the outline of Atila; *F* and *G* are large rocks nearby, and *E* another large rock where the aborigines once rested before they had a drink at Atila Spring.

According to our informants, the medicine men at Owellinna released their *kuran* [spirits] to go to Mount Conner and bring back the *wanambi*. But before doing so, the *kuran* transformed themselves into strange beings called *marali*. This transformation took place in an unusual way: the *kuran* first changed themselves into eagle-hawks; then, turning themselves completely inside out, each thrust the whole of his body through his anus. The arms then became the legs and the legs the wings of the *marali*. Each *marali* also developed two large teeth on either side of his subincised penis which, when the transformation was complete, protruded through his mouth.[15] When the *marali* reached Mount Conner, they temporarily took the shape of small butterflies, entered the home of the *wanambi*, and, by gently rubbing his body with charcoal, made him feel lazy and sleepy. Then, by lighting very small fires, the *kuran* slowly forced

Figure 7.   The *wanambi* in Atila Spring; see the text for explanation of the key

the *wanambi* into the open. As soon as the head of the snake appeared at the mouth of the spring, the leading *marali*, *E* in Figure 8, thrust a sharpened human arm bone through his nose and straddled his head and was thus able to control his movements. As the serpent emerged still farther, other *marali* sat astride his body, holding on by their eagle-hawk claws and the teeth on their subincised penes, while others took hold of his beard and whiskers. The *marali* (*G*) who sat on the tail of the *wanambi* occupied an important position: it was his duty to keep the *wanambi* horizontal so that his tail would not drag on the ground.

When all was ready, the *marali* holding onto the body of the *wanambi* carried him through the air with their wings, while the spirit controlling his head guided the mythical snake toward the Owellinna water, some fifty miles east. But as they neared the end of their journey, the *marali* on the tail of the *wanambi* became careless and, temporarily losing control, allowed the tail to drag along the ground. To prove this statement, the aborigines showed us a path of broken and uprooted trees where a local cyclone had passed through the country. This, my informants explained,

[15]   Mountford and Tonkinson (1967: 374) describe dream-spirits of Jigalong who leave the body during sleep and travel from place to place.

was where the tail of the *wanambi* had struck the ground on its way to Owellinna. The *marali*, however, still in control of the *wanambi*, guided him to a crevice in the rocky hills and, placing his head in the opening, chanted a magical song that caused the crevice to open wide enough to

Figure 8.   Theft of the *wanambi* from Atila Spring; see the text for explanation of key

admit the *wanambi* to the interior of the hill. The opening then returned to its normal size.

The *marali*, well pleased with their effort, returned to their camp, which was still in darkness, and after transforming themselves first into the *kuran* of the medicine men, then into normal people, went to sleep. For the next few days the medicine men rested, either in the hot sun or beside a large fire, so that the water which they had absorbed by their contact with the *wanambi* would escape through their skins as perspiration.[16]

At the end of that time the medicine men, waiting until it was dark, went back to the place where they had left the *wanambi*, only to find that the water had not increased according to their expectations. Again transforming themselves into *marali*, the medicine men entered the home of the *wanambi* and, by hunting him closer to the entrance, made the water flow more freely.

Figure 8 shows the theft of the *wanambi* at Atila by the medicine men of Owellinna. *A* is Atila Spring, in which the *wanambi* (*C*) once lived, and

[16]   The same method was also used by the medicine man at Henbury to release the water absorbed by the young men who had cooked a *wanambi*.

U is the stream of water that once ran from the spring before the mythical snake was stolen. *D* is the head of the snake with its mane and beard; *E*, the *marali* man who held the bone through its nose; and *F*, one of the medicine men who assisted in hunting the mythical creature out of its home with small fires. *H*, *J*, *K*, *L*, *M*, *N*, *O*, *P*, *Q*, and *R* are other spirit-men straddling the *wanambi*, and *G* is the *marali* on the tail who was responsible for keeping the body horizontal. *B*, *S*, and *T* are bloodwood trees adjacent to Atila Spring.

TANAMI. Berndt and Berndt (1950: 183) record an interesting account and a drawing of a mythical serpent associated with a well in the Tanami area in northwestern South Australia.

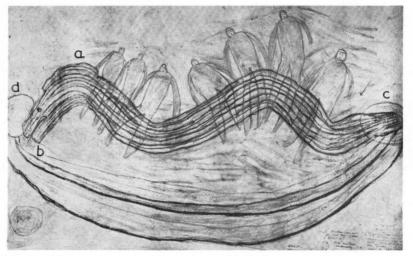

Figure 9.   Medicine men and rainbow serpent at Tjanbi Springs; see the text for explanation of the key

Figure 9, the drawing, is the work of an old Walbiri man, Munguldjungul. It depicts a mythical serpent, Jaruwari, who once camped at Tjanbi Spring near Tanami, marked *c* in Figure 9.

One day Jaruwari, hearing another rainbow serpent calling to him from Galibina (marked *a*), left his camp at Tjanbi Spring and, carrying a number of medicine men (*nori-neri*) on his back, traveled to Galibina to meet him. But on arrival at his destination, Jaruwari found that the other rainbow serpent had gone. He then continued his journey to Mung-gadura well (circle, lower left, in Figure 9), which he made his permanent home.

The crescent-shaped design below the body of the serpent Jaruwari is the rainbow (*barari*) from which the medicine men receive their power, either to heal the sick or to punish enemies.

ANERI SPRING. My notes describe a harmless *wanambi* in Aneri Spring (situated on a small claypan about four miles south of Mount Conner, point 27 on the Map, marked *a* on Plate 11).

The local aborigines can drink from this water without any precautions, and even strangers will not be attacked, although, should they become too boisterous, the mythical snake will show his disapproval by a low rumbling sound.

Figure 10. *Wanambi* at Aneri Spring

This *wanambi*, illustrated in a finger painting, Figure 10, traveled to Aneri Spring from the northern Musgrave Ranges. He made his first camp at Atila, the design in the middle of the finger painting, but, finding this place unsuitable, continued his journey until he reached the Aneri Spring, the three circles on the lower edge of the painting, and made it his permanent home. Occasionally, however, the *wanambi* left Aneri Spring and made long journeys around the base of Mount Conner. His tracks are symbolized by the large concentric circles. At the close of the creation period, the tracks over which the *wanambi* had traveled became the rocky outcrops and sandhills that now surround Mount Conner.

While making those journeys, the mythical snake often saw the stars of *kunkarangkalpa* [the Pleiades] and of *nirunja* [Orion]. The camps of these two groups of celestial beings are represented by the five small circles at the top of Figure 10.

MULTJIBILI. Three *wanambi* of entirely different temperaments live in an unlocalized group of waterholes adjacent to the Mann Ranges (point 28 on the Map).

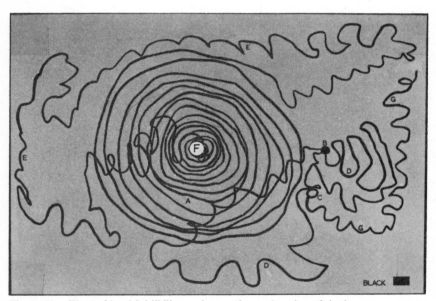

Figure 11. *Wanambi* at Multjibili; see the text for explanation of the key

One of these *wanambi*, called Muldjau, whose home is in the Wanja waterhole, marked *F* in Figure 11, often makes long journeys over the countryside; the meandering lines *E, E* and the spiral *A* indicate his track. He is not particularly unfriendly.

The two other *wanambi*, however, one named Pikari who lives in the waterhole marked *B*, right, and an unnamed one who lives in the Multji-bili waterhole, marked *C*, right, are dangerous. If an aboriginal is so foolish as to drink at either of these waterholes, the resident *wanambi* will pull him under the water and drown him. *D*, *D*, and *G*, *G*, are the tracks of these *wanambi*.

Should any aboriginal even go too near one or another of these dangerous *wanambi*, they will so confuse him with a whirlwind or blind him with a rainbow that they can easily capture and destroy his spirit (*kuran*). A rainbow in the sky, even though it belongs to some other *wanambi*, is not as dangerous as these two belonging to Multjibili.

MANDARUKA ROCK HOLE. A story is told of a conflict at Mandaruka between two *wanambi* and two women of the red-ochre totem, illustrated in Figure 12.

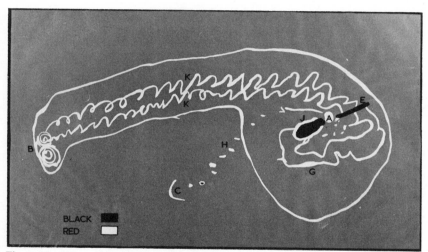

Figure 12. *Wanambi* at Mandaruka rock hole; see the text for explanation of the key

On one occasion, when the women were passing the Mandaruka rock hole at Fosters Cliffs (point 29 on the Map), they saw by the tracks on the ground that the two *wanambi* who lived there had just gone out hunting. The meandering lines *K*, *K* represent their tracks, and *B* shows where they had rested.

Meanwhile, the two red-ochre women, after blocking up the entrance to the Mandaruka rock hole, *A*, with stones, camped at *C*, where, in order to frighten the *wanambi* back to their rock hole, they made a smoke by burning their pubic hairs.[17] When the *wanambi* at *B* detected the odor of fire, they returned quickly to their rock hole at *A*.

At the same time, the women left their camp at *C* (see lines of footmarks, *H*) and attacked the *wanambi* with large sticks, *E*, but were unable to injure them in any way. In desperation, the women tried to hold the

[17] As mentioned earlier, all mythical snakes are afraid of fires and smoke.

wanambi who, at *G*, pulled themselves away without any difficulty and reentered their rock hole through a small opening which the women had missed. The aborigines claim that there are no *wanambi* at Mandaruka at the present time, nor do they know where they have gone.

The tracks *K*, *K* of the *wanambi* have since been transformed into Fosters Cliffs; the stick *E*, used by the women, into a gap in the range; and the bodies of the two red-ochre women into a pile of boulders, *J*, at the mouth of the Mandaruka rock hole, *A*.

The Friendly Rainbow Serpent at Amata

This myth was related by an aboriginal woman, Nanindja:[18]

Here is an old man living by himself at Amata [point 30 on the Map]; all the people had gone on a long way, but one young man was thinking to himself, "I want to go back and see my father; my father is a long way away."

So here he is getting up and taking his spear and walking, walking. . . . He sees a kangaroo and spears it. So he's killing the kangaroo and carrying it to the rock hole. Then he's leaving the kangaroo safe in the tree and making a fire and cooking the kangaroo here. Then he's going looking for water but the waterhole is dry. So he's eating some kangaroo and leaving some and sleeping.

In the morning he's getting up and walking, walking . . . again and seeing a kangaroo sitting, he spears and kills it. So he's cooking and eating and looking again for water at another waterhole, but it is dry too. So he's very sad and very thirsty, so thirsty he can't be eating his kangaroo. So he's walking, walking . . . and carrying the kangaroo . . . then "Ooh!" what is there? tracks of dog always going this way. . . . So he follows, follows, follows and sees . . . water here, *big* water with nice green around. Then he's drinking and drinking and coming back and sitting here by the tree. The big snake, *wanambi*, is inside the waterhole. The young man is sitting feeling sad; resting, very tired; nearly sleeping.

Then thinking of cooking some kangaroo he looks around—"Ooh"! there's *wanambi*, the big snake, in the tree looking at him. So he's sitting, not moving—too frightened—too tired—thinking "*Wanambi* will kill me today." He thinks it's too late to run so he's just waiting, waiting for *wanambi* to get him.

Then he's thinking "Why is *wanambi* quiet? *Wanambi* is just looking at me, not moving. I will cook my kangaroo." So he's getting wood to make a fire; then he's cooking and sitting down and giving some to *wanambi*. *Wanambi* eats and wants more and more. The young man gives him more and is feeling very happy. "I like *wanambi*. I want to keep *wanambi* with me," he thinks. So he follows *wanambi* to the waterhole and is building a *wiltja* [shelter] near the tree. Then *wanambi* is coming to the *wiltja* and looking in. The young man thinks "*Wanambi* would like to sleep with me." So he lights a big fire and they sleep. Here's *wanambi* curled up in the *wiltja*, sleeping.

They're living here a long time; every day the young man giving food to *wanambi*. One day the young man goes hunting, following the kangaroo a long way. Coming back in the afternoon he finds *wanambi* [the water] has gone.

Wanambi had been waiting, waiting, thinking "Where is the young man?

[18]   This myth was collected by W. T. Nichol (personal communication, 1966).

Maybe he's lost. I want to follow." So *wanambi* followed but lost the man's tracks and went another way. The young man, coming back to his camp, says "Where's *wanambi* gone?" So he follows *wanambi*'s tracks till he's near another waterhole where he sees *wanambi* has gone underground. So he's trying to pull him out by the tail. He's pulling, pulling, but it's another *wanambi*, a bad one, that's coming out and killing and eating him.

So here is this waterhole with tracks of two *wanambi*—one, the quiet one, and the other a strange and bad one.

The Cooking of a Rainbow Serpent

My field notes describe an incident at Henbury (point 31 on the Map) which is illustrated in Figure 13: when a number of young Puraia rat-men were out hunting (tracks at *J*, left center), they saw the tracks at *M* (lower center) of a young *wanambi* (which the rat-men had mistaken for a carpet snake) who had returned to its camp in a rock hole at *L* (black-and-white spiral, lower right).

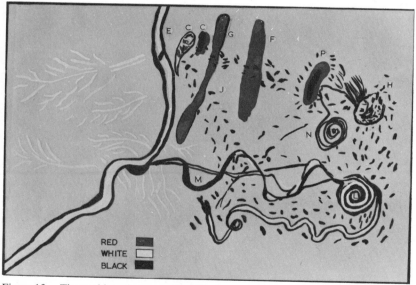

Figure 13.   The cooking of a *wanambi* at Henbury; see the text for explanation of the key

The rat-men pulled the *wanambi* from the rock hole and dragged it to *N*, then to *H* (right), where they endeavored to cook it.

They first made a fire of broom bush (acacia), but the water oozing from the body of the *wanambi* put it out. They then tried a number of other woods—desert oak, mallee, corkwood, mulga, and ironwood—but with the same result; the fire was extinguished each time by the water escaping from the body of the mythical snake. The hunters then tried samphire, a particularly fleshy-leafed plant that grows only in the swamp-lands, and with this wood they succeeded in making a fire that cooked the *wanambi*[19]

The youths carried the cooked food to their camp at *P*, where they ate most of it, the black lines on the periphery of the oval design *H* indicating where the rat-men seated themselves. Then, taking the remainder of the *wanambi* with them, the young rat-men set out for their camp at *E* (upper left). But as they were passing over a sandhill *F*, they felt their legs getting stiff and tired, and by the time they had reached sandhill *G*, they saw small snakes surrounded by rainbows traveling beside them. Long before they had reached their camp at *E*, the rat-men had discarded the remainder of the *wanambi* and were lying stiff and rigid on the ground.

When the medicine men of the Puraia saw the state of the youths, they guessed what had happened and first killed all the young *wanambi*; then, laying the youths on the ground, they extracted all the water grass from their bodies. The medicine men then placed the young men between the two large fires at *C* and *C* and kept them there until the water absorbed from the *wanambi* had been drained from their bodies as perspiration.[20] This final treatment restored them to good health.

PILTADI. A long involved myth associated with the Piltadi rock hole on the eastern end of the Mann Ranges (point 32 on the Map) deals with a quarrel between two *wanambi* and their wives.

The women had dug a trench several miles long in order to capture two large snakes for food, although the women did not know that their *wanambi* husbands, in revenge, were coaxing them to perform a useless task.

At one place among the rocky hills, the elder sister left the trench she had been excavating to get another digging stick because the one that she was using had become too short.

She had just returned to her task when she saw the large coils of her *wanambi* husband emerging from the hole she had been digging. Ter-rified at the sight, the woman threw her newly sharpened digging stick at the mythical reptile, piercing his side and injuring him severely. The wounded *wanambi*, although suffering great pain and with the digging stick still protruding from his side, chased his wife until he caught and swallowed her.

The body of this *wanambi* has since been transformed to an aged, heavily gnarled bloodwood tree, shown in Plate 13, with a dead branch,

[19]   See also Piddington (1930) for the beliefs associated with the cooking of rainbow serpents.
[20]   Compare the myth of the *wanambi* at Owellinna and the method of releasing water from the bodies of the medicine men in the subsection on Atila Spring.

marked *a*, protruding from its side. This branch was once the digging stick thrown by the wife, and the protuberances at the bottom of the trunk, marked *b*, represent the woman inside the body of her husband.

Plate 13. The bloodwood tree at Piltadi which represents the body of the elder *wanambi*

This tree is so greatly feared that no aboriginal dares to go near it, much less touch the trunk. Should anyone foolishly disobey this taboo, he becomes feverish, with pains all over his body. The medicine man, knowing the cause of his sickness, then places the sick man between two large fires until the water he has absorbed from the *wanambi* has escaped as perspiration from his body. After this treatment, the patient recovers.

The two brothers and their wives now live in Piltadi as *wanambi*, huge creatures with manes and beards and highly colored skins like carpet snakes. They are dangerous to all strangers who visit Piltadi.

When for any reason these *wanambi* become enraged, they transform themselves into rainbows, paralyze all intruding strangers, and take them beneath the waters of Piltadi.

The owners of Piltadi can drink freely at their water, although they must announce their arrival; but should thirst compel strangers to do so when there are no local aborigines to accompany them, they light fires the whole length of Piltadi Gorge as they travel and at the same time shout their names loudly to announce their presence. The fires and the shouting so alarm the *wanambi* of Piltadi that they retreat beneath its waters, thereby allowing the visitors to drink without harm.

Plate 14.   Piltadi rock hole, home of *wanambi*

Because we were strangers, one of the aboriginal owners of Piltadi, fearful that the *wanambi* might make us ill, suggested that my companion and I should not go near the rock hole until he could come with us. Later, we both stood on the edge of Piltadi, shown in Plate 14, and looked down at the black putrid water while our guardian, Tjanjundina, spoke to the great serpents beneath the water and asked them not to harm us. Tjanjundina explained that my companion, Lauri, was already his tribal son and that I, who was already a "little bit blackfellow" was the elder brother of his wife. Needless to say we suffered no harm.[21]

---

[21]   This introduction to the Piltadi *wanambi* ranks among my strangest experiences among the aborigines, yet it is not unique. Spencer and Gillen (1904: 253) were both introduced, with great solemnity, to the *wollunqua* serpent of the Warramunga tribe.

EASTERN COASTS OF AUSTRALIA

Radcliffe-Brown (1930) states that throughout the tribes of the New England tableland of New South Wales, certain waterholes (unlocalized) are taboo as bathing places. Some of these are inhabited by *karie*, rainbow serpents who swallow their victims whole; others contain a mythical creature, a *gouage*, resembling a featherless emu, which sucks down in a whirlpool anyone who dares to bathe in its waters; or another creature, a *miriwula*, which somewhat resembles a dingo.

Wentworth (Wawi)

According to Mathews (1904) the Wiratjuri tribe at Wentworth on the Darling River (point 34 on the Map) believe that a huge serpentlike creature, a *wawi*, lives in burrows in the banks of the deep waterholes. His wife and children camp nearby, but not at the same place. This mythical serpent is able to vary his size from a few inches in length to prodigious proportions. The dark streak in the Milky Way toward the Southern Cross is one of the manifestations of this mythical serpent.

It is the *wawi* who teaches the medicine men all the songs and dances for the new ceremonies. When a medicine man decides to visit the *wawi*, he paints himself entirely with red ochre and waits until there is a thunderstorm. He then follows the rainbow until he finds a deep waterhole at its end, the home of the *wawi*. Here he is met by the mythical serpent, who takes him to his home under the water and teaches him the new songs and dances. The medicine man repeats the complete ceremony many times to be sure he has learned it and then returns to his people.

When the tribesmen see him coming with his body all decorated, they know that he is returning from the *wawi* with a fresh ceremony. All the initiated men paint their bodies with colored ochres decreed by the *wawi* and travel to their ceremonial ground, where they all sing and dance together.

According to the men of the Wiratjuri tribe, it is by this means that they acquire their new ceremonies.

Barwon River (Kurrea)

Mathews (1899: 20) describes a large sheet of water several miles long, the Boobera Lagoon, on the New South Wales side of the Barwon River (point 35 on the Map). Some parts of this lagoon are deep, and in one particular place, so the natives claim, it is bottomless. In this deeper portion is the home of the *kurrea*, a snakelike monster of enormous proportions.

The *kurrea* cannot travel on dry land, so when he wishes to leave the lagoon, he forms a channel by tearing up the ground on its banks, thereby allowing the water to flow and bear him along. By this means the *kurrea* can float himself wherever he wants to go. The aborigines will point out many shallow channels around the Boobera Lagoon (dry except in time of floods) which, the natives believe, were formed by the *kurrea* when he traveled around the country during ancient times.

Should any aboriginal swim in the Boobera Lagoon, or sit on the bank fishing, or, worse still, paddle his canoe in pursuit of waterfowl, the *kurrea* will attack and devour him. The fear of this mythical serpent caused serious shortages because fish and waterfowl formed a considerable part of the aboriginal diet.

Long ago there was an aboriginal, Toolalla, of the Barwon River, who was a skilled hunter and decided to destroy the mythical snake and thereby rid the people of their enemy. So one day, armed with the best of his weapons, he stood on the bank of the waterhole and watched for his enemy. It was not long before he saw it swimming toward him. But, in spite of the fact that the weapons of Toolalla were new and sharp and that he himself was a skilled hunter, he could not injure the mythical creature.

When Toolalla saw that his weapons had no effect on his antagonist he tried to escape, but the *kurrea*, forming a channel across the plain in the usual way, followed at great speed.

The snake was gaining rapidly on Toolalla who, after making strenuous efforts, climbed a tall tree and thereby escaped. Disappointed, the giant snake returned to the Boobera Lagoon, where it is still a danger to the aborigines who fish or hunt in its waters. It is recorded that the children of the *kurrea*, called *gowarke*, resemble gigantic emus with black feathers and red legs (see Figure 3).

Narran River

During the later days of the last century, Mrs. K. Langloh Parker (1905) recorded the only information we have on the Euahlayi tribe of north-western New South Wales (point 37 on the Map).

She left behind, however, but few details of the myths of the rainbow serpent and allied creatures. She mentions that several waterholes on the Narran River are said to be inhabited by *kurrea*, crocodiles,[22] who swallow their victims whole, and by a featherless emu, *gowargay*, who sucks down in a whirlpool anyone who dares to bathe in his water supply. These

[22] Mathews (1899: 77) refers to the *kurrea* as a mythical serpent. This is likely to be correct.

creatures bear strong resemblances to the rainbow serpents described elsewhere in this survey.

Brisbane River

Howitt (1904: 398), in a somewhat confused account, states that the medicine man of the Turrbul tribe cut the stem of the rainbow where it was being held to the bottom of the Brisbane River (point 38 on the Map).[23] This was the only section of the Brisbane River where it happened, and then only when the rainbow had placed itself in a favorable position.

The aborigines believe that the rain squalls which accompany the rainbow have been sent by the medicine man (*kundri*), who can also clear away thunderstorms by throwing fire sticks at them.

Bloomfield River (Yero)

McConnel (1930: 348) describes a number of myths, some of them fragmentary, from northern Queensland. On the Bloomfield River (point 39 on the Map), where the local tribe had occupied their territory continuously for many years, a number of these myths were intact.

A rainbow serpent, the *yero*, is believed to inhabit the long, deep pools that connect the many waterholes and rapids of a stream, the Roaring Meg, that rises from a rugged mountain and flows into Bloomfield River.

It is considered dangerous to swim in these waterholes, and stories are told of men who, attempting to do so, were pulled this way and that by the *yero*.[24] This mythical creature, described as a huge eel or a serpent, is not deadly, just dangerous. It has a large head with red hair and a big mouth, out of which the rapids are said to emerge. Its body is striped in many colors. The identification of the rainbow with the *yero* explains its many-colored body and red hair.

The two storm birds, *kirwajua*, who live in the adjacent rocks, are the parents of the thunder-man, the *djaramali*. The storm bird is so sacred that no one would dare to kill or eat it. If anyone were to commit such an act, heavy rain would fall and flood the land, and everybody would be drowned.

---

[23] The reason for this was not recorded.
[24] This experience was similar to that of the young man who dived into the *bunyip* hole in the Broughton River in South Australia, told earlier.

Boulia (Kanmare)

According to Roth (1903: 29), some of the medicine men of the Boulia district of Queensland (point 40 on the Map) obtain their power through the instrumentality of the *kanmare*, a huge supernatural water snake with a manelike head of hair. It is he who drowns people. Should a man be fishing at a riverside, the *kanmare* will "point" a death bone at him, of course at such a distance and under such circumstances that the fisherman does not know that it is taking place. But as the night shades begin to fall, the victim sees the dreaded monster undulating upon the surface of the water. That night he goes to sleep as usual, but in the morning he feels sick. In the next four to five days the victim is attended by a medicine man, who removes from the patient's inside the pebbles, flint, bone, etc., that the *kanmare* put there. After this treatment the individual recovers and becomes a "doctor" himself.

Pennefather River (Andrenjinja)

Roth (1903: 10) also states that the natives of the Pennefather River, North Queensland (point 41 on the Map), regard the rainbow as a brightly colored snake who comes to stop the rain which has been willfully made by their enemies. Both the rainbow and the snake are called *andrenjinja*. The same writer also states that the Proserpine River natives have a belief that rain is made from quartz crystals obtained by the medicine men at a spot where the rainbow touches the earth.

Kabi Tribe (Takkan)

The Kabi tribe (Roth 1903: 10), at point 42 on the Map, believed that the rainbow, the *takkan*, lived in the deepest waterholes; he was regarded as being a combination of fish and snake. When visible as a rainbow, the *takkan* was supposed to be passing from one waterhole to another. He possessed terrific power and could shatter the forests and the mountains and, if he felt disposed, kill the aborigines.

Nevertheless, the *takkan* would do a good turn to one who already possessed many *kundir bonggon* [quartz crystals] in his body and who would therefore be powerful in magic.

Sometimes when one of these medicine men was asleep on the banks of the *takkan*'s waterhole, he would become aware of a prickly sensation in his limbs. This would indicate to him that the *takkan* was about to take him to his home under the water and extract the quartz crystals (*kundir*) from his body to replace them with a magic rope (*bukkar*) which would make him especially powerful in the realms of magic. The next morning when the medicine man woke up, he would be full of life and energy. Because of his dealings with the *takkan*, the rainbow-man, that medicine man would become a magician of great power.

Barron River (Kurra)

There is a belief among the aborigines of Cairns, at point 43 on the Map, (R. S. Edwards, personal communication) that a mythical dingolike creature, the *kurra*, about three feet high, lives with his wife and children in a cave under the sandy bottom of the Zumbuli waterhole. This cave extends into the center of an adjacent hill. Plate 15 shows a group of rocks on the edge of the waterhole, the largest of them being about eight feet in height, which is the metamorphosed family of the spirit dingoes who live either in the water of Zumbuli or in the cave under its surface. It is sometimes possible, if the water is clear, to see their tracks on the sandy bottom. If anyone should damage these rocks, great cyclones will issue from them and destroy everyone and everything.

Plate 15.   Waterhole of the spirit dingo, the *kurra*, at Cairns

Should the aborigines ask the permission of the *kurra*, the spirit owner, before they go fishing in the Zumbuli waterhole, he will allow them to catch all the fish that they require.

It is considered dangerous for anyone, aboriginal or European, to bathe in the Zumbuli waterhole, because he may be pulled under the water by the mythical dingo and drowned.

Sometimes during the day people swim in this waterhole and are not taken, and sometimes they are—one can never be sure. But anyone who swims at night is pulled down by the *kurra* and is never seen again. According to aboriginal gossip, the spirit dingo has taken at least two Europeans and one aboriginal boy within the last seven years.

Brisbane (Kuremah)

Palmer (1884: 291) refers to a belief from Brisbane (point 44 on the Map) in two carpet snakes, or *kuremah*, of immense size—about forty miles long—who live either in the world of the dead or on the road along which the ghosts of dead aborigines travel. These monsters are feared.

The same author also mentions certain other deep waterholes which the living aborigines will neither enter nor approach, for fear of some evil or dangerous being dwelling therein. It is likely that these are also rainbow serpents.

Darling River (Neittee *and* Jautta)

Radcliffe-Brown (1930: n. 2) records that the members of the Bakanji tribe of the Darling River (point 45 on the Map) cherish a superstitious belief in the existence of a pair of snakelike water creatures (*neittee* and *jautta*) with huge teeth, who have a special craving for aborigines.

NORTHERN TERRITORY OF AUSTRALIA

Elsey Station (Rakiniti)

There is a highly colored serpent, the *rakiniti*, with a mane and a beard, who lives in the swamps of Elsey Station on the upper reaches of the Roper River (point 46 on the Map). This mythical creature is greatly feared because, when annoyed over the breaking of some taboo, it creates violent whirlwinds which sweep the spirit of the miscreant into the air, to be destroyed by the rainbow. The aborigines claim that the bodies of their companions are never seen again, but as the nearby Roper River is infested with saltwater crocodiles, it is likely that the *rakiniti* is blamed for the disappearances of aborigines who were actually captured by these reptiles.

If, however, especially during stormy weather, the aborigines think that the mythical serpent is about, they will chant songs which will so please the serpent that he will control the rainbow and thus protect the aborigines from danger. The *rakiniti* also brings the spirit-children to the women.

Larrimah (Munga)

There is another mythical serpent, the *munga*, who lives in a waterhole about ten miles west of Larrimah (point 47 on the Map), who becomes particularly annoyed when strange aborigines visit his water supply, according to my 1942 field notes.

This serpent is armed with a long stone knife (like a sword, according to the aborigines) and a boomerang, which he can throw from remarkable distances with great accuracy. The serpent at Larrimah is highly colored and has a mane and a beard.

Roper River

My 1942 field notes also record the fragment of a myth dealing with an unnamed rainbow serpent whose home is at the mouth of the Roper River (point 48 on the Map). It too is highly colored with a mane and a beard.

The aborigines believe that if a man swims too far from shore, the serpent, making a rumbling noise, will pull him under the water and drown him. Later, the rainbow goes beneath the water and quarrels with the mythical serpent over the possession of the body. The rainbow usually wins and brings the body to the surface within a few days.

Arnhem Land (Bilumbira)

The rainbow serpents of northeastern Arnhem Land are highly colored, dangerous creatures with long projecting teeth (Mountford 1956: 351). They are reputed to be over fifty feet in length. During the dry season, the *bilumbira* live in a group of submerged rocks on the sea floor between Cape Arnhem and Port Bradshaw (point 49 on the Map). Should anyone paddle a canoe nearby, the *bilumbira* will rise to the surface and with their long teeth destroy both the canoe and its occupant.

When the wet season starts, the *bilumbira* leave their home at the bottom of the sea and create large thunderclouds in which they travel. The thunder is their voice and the lightning their tongue. The aborigines claim that during the wet season there are always thunderclouds over the home of the *bilumbira* at Cape Arnhem.

Figure 14.   The *bilumbira*, a rainbow serpent, traveling in the thunderstorm

Figure 14 illustrates a *bilumbira* serpent traveling in a thunderstorm. The pyramidal designs on either side of the painting symbolize thunderstorms "growing up." The cross-hatching on the small rectangles marked *a* and *b* indicates falling rain, and the two stingrays in the center of the rain are traveling to the swamps to give birth to their young.

Liverpool River

THE WUNUNGA. The lightning snakes or *wununga* (Mountford 1956: 366) of the Liverpool River area (point 50 on the Map), who live in the sky during the wet season, can often be seen passing from one cloud to another in the form of lightning. During the dry season, the *wununga* are dangerous snakes of the jungle who before they bite an aboriginal eat the leaves of the *memin* vine (unidentified) to make their venom more deadly. The young of the *wununga* also live in the jungle, but when they become adult they, like their parents, go into the sky during the rainy season.

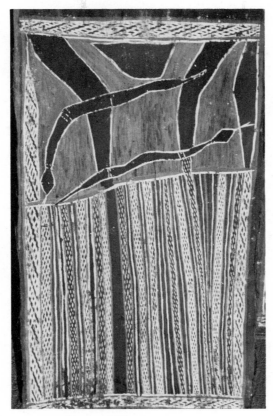

Figure 15.   Two *wununga*, Liverpool River

Figure 15 shows two *wununga* snakes passing from one cloud to another. The light gray designs at the top of the painting represent three thunderclouds, from the bottom of which rain is falling (parallel cross-hatched lines). The black vertical lines to the left are symbolical of the wet-season wind, the *bara*.

The *wununga*, although without the traditional mane, beard, and highly colored body, are still associated with the wet season with its lightning, monsoon winds (*bara*), and thunderclouds. The association between rainbow serpents and venomous snakes, however, is unusual.

THE WALA-UNDAJUA. I described (Mountford 1956: 210) another light-ning snake, the *wala-undajua*, shown in Figure 16, who sleeps in a large freshwater pool, Nandjajuba, on the Liverpool River (point 51 on the Map). As the wet season develops, the *wala-undajua* wakes up, leaves his pool, and travels across the sky in the thunderstorms. With his long arms, which are the lightning flashes, he strikes the earth beneath, splitting the trees, setting the grass on fire, and frightening, sometimes killing, the native people.

Figure 16.   The lightning snake, the *wala-undajua*, Liverpool River

The decorative painting reproduced in Figure 16 illustrates the lightning-man, the *wala-undajua*, lying across the sky. His head is at the upper right and his genitals, much enlarged, at the lower left. The mean-dering lines attached to the lightning-man are his arms, and the circles with radiating lines are the stars showing in the sky after the storm has passed.

THE NARAMA. A group of rocks at the mouth of the Liverpool River (point 52 on the Map) is the home of a rainbow serpent, the *narama*, and her sons (Mountford 1956: 211). Figure 17 shows the *narama*, second from the left, and her four sons; all are highly colored with large ears and manes but no beards.

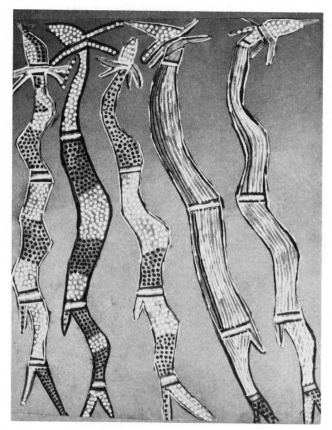

Figure 17.   The *narama* and her sons, Liverpool River

The *narama* becomes so annoyed when a stranger goes near her waterhole that she "bites" his spirit and he dies. Then, rising into the sky in the form of a rainbow, she creates clouds and rain.

Western Arnhem Land

THE GURUGUDJI. This myth from western Arnhem Land is another example of an emu who was later transformed into a mythical being with all the characteristics of a rainbow serpent. The myth describes how, at one time, two men were out hunting at Kabawudnar in Arnhem Land (point 53 on the Map), when they saw an emu which, unknown to them, was the mythical emu-man, the *gurugudji* (Mountford 1956: 212), illustrated in Figure 18. Creeping up, the hunters rushed at the mythical creature, one man grasping it by the neck and the other by the head. But the emu-man escaped, changed himself into a rainbow serpent, and swallowed the two hunters.

Figure 18.   The *gurugudji* [spirit-emu] and the two hunters

This rainbow serpent, the transformed emu-man, who appears in the sky in the form of a rainbow, is feared by the native people, because, should they inadvertently mistake him for an emu, he will swallow them as he once did the other hunters.

THE NGALJOD. The rainbow serpent called the *ngaloit* (Mountford 1956: 290) bears many resemblances to other mythical snakes in the same area: the *ngaljod* recorded by the Berndts (1970: 20) and the *numereji* reported by Spencer (1914: 290). It is evident that all the authors were referring to the same mythical creature by different names. To avoid confusion in nomenclature, however, I have chosen to use the Berndts' *ngaljod* in preference to *ngaloit*.

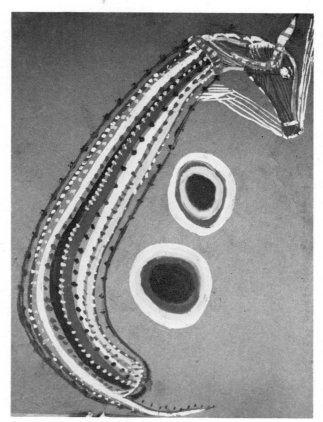

Figure 19.   The *ngaljod*, western Arnhem Land

The *ngaljod*, who lives in Gudjamandi waterhole (point 54 on the Map) only during the dry season, is highly colored and has a luxuriant growth of whiskers and long teeth, as shown in Figure 19. During the monsoon rains, the *ngaljod* ascends into the sky in the form of a rainbow. The circles to the right in Figure 19 represent boulders on the shores of the totemic waterhole.

The mythical rainbow serpents of western Arnhem Land are annoyed by the sound of children crying; there are numerous references in the myths to this characteristic, a single example of which is given in the next section.

During creation times a mythical individual, Linmarara (unidentified), decided to perform a rainmaking ceremony. He first made a rain pole, which he covered with human blood, and stuck on it lines of red and white bird down. Placing the stick in front of him as illustrated in Plate 16, the operator then chanted two songs.

Plate 16.   Chanting songs to rain pole

The first had the effect of sending the spirits of the red and white lines of the rain pole into the ground. When the same chant was repeated, the spirit of the rain pole itself went into the ground and became a mythical female kangaroo who had the power to make clouds and rain. Figure 20 is a bark painting of the mythical kangaroo-woman. She is wearing a single white feather as a headdress.

The second chant caused the kangaroo-woman to urinate over large areas of the countryside, as depicted in Figure 20. This was the rain. At the same time, the kangaroo-woman ordered the *ngaljod* to leave his waterhole at Gudjamandi and span the sky as a rainbow. The natives fear the *ngaljod* in this form, as he is many hundreds of yards long and they believe that he can, if he so desires, consume a number of people for one meal.

When we were at Oenpelli, one of the aborigines made a demonstra-

Figure 20.   Mythical kangaroo-woman urinating to make rain

tion rain pole (Plate 16) but refused to chant the relevant songs until the rain pole was heavily wrapped in paperbark and taken some distance away so that it could not hear them. Our informant explained that if the rain pole heard the songs it would enter the ground at the wrong time of the year and cause rain to fall. This would annoy the *ngaljod* so much that the storms he created would drown everyone, even the members of the expedition. In Plate 16 the pole is shown in the proper position for the chanting.

The Ngaljod *and the starving children.* This myth (Mountford 1956: 220) is associated with the *ngaljod* and a family of father, mother, and a number of children who lived adjacent to Gudjamandi waterhole, the home of the *ngaljod*.

When both parents died, the children were left in the care of a man called Wirili-up, who shirked the responsibility thrust upon him. Although he did make a halfhearted attempt to feed the children by cracking a few edible nuts, the amount he gave them was so small that the children, who were always hungry, cried continuously for more. This crying so annoyed the *ngaljod* that he rose from the bottom of his waterhole and flooded the whole countryside.

When Wirili-up saw what was happening, he deserted his charges, fled to the rocky plateau, and escaped. But the *mamalait* [children], even though they climbed the trunk of a tree as the waters rose, were finally drowned.[25] Now the tree and the children are under the water of Gudjamandi, a place everyone is afraid to go near. If they do, the *ngaljod* will attack their spirits and make them ill.

Figure 21 is a painting of the myth of Wirili-up and the starving children (*mamalait*). In the lower left-hand corner, in white, is Wirili-up cracking nuts and giving them to one of the children.

The *mamalait* climbing the tree to escape the rising water created by the *ngaljod* form the main subject of the painting.

The Berndts (1970) have recorded several other examples from the myths of the *ngaljod* in which the mythical rainbow serpent, becoming annoyed over the continuous crying of a small child, destroyed the whole party.

Northwestern Australia

Elkin (1930b: 349) has recorded additional information about the rainbow serpent myths of northwestern Australia.

FOREST RIVER (*brimurer*). In the Forest River district (point 56 on the Map), the rainbow serpent is called the *brimurer*; the rainbow is made by this water snake when it is stopping the rain. This snake lives in large freshwater lagoons. Another large saltwater snake, the *lumiri*, who lives in the same locality, makes the tides. He first emits water from his inside and then makes the tide recede by swallowing it again. The *lumiri* is closely connected with the whirlpools caused by the rush of tides in the Cambridge Gulf and the Forest River. In fact, this serpent not only makes those whirlpools but is also the ultimate source of the power of the

---

[25]   Spencer (1914: 290) and the Berndts (1970: 22) both describe similar myths.

medicine man, who obtains his quartz crystals and pearl-shell ornaments from this serpent.

HALL'S CREEK (*kulabel*). Elkin also states that among the Hall's Creek tribes (point 57 on the Map), the rainbow serpent or *kulabel* is associated with the medicine man and quartz crystals.

Figure 21. The *ngaljod* and the starving children

WALLCOTT INLET (*ungud*). In the country of the Ungarinyin tribe adjacent to the Wallcott Inlet (point 58 on the Map), Elkin calls the rainbow serpent *ungud*, a term applied to the curious cave paintings (*wondjina*)[26] found in the western part of the northern Kimberleys. A more general name, *wandjina*, has been applied to these paintings in recent years.

[26]   These have been described earlier by Love (1930: 1), Elkin (1930a: 257), Crawford (1968), and others.

UNUSUAL DEVELOPMENT OF THE RAINBOW-SERPENT MYTH

Over most of Australia, the myth of the rainbow serpent does not occupy a particularly important position in the tribal life of the aborigines, apart from the danger that it may attack if certain rites and precautions are not observed. Nor does it take any important position in the social organization of the tribes, except in an area along the northern coast.

The only possible exception to this statement is the *wollunqua* snake of the Warramunga tribe (point 17 on the Map), concerning whom, according to Spencer and Gillen (1904: 226), a number of elaborate ceremonies take place extending over many weeks.

These authors were definite, however, that the ceremonies were held for no other purpose than to please the *wollunqua* serpent so that he would stay quietly in his waterhole and not wander over the countryside, harming its aboriginal inhabitants.

In the area along the northern coast of the continent, however, extending westward from northeastern Arnhem Land (point 59 on the Map) to the Kimberley Ranges (point 62 on the Map), the beliefs associated with the rainbow serpents in their various manifestations occupy a much more important place in the tribal organization than they do elsewhere.

Northeastern Arnhem Land

The myths of the Dua and Jiritja moieties of northeastern Arnhem Land form the bases of the most important ceremonial cycles in the area. For the Dua they are the reenactment of the travels of the Djunkgao sisters in the *Narra* rituals; and those of the Wawalik sisters in four extensive ceremonies: the *Kunapipi*, the *Ulmark*, the *Mandiella*, and the *Djungoan*[27] (Mountford 1956: 278).

These ceremonies are all based on the experiences of and relationships between a great rainbow snake, Jurlungur, and the above-mentioned two groups of mythical women.

The Wawalik sisters in their travels came to a waterhole, Mirrirmina, not far from point 59 on the Map. Here the elder sister, who was pregnant, begged her companion to make a camp, because she felt that she was about to deliver her child. The younger woman quickly built a bark hut in which her elder sister gave birth to a son.

At the bottom of the Mirrirmina waterhole there lived the mythical rainbow serpent Jurlungur. The odor of the birth so annoyed him that he came to the surface, sending flashes of lightning into the sky. Then,

---

[27]   Berndt (n.d.) describes the *Djanggawar* (*Djungoan*) ceremonies of northeastern Arnhem Land.

leaving his waterhole, Jurlungur approached the hut to punish the women. When the Wawalik sisters saw the enraged serpent coming toward them, they chanted magical songs and danced many powerful dances to send him back again to his waterhole. But Jurlungur still came on and pushed his head inside the hut, where he swallowed first the child, then the younger sister, and finally the elder sister.

Figure 22.   Jurlungur and the Wawalik sisters

On the bark painting of the incident shown in Figure 22, the rectangle at the top represents the hut built by the women. Within are the two Wawalik sisters and the newly born child. Jurlungur (left) is shown leaving the sacred well, Mirrirmina. In the next position the serpent has encircled the hut, thrust his head inside, and swallowed the child. On the lower right he is returning to the sacred well of Mirrirmina after having swallowed the whole family.

The designs on the lower left represent water in the sacred well; the central parallel lines with the footmarks between them are the path of the women leading to the hut; the parallel designs to the left of the path are the blood that offended the mythical serpent Jurlungur; and those to the right, an open plain.[28]

A similar myth is associated with the Djunkgao sisters of the opposite moiety and the serpent Jurlungur.[29]

Although Jurlungur has a voice like thunder, he does not appear to be associated with either the rain or the rainbow. Only the old men of the tribe, however, can visit the Mirrirmina waterhole and drink its waters or catch its fish.[30]

Western Arnhem Land

A number of ethnologists have investigated the aborigines of western Arnhem Land. It is now over sixty years since Spencer worked among the aborigines of Oenpelli (point 60 on the Map), and his book, *Native tribes of the Northern Territory of Australia* (1914), is the best source of knowledge on that subject that we have, or ever will have.

During 1948, I led a National Geographic-Commonwealth Government expedition to Arnhem Land to study its natural history and ethnology. My research, apart from the duties of leadership, was concentrated on the art and the mythology of the aborigines of that area.

In 1970, as well as on several previous occasions, Professor and Mrs. Berndt studied the social relationships of the Gunwinggu tribe of Oenpelli to their land. Their book *Man, land and myth*, is a valuable contribution to that subject.

Although the units of research of these ethnologists are separated by considerable periods of time, and although the personnel of the tribes around Oenpelli and the approach to the same subjects have varied considerably, there is general agreement among these investigators as to the main patterns of the culture under which these people live.

The rainbow serpent, the *ngaljod*[31] (who appears to be more female than male), was responsible for creating much of the sea and the land, as well as the animals, birds, and fish that belong to them. According to the mythology, the *ngaljod* came from an unknown country to the north. Traveling underground and carrying many spirit-children inside her, she camped at Coopers Creek on the east Alligator River, where she trans-

---

[28]   The Wawalik myth and the four extensive ceremonies associated with it have been described and analyzed in considerable detail by Warner (1937: 355) and the Berndts (1970: 32).
[29]   Berndt gives a detailed analysis of this cult in his book, *Kunapipi* (1951).
[30]   C. Berndt (n.d.) also records a woman's account of the Wawalik myth. The account deals largely with the meeting of the two sisters with Jurlungur at Mirrirmina waterhole and his swallowing of the two sisters.
[31]   We are using the Berndts' *ngaljod*. In Spencer's writing she is called *numereji*.

formed these spirit-children into people. She not only formed their
bodies, she gave them sight, hearing, intelligence, and the ability to move
from place to place. She also made waterholes where the newly created
people could quench their thirst and gave the digging stick and carrying bag to the women and the spear and the spear-thrower to the
men.

The *ngaljod* is a huge creature who is always associated with water. She
drowns or swallows the aborigines who disobey her laws or break her
taboos, but befriends those who live peacefully with their fellows; she is
eternal and indestructible and is not restricted to any time or place or to
any one physical body. She can be in many places at one time to punish
offenders.

The *ngaljod*, unlike serpents elsewhere, has a strong dislike of noise,
particularly of crying children, whom she destroys by drowning as in
Figure 21. There are many references in the local mythology to these
incidents.

The aborigines of western Arnhem Land look upon their rainbow
serpent as a benevolent creator. She brought them into being, she made
their land and the creatures which provide them with food, and she laid
down the just code of laws under which they now live.

There is no doubt that the *ngaljod* of western Arnhem Land is more
powerful and important in both the secular and the ceremonial life of the
aborigines of that area than is any other rainbow serpent among the other
aboriginal tribes of Australia.

Daly River Area

In his description of the rainbow-serpent myth of the Daly River area
(point 61 on the Map), Stanner (1961: 244), quoting Radcliffe-Brown
(1926: 24), states that aboriginal mythology in many parts of Australia
gives great prominence to a being referred to as the rainbow serpent, and
that certain elements in the myth are so widely circulated that they might
form a conception characteristic of Australia as a whole, not of just a part
of it.

The elements that Radcliffe-Brown thought most essential were (1) the
rainbow is seen as a huge serpent; (2) it always inhabits deep permanent
waterholes; (3) it is responsible for rain and rainmaking, and (4) it is
associated with the iridescence of quartz crystals and pearl shells.

Although in some parts of Australia Radcliffe-Brown's comments
would be generally true, they do not fully apply to the Murinbata tribe of
the Daly River area, where Stanner has carried out so many years of
research, particularly on aboriginal religion.

The myth of the rainbow serpent Kunmanggur, of the Murinbata tribe, is confused and somewhat difficult to follow. This may be due to the fact that we are dealing with an ancient belief, which has been dimmed and perhaps distorted by the intrusion of later cults. Yet, in spite of this confusion, many of the basic elements of the rainbow-serpent myth are evident in the Murinbata beliefs.

The rainbow serpent of the Murinbata appears to be a guardian spirit; he is associated with water supplies and, with his companion Kanamgek, is believed to be the mythical source of spirit-children, animals, fish, flying foxes, rain, the deep pools of fresh water, and the general increase of nature.

During the early days of the world Kunmanggur was a huge man of prodigious strength and superhuman powers, yet with a mild and beneficent nature.

At one time, however, Kunmanggur was speared by his son Tjiminin, and severely wounded. After enduring great pain for many days Kunmanggur decided to commit suicide; so, picking up all the fire sticks in the camp and placing them on his head, he walked into the water, hoping thereby to deprive mankind of its greatest asset, fire. But before he was able to carry out his intentions, another tribesman grabbed the fire sticks from his head, and took them to the shore, and gave them to everyone, so that never again would man have to face the danger of being deprived of heat and light.

After this incident, Kunmanggur transformed himself into a fierce and dangerous rainbow serpent with sharp protuberances along his spine and a long scorpionlike tail which curved over his back. The tail ended in a hook with which he held his victims under the water until they were drowned. He is portrayed in Figure 23A.

All manifestations of the rainbow are attributed to Kunmanggur, his spittle, his tongue, and the water spat out of his drone tube. It is believed that this water contained both spirit-children (*narit-narit*) and flying foxes.

The aborigines divide the spectrum of a rainbow into three bands (violet-blue, green-yellow, and orange-red). The darkest band is usually identified as Kunmanggur, the middle as his drone tube, and the lowest band as Kanamgek, a companion of the rainbow serpent.

Five cave paintings of Kunmanggur from Stanner, given in Figure 23 are of particular interest. They show no influence of the unique x-ray art of western Arnhem Land, an example of which is given in Figure 24; the highly decorative art of northeastern Arnhem Land (Figure 22); or the almost completely abstract art of Melville and Bathurst Islands (Figure 32, shown farther on).

But some of Stanner's drawings (for example, *B*, *C*, *D*, and *E* in Figure 23) strongly resemble the art of the *wandjina* of the Kimberleys, examples of which are shown in Figures 25 and 26. The resemblance of

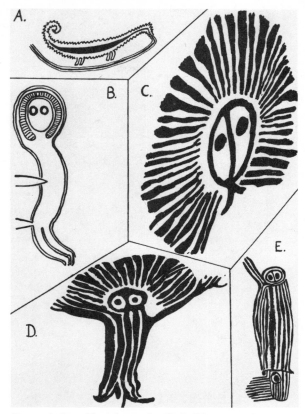

Figure 23. Cave paintings, Murinbata tribe, Daly River area

these two art forms suggests that major cultural influences must have reached the Murinbata tribe from the northwest.

On the other hand, the cave painting *A* in Figure 23 is, without doubt, an attempt on the part of the Murinbata artist to depict the rainbow serpent Kunmanggur.

Kimberley Ranges, Northwestern Australia

The *wandjina* art of the Kimberley Ranges of northwestern Australia (point 62 on the Map) soon attracted the attention of the early explorers.

During 1838, when Sir George Grey was making his famous journey along the coasts of northwestern Australia, he discovered and sketched a number of cave paintings of unusual form. Most of them depicted human figures without mouths, wearing circular headdresses with radiating lines, as in Figures 25 and 26.

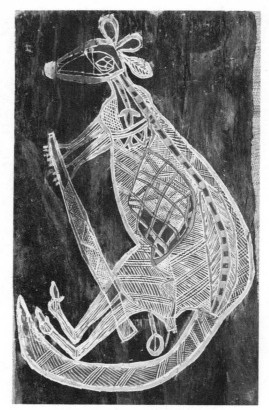

Figure 24.   The mythical kangaroo-man performing a ceremony

One of the figures illustrated by Grey (1841: 202) was shown wearing full-length clothing, with writing in some unknown language on its circular headdress.

As these cave paintings did not resemble any form of Australian aboriginal art then known, many strange and fanciful theories were advanced to account for their exotic origin. These strange guesses continued until, in 1929, almost a hundred years after Grey's discoveries, the Reverend J. R. B. Love gave an address before the Royal Society of Western Australia in which he proved conclusively that similar cave paintings adjacent to his Kunmunja mission station in the Kimberley Ranges (Figures 25 and 26) had been painted by aborigines. This address was published in July of the following year (Love 1930: 4) together with nine illustrations and much ethnological detail on these sites. Later in the same year Elkin (1930a: 257) published his data on three *wandjina* paintings he had found near Wallcott Inlet, adjacent to point 62 on the Map, with other ethnological data.

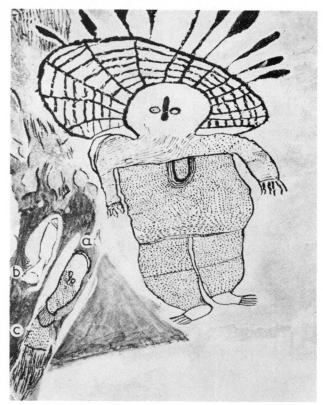

Figure 25. *Wandjina* painting, Halls Point, Kimberley Ranges (photograph by J. R. B. Love)

About the same time, the Frobenius party from Frankfurt were investigating and recording the art of the same area. Later Mrs. Agnes Schulz, one of the artists of the party, wrote an extensive paper on the *wandjina* art (Schulz 1946), which she illustrated with seventy-five paintings and a number of photographs. In the same paper she also recorded in a number of drawings the ancient art of the *giro-giro* or *dimi* paintings, about which the local aborigines had no information. These are not relevant to the subject of this paper.

Although Worms (1955: 347) described several of the *wandjina* paintings of the Kimberley Ranges, he was far more interested in the ancient *giro-giro* paintings. He illustrated about seventy of these small but decorative examples of aboriginal art, which are similar to those which I (Mountford 1937: 30) had described almost twenty years earlier. Since these paintings do not appear to be associated with the Kimberley *wandjina* art, however, they too will not be discussed further.

Figure 26.   *Wandjina* painting, Kimberley Ranges (photograph by H. Coates, courtesy of Agnes Schulz)

During 1968 Crawford produced an attractive book, *The art of the wandjina*, with over seventy illustrations in color and a number in black and white of the *wandjina* paintings of the Kimberleys, as well as many illustrations of the *giro-giro* paintings earlier described by Worms and myself. He was also able to record a number of the myths associated with the *wandjina* paintings and the methods of renovation. The value of Mr. Crawford's contribution to our knowledge of the fast-disappearing *wandjina* art of the Kimberley Ranges cannot be overemphasized.

Capell (1972) recorded a valuable series of texts associated with the Kimberley cave paintings, but these do not deal specifically with the beliefs expressed in the *wandjina* paintings.

The myths of the Kimberley Ranges describe how a number of *wandjina*, the first men, came from the north and, wandering over the earth's surface, made the present-day waterholes, rivers, ranges, and outstanding natural features. At the completion of these earthly tasks each *wandjina* painted his image, and that of other animals and plants, on the walls of a cave, then entered an adjacent deep waterhole and made that his permanent home.

The aborigines are definite that they did not make the *wandjina* paintings—they inherited them from the spirits who created the land and everything on it.

In those early times the *wandjina* not only taught the men how to make and use their spears and the women how to make their carrying bags and what food to gather, but they instituted the rules of good behavior that all must follow.

Each *wandjina* (every clan territory has one or more) controls the spirits of human babies, the creatures painted on the walls of his cave (see also *a*, *b*, and *c* in Figure 25), and the rain, on which the preservation and maintenance of life depends.

It is particularly unfortunate that since the first ethnological research by Love and Elkin on the *wandjina* cult was published, about fifty years ago now, practically all the descriptions have concentrated on the art forms and the language of the aborigines of the Kimberley Ranges, while little indeed has been written about the fundamental philosophies of the *wandjina* beliefs. This is likely to be a considerable loss to Australian ethnology, particularly as the few remaining aborigines who have been taken out of their tribal country are now old men.

As the researches of Love, Elkin, Schulz, and Crawford on the *wandjinas* do agree in general, however, we can assume that the function of the *wandjina* of the Kimberley Ranges is to ensure the periodic recurrence of the rainy season and the normal increase of the animals and plants and of the spirit-children.

Apart from the fact that the normal Australian rainbow serpent did not create any part of the Australian topography (except in three localities already mentioned along the northern coasts of the continent), and that these mythical serpents are not deeply involved in the social organization of the tribe, their attributes and duties do not vary greatly from those of the *wandjina*.

Like the rainbow serpents, the *wandjina* are associated with thunder, lightning, and rain; they punish all intruders who interfere with the totemic waterholes; and they ensure the supply of spirit-children.

THE MYTHICAL LIZARDS OF GROOTE, MELVILLE, AND BATHURST ISLANDS

It is a curious fact that although almost all the rainbow serpents on the mainland of Australia are snakelike in form, those on the two largest islands off the northern coasts, Groote Eylandt, in the Gulf of Carpentaria (point 63 on the Map) and Melville Island (point 64 on the Map), resemble lizards. They do, however, have characteristics similar to those of the rainbow serpents of the mainland.

The Geckos of Groote Eylandt

Earlier (Mountford 1956: 75), I described a family of mythical geckos, the *ipilja-ipilja*, who live in the Numarika swamp at the mouth of the Angoroko River of Groote Eylandt (point 63 on the Map). These geckos are all highly colored, and the male, who is about a hundred feet long, has long hair on his head and luxuriant whiskers.

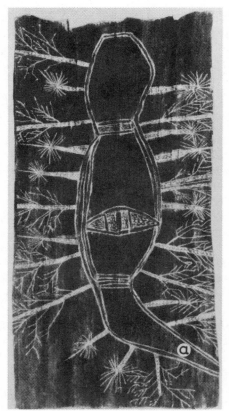

Figure 27.   Mythical gecko lizards, *ipilja-ipilja*, living in Numarika swamp, Groote Eylandt

The geckos live in Numarika swamp, shown in Figure 27, which is so sacred that should anyone ever drink from it he would surely die. The aborigines can take water from the small stream, however, marked *a* on Figure 27, that runs into one end of the swamp. The geckos, the aborigines contend, live in, not under, the waters of Numarika; they are associated with thunder and rain, being, in fact, the creators of them.

At the beginning of the monsoon season, the male gecko causes the thunderstorm by first eating the grass from the edge of the sacred swamp, then drinking large quantities of water, and finally squirting the mixture into the sky. The water makes the clouds, and the grass binds them together. As the clouds pass across the sky, the gecko roars loudly (thunder) to indicate how pleased he is with his efforts. He does not appear to be associated with the rainbow, however.

Figure 27 is a painting of the Numarika waterhole drawn in the shape of a gecko, except that the fleshy tail is not shown. The gecko and his family live in their camp, the oval design in the center of the waterhole. The waterhole is surrounded by paperbark trees and pandanus palms, those of the more spreading design being the paperbarks and those with vertical trunks and radiating limbs the pandanus palms.

Figure 28.   Mythical gecko lizards, *ipilja-ipilja*, in the sky, Groote Eylandt

The upper design on the second bark painting shown in Figure 28 represents the rain cloud created by the gecko with the rain pouring from it. Below is the gecko family: the male, the *ipilja-ipilja*, is on the left, his wife, the *guruina*, on the right, and their single child in the center.

The Maratji *of Melville and Bathurst Islands*

The lizardlike *maratji* (Mountford 1958: 155) of Melville and Bathurst Islands (point 64 on the Map) have many of the characteristics of the *ipilja-ipilja* of Groote Eylandt.

The *maratji* are highly colored lizards, the males having horns on their heads instead of hair and long projecting jaws in the place of beards, as shown in Figure 29.

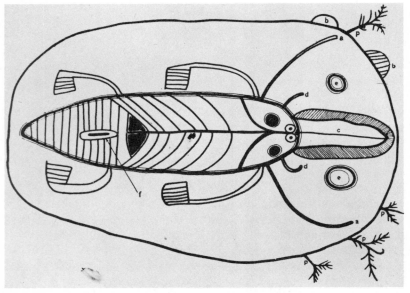

Figure 29.   Mythical lizard, the *maratji*, Bathurst Island; see the text for explanation of the key

Should any unauthorized person interfere with their home, the Maundu waterhole, depicted in Figure 30, the *maratji* become annoyed, roar loudly (thunder), and send a water spout into the air which falls as torrential rain and floods the countryside. Then one of the *maratji*, changing himself into a rainbow, travels across the land seeking to injure the offender or anyone else nearby.

These mythical lizards, who belong to the totem of Andului [freshwater], are mortal creatures who die and disintegrate like every other creature.

The *maratji* of Melville and Bathurst Islands—and there are several groups of them—are not all of the same temperament. Some are greatly feared, others are quiet and friendly.

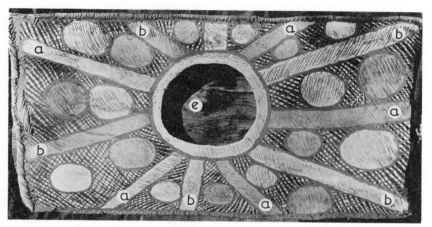

Figure 30.   Maundu swamp, Bathurst Island, home of mythical lizards, the *maratji*

Figure 29 is a drawing by a sophisticated aboriginal of a female *maratji* who lives at Maundu waterhole on Bathurst Island. She has two long horns, *a, a,* and two short horns, *d, d,* projecting from her head. Her tongue and lower jaw are indicated by *c,* her vulva by *f,* and the bubbles that rise to the surface of the water when she becomes annoyed by the circles *e, e.*

Figure 30 is a highly conventionalized design painted on a bark container, illustrating the home of the *maratji* at Maundu. The central opening, *e,* is the waterhole, Maundu; the radiating lines *a, a,* etc., are the *maratji* who live in it; and *b, b,* etc., are strips of white sand at its bottom. The darker circles indicate the water flowing from Maundu into the sea and the lighter ones bubbles that rise to the surface when the mythical creatures are disturbed by intruders.

The different concepts of the rainbow serpents in the form of lizards on Groote and on Melville and Bathurst Islands are without doubt a result of the isolation of the cultures by the water barriers that separate them from the adjoining mainland.

The effect of this isolation is clearly shown in the art forms of both localities. Even though the water barrier between the mainland and Groote Eylandt is only a few miles, the art forms of which Figure 27 is typical, are much less decorative than those of the adjacent mainland, such as Figure 22.

Similarly, the art of both Melville and Bathurst Islands is so highly formalized that it seldom resembles the objects it represents; see Figure 30. In contrast, the art of neighboring western Arnhem Land, in one place separated from Melville Island by only about fourteen miles of water, not only is entirely representational but is among the most colorful and decorative art forms of the continent (see Figure 24).

THE MYTHICAL ORIGIN OF THE STONE AXE

There is still a widespread belief among the peasant peoples of Europe, Asia, Africa, and the Indonesian islands that the prehistoric stone axes they find in the ground are "thunderbolts" thrown down from the sky during heavy storms.

The local people, unaware that these axes are human handiwork, have invented many curious beliefs about their origins. They believe that they are thrown down from the sky, that the lightning flash is made by the falling "thunderbolt," and that the thunder is the sound of it falling to earth.

In some countries it is believed that the "thunderbolt," when striking, first sinks deeply into the earth but then rises slowly over the years until it rests on the surface, and if the peasants build this stone into the wall or roof of their dwelling, it will never be struck by lightning—showing their belief in the old saying that "lightning never strikes twice in the same place."

These magical stones are also used by the local people for a number of medicinal purposes: to protect cattle from disease (by placing them in their drinking water); to prevent milk from turning sour; and to cure many of the ills of mankind.

The Australian stone axes are not associated with thunder and lightning (which is to be expected, considering that they are the tools in common use), but it is surprising to find that the aborigines of Australia, a typical stone-age hunting people, have living myths that link sky beings with thunder, lightning, and the stone axes. The Australian myths are possibly all that remain of similar beliefs once held by ancient peoples in many parts of the world.

The Lightning-Man, Mamaragan

In western Arnhem Land the aborigines believe in a lightning-man, Mamaragan, shown in Figure 31 (Mountford 1955: 141), who during the dry season lives in his waterhole Uguluma, not far from Nimbawah (point 65 on the Map).

Occasionally during the dry season in Arnhem Land, Mamaragan leaves his watery world and hunts for food among the cabbage palms beside his waterhole. Although the tops of these trees are edible, no aboriginal would even touch their trunks. If they did, Mamaragan would

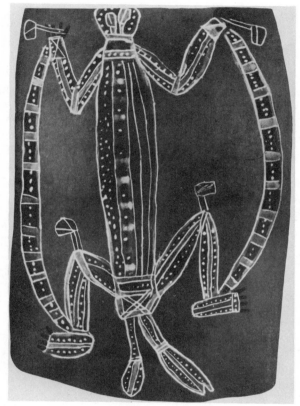

Figure 31.   The lightning-man, Mamaragan, western Arnhem Land

kill them with lightning. Further, should any aboriginal be so foolish as to throw a stone into the Uguluma waterhole, an even greater misfortune would happen: Mamaragan would rise into the sky and create thunderstorms that would drown everyone.

During the wet season, the lightning-man leaves his waterhole and travels from place to place on the top of thunderclouds. At those times he often becomes angry and roars with a loud voice (thunder), and, striking downward with the stone axes that grow on his hands and knees, shatters the trees and sometimes kills the aborigines.

Figure 31 is a bark painting of Mamaragan with the stone axes on his hands and knees. The lightning is represented by a curving band between his wrists and his ankles.

The Lightning-Woman, Bumerali

During the dry season on Melville Island (point 66 on the Map), Bumerali, the lightning-woman, together with her children, her brother, Pakadringa (the man of the thunderstorm), and Tomituka (the woman of the monsoon rains), lives quietly in an upper world, Tuniruna.

At the beginning of the wet season, the family leave their dry-season home in the sky and travel together in the thunderclouds (Mountford 1955: 141).

Bumerali, the lightning-woman, has two stone axes mounted on long crooked handles, which she carries in her hands. While traveling in the clouds with the thunder-man, Pakadringa, she strikes the ground beneath with them, destroying the trees and sometimes the native people. Bumerali also becomes angry when her children jump from cloud to cloud, and the sharp crack of thunder that immediately follows the lightning flash is the voice of Bumerali reprimanding her disobedient children. The aborigines distinguish clearly between the sharp voice of Bumerali and that of her brother, Pakadringa, the rumble of thunder.

Figure 32 illustrates the lightning-woman Bumerali. Her eyes are indicated by a, a, her nose by b, her breasts by d, d, and her feet by g, g. The crooked handles of her axes are at e, e, the axes themselves at c, c, and the "road" of the lightning flash at f.

These two living myths from northern Australia, in which the aborigines associate stone axes with thunder and lightning, are of some interest to the distribution of "thunderbolts" among the peoples of Africa, Europe, Asia, and the islands of the Pacific, but they have not, as far as we know, reached North or South America.

SUMMARY

The rainbow-serpent myths of Australia are an extension of the universal serpent myths which permeate the beliefs of all peoples, past and present.

Mythical creatures having characteristics similar to those of the rainbow serpents of Australia are recorded in many countries: in the myths of the dragons of China, of the *naga* of India, of the *taniwah* of New Zealand; in the many half-submerged myths of Europe and the ancient world of Greece and Egypt; in those of the water serpents of the primitive Bushmen of the Kalahari desert; and in those of the Indonesian and

Melanesian islands. But we can enter no further into this vast field of exotic serpent beliefs.

The rainbow-serpent beliefs undoubtedly reached Australia through the Cape York area, the only reasonable point of entry. From this locality the myths have diffused throughout the continent, remaining simple in the central area but becoming more complex on the eastern and northern coasts, where they have been exposed to external influences.

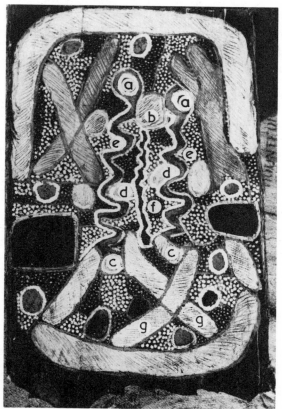

Figure 32.   The lightning-woman, Bumerali, Melville Island; see the text for explanation of the key

The fact that we have seventeen myths belonging to the aborigines in the arid center of the continent, all of which have been collected recently, has allowed us to determine with some degree of accuracy the place of the myth of the rainbow serpent in that part of Australia.

The central desert aborigines look upon their mythical serpents as living creatures who have wives and children, who can be coerced, killed, and eaten by mistake, and who, in one myth, have even been stolen by the medicine men of another tribe to increase their own water supply.

The rainbow serpents along the eastern coasts, however, from Victoria (point 8 on the Map) to Cape York (point 39 on the Map), occupy a much more important position in the magical and philosophical life of the aborigines.

The link between the rainbow serpents and the medicine men is also strong. In some localities, such as point 34 on the Map, the rainbow serpent even takes the medicine man to a place under his waterhole and spends several days teaching him the songs and dances for a new tribal ceremony.

There is also a general belief among the aborigines of eastern Australia that quartz crystals which the medicine men carry within their bodies supply them with increased magical forces. In the Pennefather River area, the quartz crystals found by the medicine man where the rainbow touched the earth endow him with the power to make rain.

When the rainbow serpent of the Kabi tribe, the *takkan*, knows that a particular medicine man has many quartz crystals in his body, he takes him to his home under the waterhole, extracts the crystals, and replaces them with a coil of magic rope (*bukkur*).

This rope, which is absorbed into the body of the medicine man, will at his command provide him with an invisible road along which he can travel, either to cure the sick or to punish an enemy.

The aborigines in Australia are unaware of the physical facts of paternity. Those in the desert believe that the spirit-children, who originate at certain increase centers, find their own mothers without any assistance.

But along the eastern and northern coasts, it is the rainbow serpents who send the child direct to its mother either in a dream or by the medium of her husband. The spirit-child, waiting until everyone is asleep, enters the body of its mother of its own accord and begins a human existence.

On the northern coasts of the continent, the importance of the rainbow serpent increases. In the northeastern corner (point 48 on the Map), the myth of the rainbow serpent in the form of the great Jurlungur forms the bases of the most important ceremonial cycles of the aborigines' rituals, which dominate both the ceremonial and the secular life of the tribe.

Further west, in the Arnhem Land plateau (point 60 on the Map), the rainbow serpent has almost reached the status of a supreme being. He is eternal and indestructible, he is not restricted to any time and place, and he is the creator of the aborigines, of the land on which they live, and of the creatures and plants that provide them with food.

Still farther west, in the country of the Murinbata tribe (point 61 on the Map), the rainbow serpent, who does not appear to be as powerful as his neighbor in Arnhem Land, is looked upon as the beneficent creator of man and of the whole of creation.

But in the extreme northwest of the continent, the cult of the ubiquitous rainbow serpent is entirely replaced by the *wandjina* cult, which centers on cave paintings and permanent waterholes. The limited distribution of this *wandjina* cult suggests that it is a comparatively recent introduction.

This contribution to the knowledge of the rainbow-serpent myth of Australia can only be regarded as a preliminary survey of the subject. The data on which it is based have been selected from the writings, over a period of almost a century, of many ethnologists. It is unfortunate that, up to the present, there has been little or no organized research to collect fuller information about this worldwide myth.

But there is time to remedy this neglect. There are many aborigines living in the more distant parts of the continent who still retain a great deal of knowledge about rainbow serpents that live in their waterholes.

REFERENCES

BASEDOW, HERBERT
  1925 *The Australian aboriginal*. Adelaide: Preece.
BERNDT, CATHERINE H.
  n.d. "Monsoon and honey wind," in *Échanges et communications*. Edited by J. Pouillon and P. Maranda. The Hague: Mouton.
BERNDT, RONALD
  1951 *Kunapipi: a study of an Australian aboriginal religious cult*. Melbourne: Cheshire.
BERNDT, RONALD, CATHERINE BERNDT
  1950 Aboriginal art in central-western Northern Territory. *Meanjin* 9(3): 183–188.
  1970 *Man, land and myth in north Australia: the Gunwinggu people*. Sydney: Ure Smith.
CALVERT, ALBERT FREDERICK
  1892 *The aborigines of western Australia*. London.
CAPELL, A.
  1972 *Cave painting myths: northern Kimberley*. Sydney: University of Sydney Press.
CRAWFORD, I. M.
  1968 *The art of the wandjina*. Melbourne: Oxford University Press.
ELKIN, A. P.
  1930a Rock-painting in north-west Australia. *Oceania* 1: 257–279.
  1930b The rainbow-serpent myth in north-west Australia. *Oceania* 1: 349–352.
GREY, SIR GEORGE
  1841 *Journals of two expeditions of discovery in north-west and western Australia during the years 1837–38 and 39*, two volumes. London: Boone.
HASSELL, ETHEL, D. S. DAVIDSON
  1936 Notes on the ethnology of the Wheelman tribe of south-western Australia. *Anthropos* 31(5–6): 679–711.
HOWITT, ALFRED WILLIAM
  1904 *The native tribes of south-east Australia*. London: Macmillan.

LOVE, J. R. B.
   1930   Rock paintings of the Worora and their mythological interpretation. *Journal of the Royal Society of Western Australia* 26(16): 1–24.
MATHEWS, R. H.
   1899   *Folklore of the Australian aborigines*. Sydney: Hennessey Harper.
   1904   Ethnological notes on the aboriginal tribes of New South Wales and Victoria. *Journal of the Royal Society of New South Wales* 38: 203–381.
McCONNEL, URSULA
   1930   The rainbow-serpent myth in north Queensland. *Oceania* 1(3): 347–349.
MEAD, MARGARET
   1933   The Marsalai cult among the Arapesh with special reference to the rainbow serpent beliefs of the Australian aboriginals. *Oceania* 4(1): 37–53.
MOUNTFORD, CHARLES P.
   1937   Examples of aboriginal art from Napier, Broome Bay and Parry Harbour, northwestern Australia. *Transactions of the Royal Society of South Australia* 61: 30–40.
   1955   The lightning man in Australian mythology. *Man* 55: 141.
   1956   "Aboriginal art of Australia," in *Records of the American-Australian scientific expedition to Arnhem Land*, volume one: *Art, myth and symbolism*. Edited by C. P. Mountford. Melbourne: Melbourne University Press.
   1958   *The Tiwi: their art, myth and ceremony*. London: Phoenix House.
   1965   *Ayers Rock, its people, their beliefs and their art*. Sydney: Angus and Robertson.
MOUNTFORD, C. P., R. TONKINSON
   1969   Carved and engraved human figures from northwestern Australia. *Anthropological Forum* 2.
PALMER, EDWARD
   1884   Notes on some Australian tribes. *Journal of the Anthropological Institute of Great Britain and Ireland* 13.
PARKER, K. LANGLOH
   1905   *The Euahlayi tribe*. London: Constable.
PIDDINGTON, RALPH
   1930   The water-serpent in Karadjeri mythology. *Oceania* 1(3): 352–354.
RADCLIFFE-BROWN, A. R.
   1926   The rainbow-serpent myth of Australia. *Journal of the Anthropological Institute of Great Britain and Ireland* 56(24): 19–25.
   1930   The rainbow-serpent myth in south-eastern Australia. *Oceania* 1(3): 342–346.
ROTH, WALTER E.
   1903   Superstition, magic, and medicine. *North Queensland Ethnography Bulletin* 5 (Brisbane).
SCHULZ, AGNES S.
   1946   North-west Australian rock paintings. *Memoirs of the National Museum Melbourne*, January: 7–57.
SMYTH, R. BROUGH
   1878   *The aborigines of Victoria*. Melbourne.
SPENCER, SIR W. B.
   1914   *Native tribes of the Northern Territory of Australia*. London: Macmillan.

SPENCER, SIR W. B., F. J. GILLEN
1904 *The northern tribes of central Australia*. London: Macmillan.
STANNER, W. E. H.
1961 On aboriginal religion: IV. The design-plan of a riteless myth. *Oceania* 31(4): 233–258.
STREHLOW, CARL
1907–1920 *Die Aranda- und Loritja-Stämme in Zentral-Australien*. Frankfurt: Joseph Baer.
WARNER, W. L.
1937 *A black civilization: A social study of an Australian tribe*. New York: Harper.
WORMS, E. A.
1955 Contemporary and prehistoric rock paintings in central and northern North Kimberley. *Anthropos* 50.

Metaphysics in a Mythical View of the World

KENNETH MADDOCK

A word I often heard during my researches in northern Australia[1] is *bolung*. It is to be heard when myths are told and when mythical allusions are made. Aboriginal speech being full of the latter—the narration of myths is infrequent in my experience—it is clear that this word is a key to their view of the world.

A point to be noticed at once is that *bolung* cannot satisfactorily be translated by an English word. Admittedly it does, in some contexts, call to mind what many anthropologists have meant by "rainbow serpent," and an additional consideration in favor of this translation is that aborigines sometimes use it when speaking English, which during this century has become their *lingua franca* (more usually, however, they say "rainbow," a rainbow being understood by them as an appearance of a snake known by the same name).

Early in my fieldwork, I came across a poetically striking example of how the term's objective correlative is imagined. Verses of the *Gunabibi* cult were being chanted in the bush outside Beswick Creek Settlement (as it then was). A word that occurred in a number of the verses was explained to me to be arcane for *bolung*; one man then added that "In raintime we look up and see him shooting light." Observations such as this fitted the usual anthropological understanding of rainbow serpents so

---

[1] I worked for about two years between 1964 and 1970 among southern and central Arnhem Land peoples under the auspices of the Australian Institute of Aboriginal Studies. In writing this paper I have made use also of data on these peoples contained in works written by Capell (1962), Elkin (1961), Oates (1964), and West (1964), but I have not sought to compare my findings and those of Capell, Elkin, Oates, and West with findings made by other writers about other Arnhem Land peoples, for example by Warner on the Murngin or Hiatt on the Gidjingali. The peoples to whom my data refer are principally Dalabon, Djauan, Maiali-Gunwinggu, and Rembarnga.

well that I soon concluded that in *bolung* I had found the local version of this reputedly common conception. In the months to follow, information came to hand to change my initial impression. It became evident that *bolung* refers to ideational realities too manifold to be understood simply as an observable phenomenon—a rainbow—or as a mythological explanation of that phenomenon—a (rainbow) snake.

The purpose of the present paper is to publish some of my data in order to show the nature of the conception and the difficulty of accommodating it within our received conceptual framework. To publish all my data on *bolung* would be tantamount to writing a full account of the traditional culture of these aborigines.[2] *Bolung*, that is to say, is as comprehensive a concept as *ungud* among some of the northwest Australian peoples (Elkin 1930a; Lommel 1952; Petri 1954).

I shall begin with some observations on the composition and occurrence of the word itself. Its world-view significance can then be examined.

Bolung may be divided into *bo* and *lung*, though whether these segments are genuinely morphemic is a question for scholars more linguistically skilled than I am.[3] The first segment (*bo*) occurs as a verb, with the meanings "to come, to go," and as a noun, with the meanings "river, milky way" (normally expressed as *bono*, *-no* being a common ending to a singular noun). It is used also as a noun to refer to certain trenches and dancing grounds made for such ceremonies as the Dua patrimoiety's *Gunabibi* and the Jiridja patrimoiety's *Jabuduruwa*. The trenches or dancing grounds thus named symbolize rivers; the other trenches or dancing grounds made for these ceremonies are called *langga* and symbolize billabongs [Australian vernacular for what would be called ponds or small lakes in England].

In the absence of a proper philology of Australian languages, one cannot be sure that *bo*, in any or all of its meanings, is related etymologically to *bolung*, but certainly there are some plausible associations between the two. Thus mythical beings of whom the word *bolung* is used are linked with water (compare *bo*, "river") and with ceremonies (for example, the *Gunabibi* and the *Jabuduruwa*) in which symbolic rivers are made. In northern regions, with their tidal rivers and striking contrasts between wet and dry seasons, one might well think of water generally and of rivers particularly as coming and going (the flow and ebb of the tides, the inundation and drying out of the countryside).[4] Capell, for example, gives the text *wa: baga balgga ga?bon* [that river flows quickly] (1962:

---

[2] Any comprehensive account of their culture would have to take notice of important changes resulting from white influence and control. I have discussed the relation between traditional and introduced components—"laws" as the aborigines call them—in another paper (Maddock 1977).
[3] It is to be regretted that West failed to complete his intended morphophonemic study of Dalabon to which Capell (1962: 98) refers.
[4] It may be recalled that Lévi-Strauss (1962: 121–8) argues for a connection between

105), which may be translated literally as "water that flood it-comes."

It might, of course, be wondered why *bolung*, associated as the concept is with water and with ceremonies in which symbolic rivers and billabongs are made, should have been built partly out of the word for river (if, indeed, it has been) instead of the word for water[5] or that for billabong. The world is said to have originally been an expanse of rainbow-colored water, so the word for water would have been appropriate enough. As for the choice between "river" and "billabong," it may be noted that in the *Gunabibi*, the ceremony associated most explicitly with *bolung*, towering figures are made to symbolize *bolung* and are taken ritually to the symbolic river, but not to the symbolic billabong. This, taken together with the linguistic likeness to the word for river, suggests that, although *bolung* is associated with water, it is especially water in the form of rivers that is meant. Furthermore, the *Gunabibi* trenches that symbolize rivers are shaped like arcs, hence like rainbows, and the images of *bolung* in ritual and rock art are elongated, hence more suggestive of rivers, rainbows and arc-shaped trenches than of billabongs or the circular trenches that symbolize them in the *Gunabibi*.

The second segment (*lung*) is not known to me to occur as a word. It does occur, however, at the beginning, middle, or end of some words. Thus it occurs initially in *lungar*, a Djauan word meaning "king brown snake" (West 1964: 43). This snake, known in Dalabon as *dadbu*, is exceptionally important in the *Gunabibi* ceremony and is symbolized therein by one of the two tall figures that I mentioned as being carried to the symbolic river. The segment occurs in an intermediate position in Julunggur, a proper name given to the water goanna (*djargar*) in the *Djunggawon* ceremony. It occurs terminally in *makayalung*, [many, big mob] (West 1964: 44).

The whole word is to be found in longer words that I shall hyphenate for clarity's sake. Bolung-bi:m (*bi:m*, "white clay, rock painting") is the name of a place with rock paintings, including a splendid *bolung* centrally depicted, and important mythical associations (see Maddock 1970b). Man-bolung-gorang (*man* is given by Oates [1964: 24, 28] as a prefix signifying one of the two neuter genders in Gunwinggu) is the name of a place prominent in creation mythology. *Bolung-gun?* means "dreaming place, totemic site," but *djang* is more commonly used. Constructions such as *gudabu-bolung* (*gudabu*, "male plains kangaroo") can be used to distinguish a mythical male plains kangaroo active during The Dreaming,

rainbow-serpent imagery and the seasonal alternation of wet and dry. His analysis has drawn adverse criticism from Hiatt (1975: 143–147).
[5] Oates (1964: 61) gives *bo:* as Gunwinggu for "water." Her linguistic researches were carried out at Oenpelli, a mission station north of where I worked, and I regret that I did not notice this point in her monograph while I was in the field. Accordingly I have not checked it for Maiali (a southern version of the language of which Gunwinggu is the northern version), but I cannot recall ever having heard the word used in this sense.

the initial epoch when the world and life were given form, from the male plains kangaroos that are nowadays to be seen in the bush and are hunted for food.

There is evidence that *bolung* is quite widely distributed as a mythical term and that it has long been in use. Dahl, a Norwegian naturalist who spent two years in northern Australia during the 1890's, reported that *barrang*, *bolongo*, and *wurrang* were used for "devil-devil" in parts of Arnhem Land (1926: 21). His *bolongo* is probably my *bolung*. The only exact localization he gave for *bolongo* puts the belief in an area west of where I worked: "a water snake, a 'bolongo,' a gigantic crocodile inhabiting a certain pool higher up the river, which killed everything that attempted to pass" (1926: 67). Traveling up the Daly River, one comes to this pool before arriving at the Flora fork.

It is a long jump from Arnhem Land to the west coast of Western Australia, but Karadjeri *bulaing* (Piddington 1930: 352, 354), *bulanj* (Capell 1962: 59) or Pulang (Elkin 1930b: 351) appear to be clearly cognate etymologically and mythologically to my *bolung*. Elkin says that Pulang is a mythical water snake identified by the Karadjeri with their rainbow serpent, who is named Maiangara. Piddington says that *bulaing* is a water snake resembling rainbow serpents in other parts of Australia except that he is unconnected with rainbows. Capell glosses *bulanj* as "rainbow serpent." The associations of meaning that I have suggested as plausible or apt for *bolung* do not carry over to Karadjeri, which has *djai* [to come]; *ja* [to go]; *muri* [river]; *nawa* [water] (Capell 1962: 53, 66, 88).

Within the actual area of my researches, *bulung* has been reported as "ashes" (Capell 1962:92) and as "ashes, rainbow snake" (West 1964: 125). West gives *bolung—polung* in his orthography—as "rainbow serpent" in the Djauan, Maiali, Rembarnga, and Buan languages (1964: 119). Dalabon, the language to which he credits *bulung—pulung* in his orthography—is the westerly form of a language of which Buan is the easterly form (Capell 1962: 92). The *u/o* distinction is not phonemic (Capell 1962: 94). I do not know of any association of meaning between ashes and rainbow serpents to explain the use of the one word for both. There is, rather, an opposition of meaning, since ashes call to mind what is hot and dry, rainbow snakes what is cool and watery.

Although analysis of the word can be suggestive, the lack of any reliable basis for etymological inquiry makes for difficulties, and there seems little point in pursuing these matters further. I shall accordingly turn to an examination of some of the contexts in which the word *bolung* is used in an attempt to show something of its world-view significance.

First, there are contexts in which *bolung* is used as a name: sometimes as though it were a proper name and sometimes as though it were the name of a class of beings (compare God, god). Where it functions as a proper name, I shall render it Bolung instead of *bolung*.

Secondly, there are contexts in which *bolung* is used to identify an attribute. It is then one of a pair of opposed terms of which the other is *du:ning*, I do not know of a proper name Du:ning or of any noun *du:ning*.

Thirdly, there is a usage related to the first but conveniently to be distinguished from it for expository purposes. *Bolung* here belongs in a series of linked terms the correlative of which is a cycle of existence posited by these aborigines.

A section of the paper will be devoted to each of these employments of the word. A final section will contain some theoretical conclusions.

BOLUNG AS NAME

There are mythical incidents in the telling of which the word is used as someone's name. "Bolung" is sometimes interchanged rather freely in these incidents with another name or names. Three short texts will bring this out, and at the same time, show something of the cosmological role ascribed to Bolung.

M_1. She was at Man-bolung-gorang (a place in the vicinity of the Katherine headwaters) too heavy with people to walk. She tried to crawl, but was too heavy. The people she carried inside her body weighed her down. Djigbei and all the other birds tried to kill her that the people might come out from inside her, but she was like stone and their spears bounced off her body. The birds decided at last to fetch Left Hand. He was in another country. They asked him to kill Jingana so that the people could come out. When Left Hand came up to Jingana he found that she had turned red in color and was wearing a headdress made from white cockatoo feathers. He took fright but managed to throw his spear, not high but low so that her anus was pierced. She jerked upwards and spewed out the people. Now she gave them their matrilineal dreamings (totems) and from there they spread out across the country.

The emphasis in this story falls on the freeing of the first humans from Bolung, also called Jingana, who had them inside her body. Another version of the story lays more stress on her universal significance as a mother figure:

M_{1a}. Jingana is mother for white men, for black men, for everything. She made us (aborigines) black; she made other men differently (as whites). She carried everything at first : snakes, kangaroos, matrilineal dreamings, dogs, birds. She put some in water, others in the desert. Everything was in her, but she spewed it all out. All things were blackfellows at first. Whitefellows call her God, but I call her Jingana, Mother. She made us. She is Jingana. She is Bolung. She carried us in her belly. A little bird speared her in the anus and then we all came out of her mouth.

This story puts before us a singular being, female in sex, who stands as mother (*na?*) to all living things. She has at least two names—Bolung and Jingana (when aborigines are speaking English they often refer to her as "Mother of us all")—and is described as having been a huge snake. The mythical or divine nature of her motherhood is shown in the absence of any reference to a husband or to how she came to have all life within her and in the extraordinary manner of "giving birth": people came out of her mouth after a spear thrown by a left-hander pierced her anus and cut open her womb. Such an apical figure may aptly be called an All-Mother by analogy with the All-Fathers best known from the literature on southeast Australia. The inability or unwillingness of this All-Mother to let out the life she contained recalls the myth fragment reported by Elkin (1961: 5) in which Iganga had people inside who could not get out until Big Kookaburra made an opening for them by throwing a spear with his left hand. Iganga is obviously cognate to Jingana and Big Kookaburra to Left Hand, whose species identity is given as kookaburra (*gorogoro*).[6]

Additional light is thrown on the All-Mother by a myth told in connection with the *Gunabibi* ceremony:

M_2. Lumaluma was Gunabibi. She used to swallow people and spew out their bones. She was the bull-roarer. The *Gunabibi* was managed at that time by a father and son named Nagorgo and a quaillike bird (*debudebu*) who was left-handed. The managers would go to meet Lumaluma, but when they called out to her, all she did was to vomit the bones of the people they had given to her. The father and son decided not to give her more people but instead to make her out of wood. When next Lumaluma spoke, the bird swung a bull-roarer to catch her voice. The bull-roarer is Lumaluma. The father and son traveled south with the bird and other companions and performed *Gunabibi* ceremonies and sang *Gunabibi* songs as they went. Lumaluma went into the salt water from this place, which is Balbonara. She is Jingana.

If M_1 accounts for the appearance of people and some beginnings of human culture, M_2 presupposes that there are people and concentrates on cultural development and diffusion in the shape of the *Gunabibi*, one of the outstanding indicators of the dual social organization. The biological bias of the first myth finds a complementary cultural bias in the second myth, but whichever way the stress lies it is clear that people must distance themselves from Bolung.

[6] Birds play a helpful role in a number of Arnhem Land myths. See, in addition to those mentioned in this paper, myths about fire and the sharing of food (Maddock 1970a: 176–185; 1975: 105–111).

M_2 introduces a new name, Lumaluma, and the being so named is given a whalelike appearance and a saltwater habitat. But at the same time she is identified with Jingana. And once again a left-handed bird acts decisively to help free mankind from a difficult female. An inability or unwillingness to spew people whole replaces, in this myth, an inability or unwillingness to give birth to them. There are some close parallels with contemporary practice. The people given to Lumaluma to swallow correspond to present-day novices; the meeting between Lumaluma and the father and son corresponds to the gathering of men and women together at a central site to await the return of the novices from their prolonged seclusion; the vomiting of the bones corresponds to the novices' actual reemergence. Had Lumaluma vomited whole those she swallowed, there would have been no need for separation from her. As it is, the *Gunabibi* ceremonies must be carried out in her symbolic presence (the bull-roarers) and not in her real presence.

Elkin (1961: 9–10) has reported a Rembarnga myth in which "the Mother, Kunapipi" traveled with two songmen and "Muitj, the Rainbow Serpent." The song-men, two in number and carrying boomerangs, may evidently be equated with the father and son from M_2, for they are described as having sung to boomerang accompaniment as they journeyed south. Muitj, male in sex and traveling underground, is to be equated with the king brown snake (*dadbu*) and rock python (*guradjadu*), males who journeyed underground while the father and son, their wives, and the bird traveled above the earth's surface. This equation is confirmed by the fact that the Rembarnga made *gumagu* or *jaramalindji* (Elkin: Yermalindji) to symbolize Muitj. These are the names of the tall figures that I mentioned as *bolung* symbols, and the king brown snake and the rock python are each so represented. That a unitary figure in one myth should turn up as a split representation in another is a familiar-enough trick of mythological imagination. But Elkin's myth lacks the separation theme, and its mother appears to have been a giver; whereas in my myths she is assimilated to those mythical females who must be robbed or otherwise mastered (M_1 has her losing the life she carries and M_2 has her losing her attribute as bull-roarer).

My first two myths, then, show a snakelike or whalelike female who is related maternally to humans and is exceptionally significant in cosmology. She goes under different names but is in some sense the same, no matter what her name, appearance, or adventures. No definite limits seem to be set to her creativity, since aborigines are inclined to credit her with whatever features of the world or culture that are unaccounted for by specific myths. No other mythic being explains so much.

In some other myths about Bolung, the name refers to a being who is not the All-Mother. Aborigines will, indeed, say that there are many *bolung*, some male and others female. It is typical for the myths to which I am now referring to depict their *bolung* as acting destructively toward some people and to have only a slight explanatory significance. One example is enough to show the type:

M$_3$. Bolung threw a stone to destroy an encampment of people who had angered him by tossing plumstones. Two lovers, who were in the bush at the time, escaped this fate. Traveling on through the bush they found a brolga's egg and took it with them to Baranggul (or Bamalagijan), but when they put it to cook in their fire it burst from the heat. Then the man cried out, "Look! A dog!" "Where?" "Over there!" "Perhaps people are following us." "No, there is no one following us." The dog was Bolung's, and when next the couple looked, the dog had vanished and Bolung himself had come up. The man tried to run, but it was too late. Bolung swallowed them both and later spewed them out at Mindjimindji (or Bamalagijan). They revived in the sun and tried to sneak away, which would have been all right except that they pinched each other, so Bolung once more swallowed them. This time he vomited them as diver ducks (or as stones or not at all).

In stories like this a *bolung*, typically referred to as "Bolung" in the narrative, acts destructively after people provoke him by some act. If a baby keeps crying or plumstones are tossed about or an egg bursts in the fire or people pinch each other, there is a risk that a *bolung* will appear to swallow and regurgitate the culprits and their companions. One might say that such myths sanction certain prohibitions of an apparently trifling nature and account for some minor features of the countryside; for example, rocky outcrops explained as the petrified remains of victims vomited or excreted by a *bolung*.

Elkin (1961: 3–5) has published two Rembarnga versions of my M$_3$. In one, two girls survived when a stone fell upon people who were tossing *damper* [native bread] up in the air and catching it as it fell. Two eggs the girls were cooking burst, whereupon a number of creatures came forth from the belly of Muitj, who was lying beneath the earth at this place. He swallowed the girls, and when they tried to run away after he had spewed them out, he swallowed them again. This tale is told in connection with the Dua moiety's *Maraian* ceremony. In the other version, "the rainbow" swallowed people who were tossing plums about at Bamalagial.

These myths (M$_{1-3}$ and Elkin's versions) show that a rainbow snake is a being from whom it is good to keep a distance. If people are originally inside her, she will not or cannot let them go, and a bird has to intervene to free them. If they go readily to her to be swallowed as part of a ceremony performed in collaboration with her, she will not or cannot regurgitate them as anything but bone, so a mother-substitute has to be made from a piece of wood. If they commit trivial transgressions, she (or he) is apt to appear and swallow them with fatal results (for them). A distinction must be drawn, however, between a situation of the kind depicted in M_1 and situations of the kind depicted in the other myths. In the former, people who had never before lived apart from Bolung were able to issue unharmed from her. This was the beginning of mankind on earth. In the latter, people who had lived apart from Bolung were destroyed by passage through her (or his) body. The moral of this sample of myths is, then, that although mankind originally came forth from Bolung, it is not possible to return without destroying oneself.

Thus far I have been considering myth narratives. These are set by definition in times past. It is true that they account for a range of natural appearances and cultural practices and hence have a present-day significance, but one is led to ask whether beings who are *bolung* are still active as distinct from having once been active. The answer is that *bolung* have remained active to this day: they are seen by aborigines and act upon aborigines, and aborigines act toward them.

The most public and obvious *bolung* appearances are as rainbows, whether arching grandly across the entire sky or curved more modestly over a billabong or in the spray of a fall. The word for rainbow is *bolung*, and the term may accordingly be accepted as having an empirical referent.

Little *bolung* are sometimes glimpsed swimming in the water. Such beings are also termed *milmilgan* and are recognizable from their spotted bodies (*bolung* images in rock art are typically splash-spotted). An intimate relation exists between one of these *bolung* and a *gudang* [clever man, magician, native doctor], since one of the latter has one of the former within him, lodged in his back or the back of his head. It passes from him into the patient he wishes to cure and returns distended with bad blood it has sucked from the sufferer. This is later vomited by the magician, who finds blood when he wakes the next morning.

A former magician told me that he saw his *bolung* for the first time while leaning over a pool of water to drink. The snake entered him as he drank the water and he feared death, but the next night he could see all the way to the towns of Katherine and Alice Springs. The gift of farsightedness is imputed to the interior possession of a *bolung* and is likened nowadays to the experience one has while watching a film, of seeing distant places. My informant lost his familiar after a methylated-spirits binge: the snake, intolerant of the fiery spirit, rose from the magician's head and dived into some nearby water. Its flight from the magician meant the loss of his curative powers.

Bolung may be heard as well as seen. Thus one evening while I was camped in the Arnhem Land Reserve with some aborigines, one of them, worried by the late return of members of our party, recalled having seen a rainbow that afternoon at a little spring and having heard it playing a *didjeridoo* [drone pipe]. Perhaps it had swallowed the absent ones? Another aborigine suggested that what had been seen might have been a *mumurijal* [child-spirit, transformed spirit of the dead]. These are not feared. A third man remarked that if Bolung called you, you had to go to him (her) and be swallowed. The attraction of the call (*bo:*) is conceived to be irresistible, at least if it is, as it were, personally directed. But if a *bolung* is calling out without calling to anyone in particular, it seems that it is possible to make one's escape. Thus a man told me that once, while fishing in a pool on the Beswick Reserve, he heard Bolung and felt the rocks shaking. He quickly left the place.

I was told that Bolung had killed three white men in the Katherine headwaters area. But meetings with *bolung* need not be fatal, even if they include swallowing and regurgitation. A man still living on the Beswick Reserve was reputed to have been swallowed by a *bolung* while busy pulling a crocodile he had killed out of the Wilton River. The snake took him beneath the water and spewed him out at a place where a number of *bolung* were performing an *Ubar* ceremony (this ceremony requires the use of drone pipes). This process was repeated several times.

The presence of a *bolung* is often remarked upon or suspected. One example: when an *Ubar* gong was being submerged in a pool of water between uses, a bystander remarked to the man who was pushing it down, "Don't put it too deep—Bolung will take it." A second example: it was remarked of some water trapped in a hollow formed by the exposed roots of a paperbark tree (*mulmu*) that there might be a *bolung* under the tree. A third example: if a stream is swollen, a *bolung* is said to be in the water.

The anecdotes I have related of meetings between man and *bolung* each affected one or a few people who had an unexpected encounter at an isolated spot. These experiences should be distinguished, on the one hand, from public appearances of rainbows and, on the other hand, from ritual meetings with *bolung*. Among the latter, two types of situation can be distinguished.

In the first type, men are genuinely, as they suppose, in a *bolung*'s presence. There is, for example, a rite that used to be performed at a certain waterhole in the Arnhem Land Reserve at the time of first rains (approximately October). A drone pipe would be blown, a lizard killed in the hunt would be put inside, and then the whole would be thrown down into the water. The *bolung*, smelling this offering, would come out to make rain-bearing winds. Because of the depopulation of the reserve, brought about by mass emigration to white-controlled centers during the 1930's and 1940's, this rite is no longer performed.

In the other type of situation, a fiction is maintained by some and believed by others that Bolung is present. It is held that *Gunabibi* novices (*gilawudi*) are swallowed by Bolung at the secret grounds to which the initiated men conduct them. When, on the first evening of a new *Gunabibi* performance, bull-roarers sound from the bush outside the general camp, this is taken to be Gunabibi herself calling out to the people. The men gather up the novices with them and run into the darkness in the direction of the "calls." The women and children are left behind. Weeks or months later, men and women converge from opposite directions upon a leafy shelter called *djabanmani*. The novices have been concealed within, and it is from inside it that they will emerge to reappear, gleaming with freshly applied blood, to their womenfolk. Gunabibi has regurgitated them.

What happens, in fact, during the performance is that novices become enlightened about the nature of the ritual process to which they are unavoidably subjected. The picture of events that they had had before being caught up into the *Gunabibi* remains valid for those who are still outsiders, but it is deeply changed for them. To be an insider is to be enlightened; "novitiate" is another name for the process of enlightenment.

Thus we have the paradoxical outcome that when a meeting with a *bolung* is planned and prepared for by the community at large, nothing is to be seen but symbols and nothing is heard but calls from concealment; yet now and again one or a few people unexpectedly meet a *bolung* face to face or hear one from close at hand. And, whereas the movement in a ceremonial setting is to go in the direction whence the calls are coming (men, novices) or to stay where one is (women, children), the tendency otherwise is to withdraw, to put a distance between oneself and the sight or sound of the rainbow snake. The ritual productive of rain-bearing winds does not fit this pattern, for there is no suggestion that the men who carry it out practice a deceit upon outsiders and there is neither a face-to-face meeting as sometimes occurs unexpectedly in the bush nor a knowing substitution of symbols for symbolized as in the *Gunabibi*. The actors in the rain ceremony put themselves deliberately in the unseen presence of a *bolung*.

The contrast between unplanned meetings that actually happen and planned meetings that do not come off can perhaps be taken as an indication that in the aboriginal view of man–*bolung* relations it is *bolung*, not man, who takes the initiative. This is in keeping with the more general fact that it is usual for *bolung* to act upon man (ordering his society, swallowing and regurgitating him, enabling him to cure), not for man to act upon *bolung*. Mythic history and living memory tend thus to convey the same view of man–*bolung* relations.

BOLUNG AS ATTRIBUTE

Bolung has appeared in the preceding section as a word that functions substantively as the name of a being (Bolung) known also under other names and as the name of a class of beings (*bolung*). The beings so referred to look like snakes and are intimately associated with water. There is, however, another use of the word in which it qualifies other words; that is, in which it names an attribute that beings have.

I came across this additional usage when asking how one was to distinguish two sorts of "animal"; for example, the sort of kangaroo that one might see in the bush and that aborigines hunt for food, and the sort of kangaroo that appears as a mythic figure and perhaps is mimed in ritual. The same name is used for them both *gudabu:* (or *gandagi*) for a male and *gandai* for a female plains kangaroo, *namar* for a male and *wuler?* for a female rock kangaroo. The answer was that the one may be qualified as *du:ning*, the other as *bolung*, though usually this distinction is implied and not expressed, since it is clear in most instances which sort of kangaroo is meant. This pair of opposed terms, *bolung/du:ning*, may similarly be used in referring to other species.

Beings who possessed the *bolung* attribute are conceived of as having been equivocally human and not-human in form and action. In addition, they are conceived of as having had certain powers of action (sometimes understood as self-transformation) that neither an ordinary human nor an ordinary not-human enjoys. Myths, for example, commonly depict their characters as like the animals after whom they are named, and yet, in the course of the story, the characters change into those very animals. Thus a Dalabon fire myth (Maddock 1970a: 176) opposes Rainbow Bird to Crocodile in a conflict over who will have fire, but it is only after Rainbow Bird has won that the pair become unambiguously animal. Crocodile had, until then, made fire and used it to cook his food; Rainbow Bird had eaten fish, lizards, and shellfish—raw, of course Crocodile, after losing fire, went down into the water; Rainbow Bird went up into the treetops. Aborigines will say of myth characters that they were like people, but the way in which myths are told shows that the characters had features of the not-human creatures that they were to become. Rainbow Bird, attempting to capture fire from Crocodile, who would not share it, would swoop down suddenly from a tree to snatch the firesticks, miss them, and then fly up again. Similarly, in rock paintings, myth characters are shown as not-human in form, albeit sometimes carrying such human paraphernalia as headdresses or dilly bags. The fire myth is typical in another way, too, for the actions of its characters were momentous for human life. Rainbow Bird, by capturing fire, was able to make it available to humans, who would otherwise have had to eat their food raw. Because these opponents were prototypical of rainbow birds and crocodiles, they explain two of the species to be seen in the world today.

Beings called *bolung* and beings with the *bolung* attribute thus exercized a creative power during primeval times. The myths about them add up to a creation picture conveyed by no myth taken singly. One may presume that such a cosmology is fluid, for the number of myths is not fixed, the telling of a myth is apt to vary from one aborigine to another, and stories or story episodes must be added to or deleted from the total body current in a community, if only because the human composition of the community changes over time and the divisions of sex, moiety, and initiation status within it prevent anyone gaining a view of the whole. The common use of the word *bolung* may be understood to convey a significant common quality of the beings of whom the word is used; the difference between the nominal and attributive uses of the word may be understood to convey a significant distinction among those beings who acted creatively in primeval times. Before discussing this distinction more closely, I shall explicate what *du:ning* means.

This word is used to qualify the ordinary members of a species, in contrast to the extraordinary prototypical members who are qualified as *bolung*. *Dadbu-du:ning* or *guradjadu-du:ning* is accordingly the sort of king brown snake or rock python that might be seen any day in the bush. It lacks extraordinariness and is interchangeable with others of its species. *Dadbu-bolung* or *guradjadu-bolung* is a snakelike being prototypical of ordinary king brown snakes or rock pythons and mentioned in myths and commemorated in rituals. The religious role these beings play gives them a certain individuality as distinct from a mere species character.

Although *du:ning* might often be translated as "ordinary," there are contexts in which "real" or "genuine" would be a better choice. One's mother, for example, can be distinguished from the other women for whom one uses the same kin term (*na?*) by referring to her as *na?-du:ning*. Here, of course, one might suspect an additional layer of meaning, namely the difference between the female from whom one was born (one's ordinary *na?*) and the female from whom the first humans came forth (Bolung, the All-Mother, one's extraordinary *na?*). Only uterine siblings would have the same *na?-du:ning*, but all persons are issue of Bolung.

The sense of *du:ning* as "real, genuine" is also, I think, to be seen in such expressions as *ga? Bolung-du:ning* and *dugula-bolung-du:ning*, where *du:ning* appears to qualify Bolung or *bolung*. I would translate these expressions as "it (is) Bolung really" and "really (genuinely) the ring-tailed opossum who has the *bolung* attribute." Having discussed the *bolung/du:ning* contrast, we may return to the contrast between *bolung* as name and as attribute. Four differences may be noted.

First, beings named *bolung* are to be thought of as a class in their own right (with subclasses, as seen in the preceding section), and there is no empirically observable animal species of which they are prototypical. Beings with the *bolung* attribute are to be thought of by contrast in relation to animal species. If rainbows and the images of rock art convey a notion of what beings called *bolung* look like, living creatures give an idea of what beings with the *bolung* attribute must have looked like in their zoomorphic aspect.

Secondly, although beings named *bolung* and those with the *bolung* attribute are significant in explaining nature and culture, for their actions formed both, the first would seem to be far more important in living experience or, more precisely perhaps, in the interpretation of living experience. They are to be seen in the sky or water, men meet them unexpectedly in the bush, and meetings with one of them are anticipated, at least by the uninitiate, every time that a *Gunabibi* is held. It would not be true to say, however, that beings with the *bolung* attribute are never called upon to make sense of people's experiences. A magician, for example, might have within him his dreaming or totemic spirit which passes from him into his patient to extract bad blood. Such a familiar appears not to have the form of the species of which it is prototypical. Thus I had a *dugula-bolung* familiar described to me as having the appearance of a short length of straw. Its action within the patient was likened to a leech sucking blood.

Thirdly, although beings named *bolung* can work beneficent effects, they often arouse fear and avoidance. To a considerable degree they belong to the class of things proximity to which is dangerous (Maddock 1974). This attitude to present-day experience is consistent with mythology's teaching about the difficulties and dangers that arose from closeness to *bolung*. Beings with the *bolung* attribute are not presented in this way. The myths often depict them as difficult or quarrelsome, but the trouble they made was for others of their kind. Clearly, then, they stand in a different relationship to humans.

Finally, beings named *bolung* are associated more with nature and common experience, while beings with the *bolung* attribute are associated more with culture and hence with particularism. Thus Bolung is mother to all: that is, she stands in the same relationship to everyone. Classes and matriclans, which are not localized and the members of which are widely dispersed, are imputed to her. The rains which renew the earth are from *bolung*, and rainbows arching across the sky make *bolung* visible to everyone. Anyone might meet a *bolung* face to face, and, as will be seen in the next section, everyone contains a *bolung*. Bolung (or *bolung*) myths and anecdotes are, of course, located spatially, but these beings seem not to be territorially definitive in the way in which beings with the *bolung* attribute are. The latter are thought of especially in relation to the paths they traversed, which form a mythic network right across the countryside; to the named places at which they acted while traveling; and to the patriclans of which they are the dreaming or totemic spirits.

BOLUNG AS PHASE

The aborigines posit a cycle of reincarnation in which a spirit passes through a succession of phases. In one of these it is a *bolung* or, more particularly, a *mumurijal*. This latter word makes an empirical reference, for it is compounded from *mumu* [eye] and *rijal* [nerve, tendon] and, from what aborigines say, appears to mean the optic nerve. To understand this aspect of *bolung* it is necessary to consider the life–death cycle and its connection with ritual.

Child-spirits, as we may call the *mumurijal*, live in water and may show themselves over a river or a billabong as rainbows. The entry of one of these into her body is necessary if a woman is to bear a child. The spirit that so penetrates the mother becomes the spirit of the child. I was told that the child-spirit enters a woman through her back. It appears at that moment to be like a particle of matter, small and hard, and a man with whom I was discussing child-spirits claimed a resemblance between it and a dried split pea that he noticed lying on the ground near us.

The spirit of a person is his *waral* or, in aboriginal English, "spirit" or "shade." "Shade" is here to be distinguished from a person's shadow (*djulu*). The latter is also understood to lead an existence independent of the person (or animal, tree, etc.) whose shadow it is, but the notion of reincarnation is not extended to it. After a person dies his *djulu* lives on, but the aborigines take next to no interest in it, and I know of no observances directed to it. It is said to go to live among rocks, but I have also heard it suggested that it might become a fish. The *waral*, on the other hand, is conceived of as skeletal in appearance, and the little stick figures to be seen at many rock-art sites are *waral* representations. After a person dies, his *waral* wanders in the bush and may appear to his survivors in dreams, perhaps transmitting curative power to them, or even in waking life, as when a person who has lost his way may be guided in the right direction by a kinsman's *waral*. The spirits of the dead are not feared, but one who is neglected may take its mild revenge by spoiling the chanting of verses at a ceremony or making the singers forget the words or lose their tune.

The spirits of the dead are unable to enter into women again unless they are first transformed into *bolung*. This returns them to the water-dwelling child-spirit phase of existence and is ritually effectuated. If the deceased belonged to the Dua moiety, a *Gunabibi* should be performed for his *waral*; if he was of the Jiridja moiety, then a *Jabuduruwa* should be held. These are postmortuary cults: that is, they are celebrated after the rites of primary and secondary disposal have been completed, though nowadays, when it is usual for aborigines to die in hospitals and to be buried in a municipal graveyard, they are rarely performed. Ideally a *Maraian* would also be performed for the spirit some time after the *Gunabibi* or

Jabuduruwa, but in practice the number of ceremonies for a spirit (and indeed whether any at all are held) depends on whether the dead person is survived for long enough by kinsmen sufficiently active and interested to make the arrangements.

When one of these cults is celebrated for a spirit of the dead it is called *djagulba*. This word would appear to be connected with *gulba* [blood], but I was unable to discover that the aborigines gave *djagulba* any signification apart from its meaning of a cult celebrated for the dead. The same ceremonies can be performed without serving a postmortuary purpose, and in that case they are described as *wiridji-du:ning*. *Du:ning* here qualifies *wiridji*, which the aborigines say means "business" (vernacular for "ceremony"), but I am unsure whether it should be understood as expressing "real, genuine" or "not-*bolung*" or even something else again.

The transformation effected by the appropriate ceremony or ceremonies not only moves the spirit from being *waral* to being *mumurijal* or *bolung*, it also changes its color, shape, and habitat. From white or black, according as its moiety is Jiridja or Dua, it becomes rainbow-colored; from an anthropomorphic stick figure, it becomes snakelike; and from wandering in the bush, it becomes settled in the water.

The spirit is now once more in the prebirth phase of its cycle, but whether it enters a woman again usually depends on itself. Reincarnation does not appear to be conceived as following inexorably upon transformation into a child-spirit, though it is the only direction in which the spirit can move if it is to change its state of existence. The only exception to this freedom is when a rite is performed to stimulate the flow of child-spirits into women, since such a rite must by definition be conceived of as operating coercively. There is a child-spirit increase center near the town of Mataranka, and a rite was performed at it during the 1950's in an attempt to offset the then-high mortality rate among aborigines. The steady rise in population since then is credited to that performance. But the rite has not been performed more recently, and, in general, the aborigines among whom I worked put very little emphasis on increase ritual. Fertility in animals and men is evidently something that can as a rule be left to itself. Though coordinated human effort is needed to make child-spirits of the wandering spirits of the dead, the unforced volition of the child-spirits is relied on, except in abnormal circumstances, for the next phase of existence.

CONCLUSIONS

It is nearly half a century since Elkin (1930a: 258) remarked that the *wondjina* paintings of northwest Australia "are bound up with the organization and beliefs of the tribes concerned, and so will not be fully understood until these are thoroughly studied." The figures shown in these paintings are, as Elkin appreciated and as Lommel (1952) and Petri (1954) have thoroughly demonstrated, bound up with the *ungud* conception, a notion strikingly like that of *bolung*. The two are semantically complex and need to be explained in the light of the organization and beliefs of the people among whom they are current. Indeed, it is in the course of studying their organization and beliefs that one comes to see how far-reaching and pervasive these concepts are; and, conversely, it is in trying to plumb the conceptual depths lying beneath these words that one is led ever further into organization and beliefs. It is questionable, however, that anything like a full understanding can realistically be hoped for, let alone achieved. Why this should be so can perhaps best be seen by considering the question of translation.

I think it will now be clear that the word *bolung* points us to a pattern of thought and imagery. The northwest Australian word *ungud* points us to an analogous pattern. An Ungarinyin or Unambal speaker should, therefore, understand *bolung* if it is translated to him as *ungud* and a Dalabon, Djauan, Maiali, or Rembarnga speaker should understand *ungud* if it is translated to him as *bolung*. The speakers of these languages conceive of perceived realities very similarly. But English does not, so far as I am aware, have words to symbolize *ungud*-type or *bolung*-type patterns of thought and imagery. These aboriginal words have accordingly to be explained rather than translated. It is even the case that English does not contain indigenous notions corresponding to all the elements out of which these imaginative constellations are composed. Snake and rainbow, yes, but rainbow snake or child-spirit or All-Mother? *Ungud* and *bolung* capture like elements in like structures (see my "Introduction" to this volume for an account of *ungud*).

Granted that there is a translation problem, along what lines might one try to understand such a concept as *bolung*? Three lines come to mind as worth following, and I shall sketch them here, though I am not yet ready to develop them systematically and must accordingly admit that they might turn out to be dead ends.

A first approach would be to lay stress on the cyclicity embedded in the concept and to draw attention to the role of cyclical thinking in aboriginal thought generally. Thus human spirits are conceived of as engaged in indefinitely repeated rounds of existence; there is a cycle of the seasons marked by the presence or absence of rain and rainbows; and subsection systems, introduced as we have seen by the All-Mother, are descent cycles. The curvilinear imagery of snakes and rainbows might be considered apt to express the abstract notion of cyclicity. The *bolung* concept, then, harmonizes intellectuality and affectivity in a harmony of cycles and curves.

A second approach would draw attention to the unity of past and present as expressed in relations of analogy and inversion between mythic history and the constructions placed upon present-day experiences. The one, we may say, is constructed in the light of the other. Thus M_1 might be understood as an imaginative reconstruction of conception doctrines. The All-Mother corresponds to the waters in which child-spirits dwell; the people within her to the child-spirits in the water; the spearing by which the people were enabled to issue forth to the act of sex which is paired with the entry of a child-spirit as necessary for the bearing of children (alternatively or additionally, the spearing might be held to correspond to the child-spirit's entry). There would thus be parallel series of elements that can be substituted for each other: All-Mother + first people + spear + n = water + child-spirits + penis + n. M_2 might similarly be put in relation to *Gunabibi* ceremonial, with swallowing and regurgitation in the former corresponding to the rites of entry and exit in the latter, snake to bull-roarer, real presence to symbolic presence, victims reduced to their bones to novices freed from their illusions, and so on. Stories of the type of M_3 would be seen as imaginatively reconstructing such putative experiences of the present day as swallowing a *bolung* or being swallowed by one. It would, of course, be unnecessary to ask which comes first, myth or interpretations of experience. The two exist contemporaneously and can best be understood as forming in relation to each other, with each serving as a model for the other. If one takes this view, then one is better able to understand the fact of change in aboriginal thought and imagery, for myths and interpretations of experience offer well-nigh inexhaustible possibilities for kaleidoscopic combination and recombination.

A third approach would direct attention to the logical and grammatical peculiarities of the word and would seek to develop an explication of *bolung* or *ungud* and other such notions along the lines Lévi-Strauss (1950: xlix–1) suggested for *mana*:

En d'autres termes, et nous inspirant du précepte de Mauss que tous les phénomènes sociaux peuvent être assimilés au langage, nous voyons dans le *mana* . . . , l'expression consciente d'une *fonction sémantique*, dont le rôle est de permettre à la pensée symbolique de s'exercer malgré la contradiction qui lui est propre. Ainsi s'expliquent les antinomies, en apparence insolubles, attachées à cette notion, qui ont tant frappé les ethnographes et que Mauss a mises en lumière: force et action; qualité et état; substantif, adjectif et verbe à la fois; abstraite et concrète; omniprésente et localisée. Et en effet, le *mana* est tout cela à la fois; mais précisément, n'est-ce pas parce qu'il n'est rien de tout cela: simple forme, ou plus exactement symbole à l'état pur, donc susceptible de se charger de n'importe quel contenu symbolique? Dans ce système de symboles que constitue toute cosmologie, ce serait simplement une *valeur symbolique zéro*, c'est-à-dire un signe marquant la nécessité d'un contenu symbolique supplémentaire à celui qui charge déjà le signifié. . . .

I would not wish to commit myself to the applicability of this view in its entirety to the concept of *bolung*. It is important that *bolung* is a being or class of beings as well as an attribute of certain beings, which is as if *mana* were a person or class of persons as well as an attribute that some persons can possess. The point is merely that the difficulty of translating *bolung* into our language (as contrasted to the ease with which it could probably be translated into some, at least, of the other aboriginal languages) is due not only to the fact that it refers to a semantic configuration unlike any to which any of our words refers, but is perhaps a result also of its special symbolic function in verbal (and visual) communication. To include *bolung*, *ungud*, and other aboriginal equivalents in a comparative study of thought symbols and their functions in, say, Melanesian or Polynesian cosmology might yield rich rewards to whoever cares to explore uncharted coastlines.

REFERENCES

CAPELL, A.
   1962 *Some linguistic types in Australia*. Sydney: Sydney University Press.
DAHL, K.
   1926 *In savage Australia: an account of a hunting and collecting expedition to Arnhem Land and Dampier Land*. London: Allan.
ELKIN, A. P.
   1930a Rock-paintings of north-west Australia. *Oceania* 1: 257–279.
   1930b The rainbow-serpent myth in north-west Australia. *Oceania* 1: 349–352.
   1961 Maraian at Mainoru, 1949. II. An interpretation. *Oceania 32: 1—15*.
HIATT, L. R.
   1975 "Swallowing and regurgitation in Australian myth and rite," in *Australian aboriginal mythology*. Edited by L. R. Hiatt. Canberra: Australian Institute of Aboriginal Studies.
LÉVI-STRAUSS, C.
   1950 "Introduction à l'oeuvre de Marcel Mauss," in *Sociologie et anthropologie*. By M. Mauss. Paris: Presses Universitaires de France.
   1962 *La pensée sauvage*. Paris: Plon.
LOMMEL, A.
   1952 *Die Unambal: ein Stamm in Nordwest-Australien*. Hamburg: Hamburgisches Museum für Völkerkunde.
MADDOCK, K.
   1970a "Myths of the acquisition of fire in northern and eastern Australia," in *Australian aboriginal anthropology: modern studies in the social anthropology of the Australian aborigines*. Edited by R. M. Berndt. Nedlands: University of Western Australia Press.
   1970b Imagery and social structure at two Dalabon rock art sites. *Anthropological Forum* 2: 444–463.
   1974 Dangerous proximities and their analogues. *Mankind* 9: 206–217.
   1975 "The emu anomaly," in *Australian aboriginal mythology*. Edited by L. R. Hiatt. Canberra: Australian Institute of Aboriginal Studies.
   1977 "Two laws in one community," in *Aborigines and change: Australia in*

the 1970s. Edited by R. M. Berndt. Canberra: Australian Institute of Aboriginal Studies.

OATES, L. F.
1964   *A tentative description of the Gunwinggu language (of western Arnhem Land)*. Sydney: Sydney University Press.

PETRI, H.
1954   *Sterbende Welt in Nordwest-Australien*. Braunschweig: Albert Limbach.

PIDDINGTON, R.
1930   The water-serpent in Karadjeri mythology. *Oceania* 1: 352–354.

WEST, L.
1964   "A sketch dictionary of Dalabon and related languages of central Arnhem Land." Unpublished manuscript, Australian Institute of Aboriginal Studies, Canberra.

The Fecal Crone

IRA R. BUCHLER

> . . . all the lot—all the whole beehive of
> ideals—has all got the modern bee-disease,
> and gone putrid, stinking. And when the ideal
> is dead, putrid, the logical sequence is only
> stink.
>
> D. H. LAWRENCE

> Poetry is not a turning loose of emotion but an
> escape from emotion; not an expression of
> personality but an escape from it.
>
> T. S. ELIOT

One of the codes through which human societies formulate and com-
municate the system of differences that separates them from other animals concerns the selection and preparation of food for ingestion: in
mythic thought and ethnological theory, the transition from raw to
cooked symbolizes one modality of the passage from their species to our

This essay is dedicated to the memory of my father, Sidney S. Buchler, and the future of my
daughter, Neilyn Celine Buchler, who were denied the chance of meeting one another: with
feelings too deep to express.

The initial research upon which this essay is based was supported by a Special Fellowship
from the National Institute of Mental Health for the study of structuralism and mythology at
the Laboratoire d'Anthropologie Sociale, Collège de France, under the sponsorship of
Professor Claude Lévi-Strauss. I would like to express my gratitude to Professor Lévi-
Strauss, M. I. Chiva, J. Pouillon, and other members of the Laboratoire for their generosity
and hospitality during the 1971–1972 academic year. A particular debt is owed to Barbara
Buchler and Raymond Fogelson for their penetrating and demanding criticisms of various
drafts of this myth. The results presented in this study are partial and incomplete, as they
merely represent the first step toward a structuralization of the Murngin corpus and,
eventually, a structural synthesis of Australian mythology and praxis. Within this myth there
are innumerable possibilities whose internal coherence emerges only in relationship to
other myths that we have been unable to incorporate.

The preliminary research upon which these studies are based was made possible by
two deeply appreciated grants from the Wenner-Gren Foundation for Anthropological

culture.[1] There is a puzzle contained on the other end of this operation that conjoins human groups and other manifestations of the animal kingdom, mythography's alimentary solution to Newtonian law: whatever goes in must come out. A concern with culinary style and interpretation can mask neither the smell nor the substance for which good smells and subtle flavors are destined by the digestive and excretory processes of the organism. And if the principles for selecting and processing what goes in have provided a rich repast for the logic of myth, then what comes out may provide a tasty nutriment for ethnological thought.

The semantic verity of shit[2] is neither exhausted by a catalogue of its objective properties nor wholly contained in the relational proposition: what cooking and eating seeks to render culturally disjoint, digestion and excretion naturally conjoins. For shit, or excrement, or faeces, is never apprehended as a discrete relationship with a *culture's texts*, it is in a metonymical relationship with other things, and in the passage from metonymy to metaphor, which provides the prior conditions and fundamental harmony of mythical thought, its signification transcends its process of composition within codes on either end of the alimentary canal.

"Shit," rather than the more delicate locution "faeces," has been selected in metaphorically relating domains of classification and activity, as it is shit and not faeces, at least in American English, that is an item offered on our logic-menu, in utterances such as (1) "That's a bunch of

---

Research: one devoted to ethnoentomological aspects of mythology and the other concerned with the syntactic properties of mythological discourse.

In order to suggest the deeply felt and global character of the myth(s) to which this work is consecrated, we can call forth, at the outset, the words of the Australian naturalist and ethnographer, Charles P. Mountford:

Any white man who has travelled alone with a group of aboriginal men, in places far removed from the haunts of other white intruders, will have soon become aware of the close personal links between these people and their country and the affection which they feel toward it. Everything that they see about them is reminiscent of their creation and proof of the authenticity of the ancient stories: the hills, the rocks, the conformation of the land, the waterholes, the trees and even, in some places, the grass between the trees (Mountford 1972: 10).

[1]   This passage, as we now understand from the structural studies of C. Lévi-Strauss (1969a) and the Amerindian texts upon which they are based, is inseparable from those other systems of differences within and between cultures, which are metaphorically and metonymically related to culinary codes (on stench, cf. Lévi-Strauss 1969a: 175–185; 1973a: 209–210 [excrement], 362 [excrement, menses, and honey]; 1971b: 287–314 ["Du bon usage des excréments"]; and elsewhere). A concern with menstrual blood is apparently the central concrete element of a recent critique of structuralism (*Times Literary Supplement* 1974). And the most recent demonstration of the jejune nature of the criticisms concerning the handling of concrete data in structuralism is provided by comparing their ethnographic analyses with Lévi-Strauss's decomposition and recomposition (1973a) of clam siphons, dentalia shells, and goat horns, and other Bella-bella and Chilcotin things.

[2]   An ethnographic interpretation of the Maenge (East New Britain) category of the rotten, in which faeces, food, old women, snakes, and other elements ordered in this study are analyzed, has been provided by F. Panoff (1970). This work, as well as psychoanalytic variants on faeces (e.g. Freud 1908, 1917), will be considered in a future, more inclusive synthesis of the Murngin corpus. For an African fecal doppelgänger see Sapir 1977.

shit" and (2) "It's all about who gets to do the shit jobs." Perhaps it is the association of shit in our metaphorical stew with the rotten, the dirty, the low, non-sense, that underlies ethnology, turning a mythic necessity into a ritualized virtue, preferring serial metonymies such as sections and subsections rather than metaphorical operators like shit in the interpretation of Australian ethnography (cf. below). Alan Dundes (1962) sounded a general alarm over a decade ago, and still we prefer corporate groups and clans to excrement: poor taste. But utterances are not texts (Barthes 1972b: 136) and meaning emerges in the multiple paradigmatic interrelations between what appear to be experientially discrete codes within the ensemble of significant orders that become intelligible when a culture's texts are stacked (cf. Boon 1972: 84–89; Geertz 1973: 26). And it is this notion of stacking texts that paradigmatically differentiates the path to meaning which we pursue from American approaches to semantics within anthropology variously known as componential and formal analysis. One more or less rules out metaphor and insists upon an absolute contrast between content and form, whereas for the other the movement to or from metaphor is very nearly everything and all mythic contrasts are, at the same time and in terms of the fundamental paradox of logical types, decided and undecided, products of a quixotic synthesis of systems of differences.

The mutually substitutable and correlative contrasts myth/metamyth, object language/metalanguage, content/form, refer to mythically separable ways of ordering experience that are dialectically conjoined by the elementary principles of selection and procedures of logical deduction which they both employ (cf. Lévi-Strauss 1971b; T. Turner 1973: 357–361).

An issue of substantial significance in structural analytics concerns the relationship between the environment in which myths live and the image of the world which they express. Lévi-Strauss (1969a, 1973b) has suggested that this image, derived through a continual process of composition from ethno-bases, which seeks on a transcendental plane to deduct the principles of coherence of the system of differences that it unfolds, is already inherent in the structure of the mind.

... *l'esprit,* delivered over to a tête-à-tête with itself and escaping from the obligation to compose with objects, is itself in a way found reduced to imitating itself as object . . . it thus confirms its nature of a thing among things . . . (Lévi-Strauss 1964: 18; my translation).

Those other things thru which myths organize and recognize their logical processes are pieces of an ecology, inner and outer, that is already structural in nature and culture: articulated myths are *eo ipso* metamyths, just as metamyths are myths. The myth/metamyth, emics/etics contrastive puzzles are partial productions of a mythic subject/object dilemma that is equally at the base of mythological and ethnological thought. The structural approach to meaning is neither a dressed-up form of idealism nor mentalism: it is firmly rooted in materialism and is, in consequence, a close kin of neo-Marxist thought (cf. Godelier 1970, 1972; Terray 1972; Wilden 1972).

A particularly apposite example is provided by the conception of knowledge as production in Marxist cosmology (Althusser and Balibar 1970: 34–35; Terray 1972), a position that is closely related to Lévi-Strauss's efforts to synthesize the basic, mythic contrasts of the empiricist conception of knowledge in the "Overture" to *The raw and the cooked*, as well as in more recent deductions and productions (cf. Lévi-Strauss 1973b). Geras's assessment (1972: 63–64) outlines some of the epistemological convergences:

The structure of the empiricist conception of knowledge is defined, according to Althusser, by a small number of central concepts: those of subject and object, of abstract and concrete, and of the given. The starting point of the knowledge process is conceived as "a purely objective 'given' ", i.e., as something immediately visible and accessible to direct observation. But since what *is* so given is supposed to be the real (object) itself, the concrete, the starting point for knowledge must be concrete reality. The subject must perform on the latter an operation of abstraction in order to acquire thereby a knowledge of it. This is empiricism's first mistake: it takes the initial object or raw material of theoretical practice to be reality itself.

The various realizations of the subject/object dilemma through which we build up our paradoxes—etic/emic, content/form, their myths/our metamyths, empirical/transcendental deductions—are synthesized by structural and neo-Marxist thought in the unfolding of the material foundations of their uncertainty axiomatics.[3] The empirical deductions formulated by mythic thought are the food upon which ethnological praxis nourishes itself in the formation of transcendental deductions which, in turn, are the empirical deductions for further transcendental deductions in a ceaseless exchange between content and form (Lévi-Strauss 1973b; Durkheim 1957: 227-228).

Despite these fundamental convergences, a minimal difference which makes all the difference between structural and neo-Marxist thought remains, and the contours of this difference are nicely outlined by Godelier:

[3]   Compare Barthes (1972a: 159):
". . . if we penetrate the object, we liberate it but we destroy it; and if we acknowledge its full weight, we respect it, but we restore it to a state which is still mystified. It would seem that we are condemned for some time yet always to speak *excessively* about reality. This is probably because ideologism and its opposite are types of behavior which are still magical, terrorized, blinded and fascinated by the split in the social world. And yet, this is what we must seek: a reconciliation between reality and men, between description and explanation, between object and knowledge."

Marxism is not a philosophy of history, or a "model of history." History is not a concept that explains, but that one explains. Marxism is above all a theory of society, a hypothesis regarding the articulation of its internal levels and the specific hierarchical causality of each of these levels. Marxism assumes both the relative autonomy of social structures and their reciprocal relation of *referring back* to a system of *constraints* which determine in the last analysis, but which are never directly visible, and which express the conditions of production and reproduction of the material basis of social existence. Developing the theory of these structures, their articulations, their causality and the conditions necessary for them to appear and disappear, signifies making history a science and developing it as such, as provisional synthesis and conclusion, as "reproduction of the concrete by means of thought" (1972: xxviii–xxix; cf. "all the positive determining factors . . . " [Godelier 1971: 95]).

That the mode of production determines the character of political, social, and intellectual life implies a mythic contrast within neo-Marxist thought: between a cause and its consequence (cf. Thompson 1961: 272 on biological causality). And it is upon the edifice raised on the basis of this distinction that structuralist and Marxist thought part company. For the former, there are no privileged orders of experience, whereas for the latter, one order determines—directly or dialectically—everything worth determining. We provide a mythic proof in this essay that interpretations predicated on the cause/consequence contrast of historical materialism are variants of the mythical matrix of groups whose fundamental determinants they purport to explain. The distinction between a cause and its consequence emerges as yet another expression of a mythologized distinction between *they*, whose thought and activities are interior to an order of orders and are therefore mystified puppets of it; and *we*, who are exterior to these orders and are *in consequence* in a privileged position to determine its determinants. Mythological analytics decomposes the primitive paradox of the neo-Marxist critique of structuralism: that it assumes an absolute ordering external to mythological universes and a privileged position within them (cf. Kroeber 1952: 107). In the phenomenology of Merleau-Ponty (1964: 276), the locus of the fundamental Marxist drama is not in determinant relationships between superstructures and infrastructures or between men and things, but rather in a choice, built into the logic of situations, between revolution as action and as truth. Depoliticizing this formulation, deleting the "revolutionary" qualifier, brings us a bit closer to home on the condition that we neutralize the action/truth diacritic. Divided in some matters, overdetermined synthesis in others: the theory of theoretical practice (Althusser 1970: 209, 266, 272).

Myths, in a sense, are in neither language nor culture: they are multidimensional assessments of orders of differences that define the interrelated distances within and between culture(s) and language(s); they are not in but articulate between and are more perspectives on another and less descriptions in themselves (Lévi-Strauss 1971b: 577). As myth is a type of speech, a discourse between, it can be defined, not by the object which its message conveys, but by the manner in which a message is conveyed, by the appropriation of matter for "social usage" (Barthes 1972a: 109), or the distribution of social usages as matter. As a language in which it becomes possible to speak about language, myth may either be mythologized as a second-order semiological system (Barthes 1972a: 114), or as a language behind language: subsequent or prior, it preserves the illusion of distance, to compose with objects what it seeks to decompose in relations. A text, like yet another mirror, provides a metonymical ordering of things drawn from particular angles: the internal coherence of the pieces, language-objects that experience suggests and reasoning derives, emerges as a process of refraction: angles between refracted codes and the perpendicular (the angle of, case for flexible inflexions) to the texts *as myth* at the point of incidence. The angle of these angles between orders is the production of depoliticized speech: seeking to impoverish the historical qualities of things, myth removes "from things their human meaning so as to make them signify a human insignificance" (Barthes 1972a: 142–143) in reconstituting the fundamental harmony of mythical thought.

The problem of the meaning of an old woman's shit, and the metaphorical uses of shit in the passage from stinking and thinking, dissolves into a consideration of constituent elements: old, woman, shit (and faeces), and their combinatorial relations with other building blocks in (Australian: "Murngin") mythical thought and ritual practice. We are immediately confronted with the idea of a myth, which refers either to a particular text, metonymizing elements drawn from a multiplicity of ensembles, or to a metaphorically derived set of relations of relations that obtain between a group of texts. It is undecidable whether these relations are in the object language or the metalanguage which decomposes and recomposes the set: a doubly reflexive conjunction of thought processes rules out the necessity of a mythologized arbitrator to sort out the treasure (cf. Lévi-Strauss 1969a: 13–14). To provide correlative contents for these forms: the Freudian interpretation of Oedipus (Lévi-Strauss 1955) is a variant—neither archaic nor derived, and the neo-Marxist interpretation of Lévi-Strauss's study (1969b: 168–196) of Murngin exchange by Godelier (1970: 344–346) is, simultaneously, a variant of structuralism and Marxism: it poses the problem of a relational synthesis, rather than the promise of a unique solution.

Within *a* culture, mythical thought poses differences between categories of natural beings—things given in nature and used in culture—that are played out as distances between categorically disjoint, intracultural variants: for example, old men/young women, young men/old women. The task of myth analysis is to decompose the ranking of these

elementary categories, on various axes, in order to recompose their analogical relations with orders that appear to be experientially distant.

Structural analysis of myth-o-logics is concerned with (1) establishing
relations of contrast between empirical categories, (2) determining the
right distance between these categories, and (3) unfolding relations between relations: (1) corresponds to the problems that myths construct
and the alternative ethno-bases through which these problems are organized and expressed; (2) corresponds to the solutions (to [1]) that myths
derive; (3) refers to transcendental deduction (Lévi-Strauss 1971a), in
which mythical thought ceases the process of composition with things, the
particular concern of ethno-science, in order to compose its internal
order, now with relationships behind the relations with which it started
and to which it returns. The demonstration of relations of contrast (1)
frequently depends upon the logical procedure that has been referred to
as empirical deduction.

Empirical deduction occurs whenever a myth attributes a function,
value, or symbolic meaning to a natural being because of an empirical
judgment durably associating the being with the attribution. From a
formal point of view the correctness of the empirical judgment is irrel-
evant (Lévi-Strauss 1971a: 3).

To anticipate several possibilities from the Murngin corpus, the lust of
old women, the sensitivity of the rainbow serpent to female odors, the
attribution of a certain generosity to the *wiridwirid* [tail-tail] rainbow
bird, and the assignment of a deceptive and gluttonous nature to the
frilled-neck lizard all exemplify the process of empirical deduction. This
type of procedure has its base in the perception of both cause–effect
contiguities and similarities (Lévi-Strauss 1971a: 19). The necessity that
lies behind the empirical deductions proposed by mythic thought is
imponderous unless some attention is lavished upon the possible objective properties of those objects from which myths compose themselves.
An instance of a judgment in which aspects of ethnozoological knowledge
are contained, somewhat obliquely, in a particular text, will provide the
pretext and context for introducing the reptilian luminary of our reference myth: first the advance publicity.

THE RAINBOW SERPENT

A major creature in Australian mythical thought is that legendary
chromatic snake, the rainbow serpent, widely associated with water,[4]

---

[4]   Without wishing to invoke the roster of names or properties of the sacred serpents known
to mythology, a few should be mentioned: (1) Damballah-wedo, the serpent god of Haitian
voodoo. Associated, like the rainbow serpent, with water (rivers, springs, and marshes; see
Métraux 1972: 104–105), Damballah is white: fully luminous and devoid of any distinctive
hue, he is all hues. (2) The Great Horned Serpent of the Pueblos: Palülükon (Hopi),

death, medicine men, and quartz crystals (Radcliffe-Brown 1926, 1930; McConnel 1930a; Elkin 1930; Mead 1934; Lowenstein 1961; Eliade 1973; cf. Durkheim 1957: 285–288, 292). With characteristic foresight, Radcliffe-Brown noted that

My studies of Australian beliefs have led me to the conclusion that this particular myth is one of the most important of the mythology and that fuller knowledge of it is necessary in any attempt we may make to understand the Australian conception of nature. . . . This myth is a belief in a gigantic serpent which has its home in deep and permanent waterholes and represents the element of water which is of such vital importance to man in all parts of Australia. The serpent is often regarded as being visible to human eyes in the form of the rainbow. The Rainbow serpent as it appears in Australian belief may with some justification be described as occupying the position of a deity, and perhaps the most important nature deity. In some tribes it is the object of a definite cult either as part of the totemic cult or as part of the cult of the initiation ceremonies. In a considerable number of tribes it is the chief source or one of the chief sources of the magical powers possessed by the medicine-men (1930: 342).

The rainbow serpent appears in the story of the Wawalik sisters and is the basis of four major ceremonial cycles: the *Djungguan*, the *Gunabibi*, the *Ulmark*, and the *Marndiella* (Mountford 1956: 278–279; Warner 1958: 248–259, Berndt 1951). The myth is said to be "of extreme importance to the Murngin and is always present in their thinking" (Warner 1958: 248).

A cult of the serpent was an element of the *Bora* [initiation] ceremonies of the New South Wales tribes, and although he is not the Victorian tribes' *bunyip* by another name, the people of Melbourne district associate the great snake Myndie with death and disease and fear greatly to intrude upon his waterhole. These associative beliefs have been reported in North Queensland (McConnel 1930a) and Western Australia (Elkin 1930; Piddington 1930). The men's age grade is a snake and a purifying element, and the sociological women's group is the unclean group. The male snake-group, in the act of swallowing the unclean group, swallows the initiates into the ritually pure masculine age grade: from mystification through ingestion to intelligibility in defecation is the path that we are set upon (LaBarre 1968: 10, 32).

The snake is the fertilizing principle in nature according to Murngin symbolism: this explains why, according to the principal ethnographer, it

Ko'lowisi (Zuni), Awanyu (eastern Pueblos) (Smith 1952: 214; cf. Stevenson 1887). (3) Kukulcan (Maya), Quetzalcoatl (Nahuatl) (Nuttal 1901: 68–71; Vaillant 1962: 56, 133, 140, 142–144, 148, 152, and Plates 22, 53, and 63). Some of the more recent interpretations of M_{1-2} (see Appendix) include Munn (1969) and Layton (1970); and Arndt (1965: 241, 255–256) has given us a useful interpretation of the legend of Kunukban, the black-headed python (*Aspidites m. melanocephalu*) of the Ord Victoria region of northwest Australia, a legend that reveals a penetrating appreciation of snake locomotion and regional geomorphology (cf. Von Brandenstein 1972). A good idea of the innumerable aspects of the rainbow serpent and his kin, in their various transformations, that we have not mentioned, is provided by Robinson (1956).

is identified with the men's group rather than with the women, with whom it is mythically associated; otherwise one would suppose that the male principle, being identified with the positive higher social values, would be associated by the Murngin with the dry season, the time of the year of high social value (Warner 1958: 387).

Lévi-Strauss points to the series of significant contrasts constructed by the mythological system and the mode of representation that it employs; he suggests that the primacy of the infrastructure presents native thought with a contradictory logic and outlines the process thru which the internal undecidability of the logical procedures disguises itself to itself (Lévi-Strauss 1966: 93–94).

Although natural phenomena are not what myths seek to explain, but are rather "the *medium through which* myths try to explain facts which are themselves not of a natural but a logical order" (Lévi-Strauss 1966: 95; original emphasis), the selection of certain natural phenomena and the exclusion of others in the stories that myths convey is critical in making that logical order intelligible. A structuralism that does not depart from its foundations in materialism must sort out the distinctive properties of the material from which it is built, seeking intelligibility in the multiple interrelations of seemingly disparate orders located on different levels rather than assigning any particular organization of content a privileged position.[5]

We know that the Wawalik sisters, "by their uncleanness" (Warner 1958) polluted the waterhole of Yurlunggur, the rainbow serpent. The polluting substance, in different variants, is either afterbirth or menses: a distinctively female emission to which empirical deduction attributes a foul odor: stench.[6] Despite the observation that this pollution was olfactory in nature, analysts have not attempted to relate this selection of mythical thought to ethnozoological knowledge and have, in consequence, failed to utilize this judgment in a true reasoning process. If ". . . what we are doing is not building a theory with which to interpret the facts, but rather trying to get back to the older native theory at the origin of the facts we are trying to explain" (Lévi-Strauss 1968: 351), then we must ask, at the outset: why a snake, why a smell? After all, the

---

[5] With reference to Kariera sections, Von Brandenstein (1970a) has taken to pieces the analytic assumption that the meaning of sections is exhausted by their use in ordering alliances or by some restricted construction of the totemic operator.

[6] Compare Lévi-Strauss (1969a: 270): ". . . stench is the natural manifestation, in an inedible form, of femininity, of which the other natural manifestation, milk, represents the edible aspect." In Middle America, the unmarked value of sex—maleness/femaleness—is derived from the menstrual cycle, which is a sign for this value. "Women are better than men in that sense. They don't have to jump into an abyss. They have their own abyss. Women menstruate. The Nagual told me that that was the door for them. During their period they become something else . . . there is a crack in women, a crack that they disguise very well. During their period, no matter how well-made the disguise is, it falls away and women are bare" (Castaneda 1977: 50–51).

Australians have at their disposal a wide variety of reptiles that, on *a priori* grounds, could play the role attributed to the rainbow serpent, and this serpent might have been offended by the sight of the Wawalik sisters, the sound of their activities, the taste of the polluting substance: *a posteriori*, the judgment is conjointly constrained by a group of empirical deductions contained within the corpus of Murngin myths. From Radcliffe-Brown to contemporary interpreters, the normative path has entailed turning out to those other things with which the rainbow serpent is associated, rather than turning in to the identification and empirical assessment of sensory processes. The story of the Wawalik sisters reduplicates the message, signaling the selection of an olfactory code:

When the menstrual blood dropped into the pool Yurlunggur smelled the odor of this pollution from where he was lying in the black water beneath the floor of the totem well. His head was lying quietly on the bottom of the pit. He raised his head and smelled again and again (Warner 1958: 252).

The Australian zoologist Eric Worrell has identified the rainbow serpent as a water python (*Liasis fuscus* Peters) that is sometimes found in saltwater mangroves and in all far-northern watercourses that eventually empty into the sea. This python grows to a little over ten feet, is a rich glossy brown with an apricot belly, and prefers a cuisine of reptiles, as well as birds and mammals (Worrell 1966: 99, Plates 34, 36, 63). Pythons kill their food by constriction, swallowing their dinner whole without preliminary sliming, often disgorging to obtain a better hold.

Like other snakes, the rainbow serpent lives by smell, for the other sensory processes are rather weakly developed: (1) the eyes are not adapted for long-range focusing, focusing is not fully automatic, and eye movement is restricted; (2) snakes have no external ears and feel vibrations rather than hear sounds; (3) the bifurcated tongue is not developed for the function of tasting, food is tested by scent. In matters of smell, however, they are masters:

The olfactory senses, which seem to be the most developed of the senses in a snake, are somewhat complicated in arrangement, being a combination of nostrils, tongue, and an organ lying in front of the palate known as Jacobson's organ. Traces of this organ occur in most mammalian embryos, including that of man, but persist only in snakes and lizards (Squamata). The nostrils can be used independently, while the thin bifid tongue, normally enclosed in a basal sheath beneath the glottis, is used as a sensory organ to take particles from the air for testing in the paired Jacobson's organs . . . (Worrell 1966: 86).

The empirical deduction that makes the rainbow serpent a master of olfaction (as well as water), a passive gourmet of bad smells, allows the coherence of other empirical judgments in the Murngin corpus to unfold conjointly. Another reptilian deduction in Murngin mythology internally confirms the criterial nature of olfaction and provides a fleeting and partial taste of a transcendental logical procedure.

Human faeces are in a metonymical relation with turtles and tortoises in a number of Murngin myths (M_3, M_8; see Appendix for a list of the myths), and faeces, unlike menses and afterbirth, is a sexually undifferentiated bodily emission (physically that is: mythically aligned with relatively older men and their natural shadows; cf. below). What do turtles and tortoises have to do with fetid things that would make this relationship intelligible, contrasting turtles and tortoises on the one side and water pythons on the other? Worrell's observations (1966: 10–14) suggest that these myths knew what they were doing:

> In some of the stronger-smelling species the scent-glands in the bridge of the shell are first chopped out before cooking.
>
> The scent-glands are situated on both sides of the tortoise, in the anterior and posterior of the bridge. In Australia only some of the long-necked species produce an odour strong enough to be objectionable to man, although the glands are present in all species. It seems likely that all species produce an odour that can be detected by their normal enemies. The fear odour is released only when the tortoise is molested, and probably a barrier of smelly water can be spread in times of danger (Worrell 1966: 12).

> The Hawksbill (*Eretmochelys imbricatabissa* Rüppell) is largely a fish-eater, and not considered particularly palatable. North Australian aborigines, however, do eat this species after removing scent-glands, or "poison-bags" as they call them (Worrell 1966: 11).

The rainbow serpent, a good consumer of smells, is associated with female bodily emissions related to reproductive processes, whereas a turtle (or tortoise), a producer of bad smells, has to do with sexually undifferentiated bodily emissions (the production of large quantities of faeces, for offensive or defensive purposes, is attributed to both male and female characters: cf. below) related to digestive processes. Australia's most significant nature diety is a dialectical cross-cousin of human faeces.

THE MURNGIN PUZZLE

These are not peripheral issues, nor do they represent a retreat to the land of the lotus-eaters! Quite the contrary. Although we cannot provide a definitive proof in this essay, our thesis is that a wide variety of ethnobases are directly relevant to one of the more refractory puzzles in the anthropologist's bag of tricks, the Murngin problem. The Murngin problem refers, of course, to the Murngin exchange system; and alternative solutions of this puzzle have been organized, without exception, in terms of a group of separable, although related, ethnological constructs: rule of marriage, sections and subsections, kinship nomenclature, descent lines/local lines, and so on.

In view of a recent inquest, a resolution of the confusion surrounding this major analytic problem in social anthropology would appear to be highly problematic (Barnes 1967; Maddock 1970a). Does this confusion stem from the inadequacy of the ethnographic information at hand, the paradoxical properties of the exchange system, or the ethnological constructs through which solutions have been organized and expressed? An intent of this essay is to provide a partial demonstration that this confusion derives more or less directly from an exclusive reliance upon the analytic lexicon of social anthropology (cf. Maddock 1970a: 89).

The Murngin exchange system is a system of generalized (asymmetric) exchange that presents the appearance of a system of restricted (symmetric) exchange. Typologically, the system is medial to the Kariera and Aranda games, differing from the former in form and from the latter in function (Lévi-Strauss 1969b: 168, 190).

The various groups of people that populate the northeastern regions of Arnhem Land, known traditionally and collectively as the Murngin, have eight subsections, like the Aranda, although the subsections do not function as they do in Aranda: rather than eliminating cross-cousins from the class of possible spouses, they retain them. Unlike Kariera, with a symmetric exchange system, the Murngin, although they appear to function as if they have a section rather than a subsection system, prescribe marriage asymmetrically, although they revive the conditions of bilateral exchange: in the lexicon of genealogical specifications, MBD is ruled in as a preferred spouse, whereas FZD is ruled out. The locus of the paradox is medial to the rule of marriage and the operation of the subsection system, for a man has a choice between two subsections which comprise one section. Proposed solutions to this anomaly by Lévi-Strauss (1969b), seconded by Dumont (1966: 244–249), are based, to a certain extent, upon Elkin's distinction (1932–1933) between regular and alternate (straight/oblique; Dumont 1966: 246) marriages, which, in Lévi-Strauss's hypothesis, alternate in a male line with the generations, harmonizing the individual marriage rule and the rule of marriage and filiation in the vocabulary of sections. The doubling of the masculine cycle appears to annul the specific effects of a system of subsections[7] and poses the problem of establishing the relationship between two systems of differences, a difference in the class mechanism and a difference in marriage preferences (Lévi-Strauss 1969b: 174). This solution provides a means of synthesizing the logical problems posed by construing the

[7]   "If Aborigines manipulate kinship categories, marriage rules and subsections, they do so in the course of creating systems, many of whose elements are not phenomena of kinship" (Maddock 1970a: 89).

system through the lexicon of restricted exchange with a grammar of generalized exchange (cf. Lévi-Strauss 1969b: 186–190).

Our concern is at once more restricted and more general than prior interpretations of the Murngin puzzle. More restricted in the sense that certain differences (principles of kinship nomenclature, subsections) through which generalized exchange is organized and played out—the mechanics and categorical base of the game—are not a matter of direct concern. This restriction stems in part from pragmatic considerations: the inspired *bricolage* that has given us variant but apparently equally unacceptable solutions to the Murngin exchange system has been exclusively expressed through ethnological constructs. My thesis has two aspects. First, these solutions are neither right nor wrong, nor are they rankable in view of their relative truth value. As they involve a seemingly endless play of combinations and recombinations of essentially similar elements, they are mythical variants, *bricolage*—for ethnologists, a group of transformations. My second point, closely tied to the first, derives more or less directly from the structuralist notion that the meaning of any paradigmatic set (e.g. the analytic, kinship constructs previously used to apprehend Murngin exchange) is contained not exclusively in the rules of formation which produce that set, but rather in the multiple interrelations between that set and other sets (cf. Terray 1972: 141), which is defined by simultaneity rather than causality. Meaning, in consequence, is a matter of internal coherence, the transcendental deduction of mutually convertible significations on a variety of levels. A perspective of this sort invites the possibility of admitting elements other than those pertaining directly to "kinship and marriage," in order to assess indirectly the multiple refractions and mythical constructs through which one aspect of the Murngin system—as conceived of by ethnological theory—is expressed: the formula of asymmetrical intermarriage. Rather than proposing yet another ordering for the same group of elements, the asymmetric formula is selected from the group and brought into play in relationship to other elements that have not been traditionally regarded as proper concerns of kinship theory. Although it is one among many things, some anthropologists regard the elementary relationship that we have selected as the fundamental puzzle in the Murngin controversy:

Now though much of the controversy has been due simply to misunderstandings and a lack of consistency and uniformity in notating and interrelating the subsection categories (Barnes, 1967: 9–26) and in handling the "kin" categories in relation to whether they are patri- or matri-determined (Maddock, 1970), the core of the controversy, the asymmetry, remains. Again, although with Maddock's article (above) the datum of MBD marriage disappears in favor of a marriage between Ego and the mother's mother's brother's daughter's daughter (MMBDD) and the Murngin (or Wulamba) are not now as exceptional as they had seemed to be, the asymmetry is still there, and so is the problem of what it is all for (Burridge 1973: 141).

Taking a single Murngin myth as a point of departure and reference ("The story of the Wawalik sisters"), I will demonstrate the manner in which the choice of a modality of exchange is refracted in multiple orders of signification. Refracted in the sense that the structural schema underlying Murngin beliefs about bodily emissions (faeces, menses, vomit), natural elements (fire, water), the classification of meat (fatty meat/bad meat) and persons (young/old, male/female), cultural (initiation rites, the exchange of access rights in land) and natural (wet/dry) periodicity define conceptual dilemmas that are soluble only in terms of the admissibility of an asymmetric distribution of food and women as a synthetic operator. The mythologically embedded constraints therefore define asymmetry, in variant expressions, as the right distance between a group of mutually convertible sensory contrasts.

Our intention is subversive only for those who regard the proper study of kinship as given, at the outset, by the analytic constructs of social anthropology. But we already know, from the work of Von Brandenstein (1970a),[8] that the meaning of section in Kariera is neither exhausted by nor solely reducible to a discourse whose lexicon is selected from alliance and descent theory: sections encode a global conception of order. Within this global construction, there are no privileged relationships, orders of priority: the affinal operator does not provide an automatic access to the cosmology within which it is embedded. This form of composition, style in search of a cosmological intelligibility, to identify with the acute sensibility and logical power of its object, whom it seeks to serve as exegete and advocate thru the point-counterpoint of concrete differences and formal affinities, does not seem too distant from the aboriginal premise of existence-potentials (possibilities), with concrete creatures and phenomena, beliefs and actions as realizations. And it is the return from the discontinuous to the continuous thru the dreaming that is the gift of initiation into the sacred rituals and mythical thought: the essence of the nonappearing (cf. Elkin 1969: 87–88; Ashley Montagu 1937: 336).

This is neither more nor less than a slightly different way of coming at an old problem: the choice between a restricted kinship operator in the style of Lévi-Strauss (1965, 1969b); Goodenough (1970); Scheffler and Lounsbury (1971); and Scheffler (1972); and a more inclusive mythic operator in the style of Lévi-Strauss (1966), Leach (1967), Geertz

---

[8] "Apparently Aboriginal tradition has carried into our times only the relics of a prehistoric, perhaps once universal, concept of world order. This world order ruled totemism as, perhaps, mathematics rule technology today" (Von Brandenstein 1970a: 47). This study continues a quest for a more global intelligibility associated, within ethnology, with such names as Durkheim and Mauss (1963), C. Lévi-Strauss, R. Needham, and E. R. Leach. Ethnological neglect of another dimension of Australian systems, political strategy and manipulation, has been equally profound (cf. Hart 1970: 302; Barnes 1965: x).

(1966), and Geertz and Geertz (1975), a strategic retreat from the ethno-graphic goal of global intelligibility, or an immersion within it, buried under pragmatics as a thing apart, or resurected mythically, dispersed in a continuous field.

A related concern is to provide a demonstration, however partial and tentative, of the mutual convertibility of myth and ethnographic interpre-tation. Mythology and ethnology are, by this mode of reckoning, relative terms rather than absolute categories: they are the interlocutors in a dialogue that seeks to neutralize the difference between the logic of the concrete and the language of the abstract. My specific thesis is that materialistic interpretations of social arrangements and cultural solutions are well-defined variants of the myths of the groups of people whose classifications they attempt to explain.

As an aside, which is as central as anything can be, we use "we" neither to upgrade me, by appropriating the royal form, nor to degrade he (she) by allocating the message solely to the other: rather inflexively: that he in me that reflexively derives am I (they are) without them, I merged with he, us against them, back to go.

It's true I have not spoken yet. In at one ear and incontinent out through the mouth, or the other ear, that's possible too. No sense in multiplying the occasions of error. Two holes and me in the middle, slightly choked. Or a single one, entrance and exit, where the words swarm and jostle like ants, hasty, indifferent, bringing nothing, taking nothing away, too light to leave a mark. I shall not say I again, ever again, it's too farcical (Beckett 1965: 354–355).

SOMETHING SMELLS FISHY

> In vials of ivory and coloured glass
> Unstoppered, lurked her strange synthetic perfumes,
> Unguent, powdered, or liquid-troubled, confused
> And drowned the sense in odours. . .
> T. S. ELIOT, *The waste land*

M_1 *(Yirrkalla): The Story of the Wawalik Sisters*

The Wawalik sisters came from a locality far away to the west. As they traveled they collected and named all the yams. They are *arituna*, black inside; *jakwa*, white inside; *mawoka*, milky white inside, with a black stem; *dilkaruu*, with hair from its roots like a beard; *wunga-rapu*, red inside with black roots; *kungari*, a large round yam that must be soaked all night to make it edible; and many others. The sisters also caught and named a number of the food animals and reptiles—the kangaroo (*karitjimba*), the lizard (*tjunda*), the bandicoot (*warnt-kura*), the blan-ket lizard (*baltjira*), to mention but a few.

When they reached a waterhole called Mirrirmina, the elder sister, who was pregnant, begged her companion to make a camp because she felt that she was about to give birth to her child. The younger woman quickly built a bark hut, placed her sister inside, then lit a fire to cook the yams. No sooner had she placed them on the fire, however, than they all came to life and ran away. Again she tried to prepare a meal, this time placing the dead animals and reptiles on the coals, but they too, came alive and escaped into the forest. Both of the Wawalik women then retired into the hut, and soon afterward the elder sister gave birth to a son.

In the bottom of the nearby waterhole, Mirrirmina, lived a huge mythical brown python called Jurlungur (nonsacred name, *witik*). The odor of the blood of the birth so annoyed him that he first came to the surface and sent flashes of lightning into the sky and then, leaving his waterhole, approached to punish the women. When the women saw the enraged serpent approaching, they sang many magical songs and danced many powerful dances to send him back to his waterhole, but he still came on. In desperation, the women went inside and blocked the openings of their hut with bark and leaves to keep Jurlungur at bay. But the serpent pushed his head inside and swallowed the child, then the younger sister, and finally the elder sister. He returned to the waterhole but later came again to the surface and regurgitated the women and child, whose bodies are now large rocks (Mountford 1956: 278–279; cf. McCarthy 1960: 425–427 for a myth which associates the origin of ninety-two string figures with the wanderings of the Wawalik sisters).

Warner (1958: 250–259) gives a more extensive version of the myth of the Wawalik women. We provide a summary of the more detailed version:

M₂ (Murngin): The Wawalik Women

M₂ (Murngin): The Wawalik Women

The Wawalik women walked from the interior to the Arafura Sea. The older sister carried her male child; the younger sister was pregnant. Before they left, they had incestuous relations with their clansmen. On their way they gathered and named all the plants and animals that are in the Murngin country today. As they went along, they named the country. After the child was born, they moved on toward the sea, naming all the clan territories and localities.

They stopped at the great Mirrirmina [rock python's back]. The older sister made a fire with her fire drill. The animals and food jumped out of the fire as they were being cooked and jumped into the Mirrirmina waterhole. The older sister's menstrual blood fell into the sacred waterhole as she was gathering bark to make a bed for her sister's child.

The python smelled blood and opened the bottom of the well by throwing the stone which covers its base onto the land near the women's camp. The python crawled out of his well, sucked some well water into his mouth and spit it into the sky. He hissed to call for rain. A cloud formed in the sky and the totemic well water rose and flooded the earth. The cloud grew larger and it started to rain, harder and harder. The women hurriedly built a house and went inside.

The older sister sang and danced around the house; the younger sister stayed inside. All the snakes in the land came and formed a circle around them, for they had heard the call of their father, Yurlunggur. It was night and the women did not see them. They sang the Dua subsection names. They sang the *garma* songs[9] first,

---

[9]   "All the water holes found in the territory of a clan are divided into two classes: they are either garma wells or narra (ranga) wells. The first are totemic but not sacred; they were made by the lower order of totems, whose emblems may be displayed in camp and seen by the women. The narra wells are always sacred; they were made by the higher wongar totems,

then the songs of the *Marndiella*, the *Djungguan*, and the *Ulmark*. The rain came down harder and harder.

The women sang Yurlunggur and menstrual blood. When Yurlunggur heard these words he crawled into their camp. They had suddenly fallen into a deep sleep from his magic. Before swallowing them and their sons, he bit the nose of each and made the blood come. He stood very straight, like the trunk of a high tree: he reached as high as a cloud and the flood waters came up as high as he did. (In some versions, after swallowing the women, the rainbow serpent flies over the country and names the various territories). When he fell, the water receded and there was dry ground. While he was high in the sky and had the two women and children inside him, he sang all the *Marndiella*, *Djungguan*, *Gunabibi*, and *Ulmark* ceremonies.

In another version (Berndt 1951), the women carried stone spears and put the various animals and yams that they gathered in their large *bulpul* [dilly bag]. Julunggul, the rock python or rainbow serpent, is said to be the headman of the animals, birds, and vegetables. This variant attributes the pollution of the well to the python, who creates rain which washes the coagulated blood from the ground into the well (Berndt 1951: 22). In some interpretive comments, the python's entry into the sisters' hut is associated with a penis entering a vagina: prior to ingestion, Julunggul sprays the Wawalik sisters with a salival substance, *ngal*, which is a term also used to denote semen.

SERPENTINE DECLENSIONS

1. The gecko of Groote Eylandt, *ipilja-ipilja*, lives in a swamp and is described as "a huge, highly-coloured lizard, about one hundred feet long, with hair on his head and whiskers" (Mountford 1956: 75). The gecko's waterhole is sacred and anyone foolish enough to drink from it will surely die. The gecko is the master, like the rainbow serpent, of thunder and rain. The gecko makes thunderstorms by eating grass from the edge of the sacred swamp, drinking large amounts of water, and spitting them both into the sky. The water makes the clouds, the grass binds them together. The sound of thunder is the gecko roaring to express his pleasure. Both the gecko and the rainbow serpent are greatly feared, punish intruders with sickness and death, are polychromatic, have hair and whiskers, and make a roaring noise.

2. The emu is also associated with the rainbow serpent in the form of the emu-man, Gurugadji (Oenpelli: Mountford 1956: 212–214), who

---

whose emblems are ranga (higher emblems) and can be seen only by the initiated young men after the age of puberty" (Warner 1958: 20).

"The garma totems are all lower than the rangas (high totems). The rangas are preponderantly connected with the myths of the two sisters, but the garma generally are not" (Warner 1958: 401).

was captured by two men who crept up on him, one seizing his head, the other his neck. The emu-man escaped by changing himself into a rainbow serpent and devouring the two hunters. The transformed emu-man now appears in the sky in the form of a rainbow and is greatly feared.

The rainbow serpent and the emu are associated, in some accounts, as parent and child, which makes a featherless emu a kind of water snake and therefore a master of water. These remarks are cited in Radcliffe-Brown (1930: 344) and attributed to Mrs. Parker's *The Euahlayi tribe* (see Parker 1905; Stow 1953; Yularai: R. H. Mathews, in *Folklore of the Australian aborigines* [1899], refers to the *gauarge* as the children of the *karia*):

Certain waterholes are taboo as bathing places. Some of these are inhabited by *karia* which swallow their victims whole. Others contain a mythical beast known as *gauarge* [spelled Gowargay by Mrs. Parker], which is described as like a featherless emu which sucks down in a whirlpool anyone who dares to bathe in one of his holes.

3.   An Oenpelli myth associates the rainbow serpent and the kangaroo by making the kangaroo the master of the master of rain (the rainbow serpent) (Mountford 1956: 218).

In Melanesian mythical thought, yams—assiduously collected and lexically filed by the Wawalik sisters—are frequently associated with masculine sexual symbolism (Wik-Mungan, Trobriands, and so on): the bottom part is similar to the scrotum, the top part is like the male sexual organ, and the small roots attached to the bottom are thought analogous to pubic hair) McKnight 1973: 199–200; cf. McConnel 1931–1932: 11). The possible relationship between yams and (female) stench is suggested by the final (Wik-Mungan) step in yam processing: when a quantity of yam pulp has been collected, a woman may sit on it to press out all the water. The Wik-Mungan are suspicious of cooked yams.

Two women on the margins of culture create culture by constructing the differences that make a difference and assign this lexical discontinuity to now discrete members of the animal and vegetable kingdoms. The constructivist function of the sisters, in some variants, includes, as well, the assignment of place names, the formulation of a mythic geography. This categorical unfolding is reduplicated in the form of a dialectic: the givers of ritual language, a feature differentiating nature and culture, bear children who are in nature *in extremis*: they are born to be ingested rather than encoded. The signification that is lost is regained by transposing it in terms of a mineralogical order: the Wawalik sisters are vomited, memorialized in the form of stone landmarks.[10]

Reduplication, in this instance carried to the "third power," empha-

[10]   Compare further on a consideration of the inverse association of stone memorials and stench.

sizes and reemphasizes a meaningful serial intent, suggesting the sign character of prior selections, pointing emphatically to areas of meaning within a text as possible metaphorical operators between texts (cf. Lévi-Strauss 1969a: 339–340; Jakobson 1962: 541–542). The story that the myth conveys constructs sequences (not schemata) in which filling is always followed by emptying of one sort or another and the emptying produces the major categorical kingdoms within culture and between culture and nature: animals, vegetables, minerals, and humans, as shown in Figure 1. In order to demystify the necessity of selections underlying reduplicative sequences, we must effect the transition from principles of serial composition to metaphors of multidimensional decomposition: thus, a tale of turtles, faeces, and an old woman.

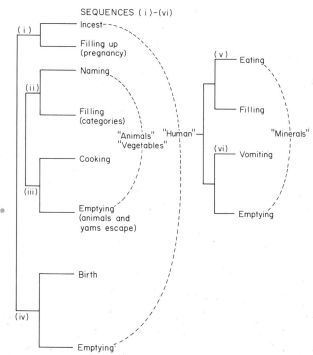

Figure 1. Aspects of linear reduplication: the wandering Wawalik sisters

M₃ (Murngin): The Old Woman and the Turtle Flipper

All the men of the Gwiyula clan harpooned a turtle and brought him to the shore and ate him. They cut the turtle up and cooked it first. They gave a piece of meat to everyone, with the exception of one old woman; they didn't give her anything but a flipper.

"Where is the real meat?" she said. "How can anyone find fat on a turtle flipper? You men are very greedy."

She threw the flipper away. You can see the stone there in the Gwiyula country today where she threw it.

The old woman sat down on a log over a fresh pool of water. She defecated in the water so that the people could not drink it. The water is still bitter and impossible to drink and no one drinks it even today.

She came back from the pool and picked up a firebrand. She made a huge fire almost the size of a bush fire in the springtime. She picked up some of her defecation and threw it in the fire by the handful. All the people smelled a foul odor. Everyone ran after her. She ran and ran and fell down. There is a stone there today in that country. It looks like a woman on her knees with her head in her hands.

Sickness came everywhere after this. The odor of this woman's excrement in the fire had killed everyone in the world. All the black people had died.

There was one man who did not die. He came from the Marungun clan's country and had the Yaernungo tongue. His wife was dead, and all his children and relatives, except one young woman. The girl made a paperbark raft and got out on the water of a large lake so that she did not die. The man came from the Marungun country to the Gwiyula and saw that all the little girls and boys and men and women and dogs were dead.

When the man saw them he started to cry. He went looking for his own relatives and while he looked he thought they must all be dead. He went further and saw a fire. "Ah, someone has made a fire. Someone must be alive," he said. He came to the shore of the lake and swam across the water to the other side, where he found a small fire burning. There was no one there. Someone called out to him from among the trees, "Oh, is that you, father? Where is my mother?"

"She is dead," he said, "and everyone in the world is dead except us."

She said, "Let us make a canoe and cross the ocean and go to the other side of it and maybe there will be someone alive there."

The old man said, "No, we must stay here."

They stayed there. It was that Maipi, in the Naladaer country near the Daiuror country. The father and daughter slept separately in different camps. Next day the father went to look for more people, but in all the clan countries he found only corpses. That night he came back. "My daughter," he said, "no one is alive. There are only corpses."

She said, "There is nothing we can do. We can only stay here."

The old man said, "Where did this sickness come from?" He said, "I am going to sleep and dream and it may be I can find out."

The daughter said, "I think, father, it would be better if we made only one camp."

The father said, "All right."

The woman had gathered some lily bulbs and killed some iguana lizards. They ate them, then went to sleep. The father, late in the night, said, "Daughter, I'll tell you a good way for us to do."

She said, "What?"

He said, "You can camp close to me."

She said, "All right, father."

He made a brush lean-to. They slept. When the woman went to sleep the father touched her. She awakened and the man copulated with her. She did not object. The father said in the morning, "You are going to be my wife now because there are no more people in the world and we must make children."

After a while the girl was pregnant and soon a baby was born. It was a girl baby. Soon a second daughter was born, and after a while, two more, first a male child and finally a second male child, were born. The seasons went by and the children all grew up. The father gave his oldest son the two daughters. He said to his son, "I am your *gawel* [mother's brother and father-in-law] now. You are my *waku* [sister's son and son-in-law]. He turned to his young son and said "I'll call you *kutara*."

He thought that when his first son had a daughter, his second son could marry her, which would make everything straight again in the relationship system (*guratu*). All these people were Dua moiety, but the old man, by giving his children different relationship terms, had turned the *guratu* about and made some of them Yiritja. The old man and his daughter died and the new sons and daughters made a new people (Warner 1958: 528–530).

AN INTERIORIZED CUISINE

If, on a provisional basis, "old woman" can be read as one who no longer menstruates ("if you remove the maternal element from femininity, what is left is stench" [Lévi-Strauss 1969a: 271]), and from M_3 we know that defecation (+ fire = faeces smoke) is a method of destruction, of undercutting the demographic and categorical base of proper conjunctions, then it follows that menstruation, which signifies that one can produce life, can be contrasted with defecation, for whereas the latter uses fire as a means of destruction, the former has to do with water as a consequence of reproduction (realized or aborted).

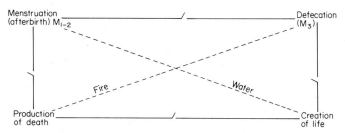

Figure 2.   Life and death: a dorsal and ventral interpretation

As faeces is transformed food and menses (urine: cf. below) is transformed water, Figure 2 may be read as follows: transformed food:production of death::transformed water:production of life. Both transformed food and water are, in turn, realizations of interiorized cooking, products of an infracuisine. Urine and faeces are completed digestive processes. Menses and vomit, on the other hand, are abortive processes: the former, an abortive reproductive cycle, the latter, an abortive digestive process, as illustrated in Figure 3. Following our noses, we have proceeded from a natural being of very nearly absolute luminosity to human bodily emissions of relative viscosity. Some mythic realizations of interiorized cooking in American English include (1) she had a bun in the oven (pregnancy); (2) the raw data was thoroughly digested (cooked just right) by the scientist; (3) it was only a half-baked idea. Ideas that are not well-cooked are, as we all know, a bunch of shit: no shit.

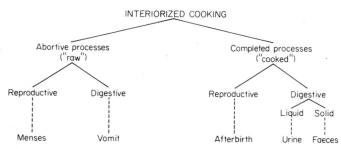

Figure 3.   Aspects of interiorized cooking

So far we have at least four empirical categories that refer to bodily emissions: (1) faeces, (2) afterbirth, (3) menses, and (4) vomit. An Oenpelli myth (Mountford 1956) associates the origin of rain with a female kangaroo's urine, and a Murin'bata[11] myth associates the origin of waterholes in the Rambu plains area with the sputum of Rambu, who also produced a good deal of vomit and semen (Falkenberg 1962: 87). Ferenczi (1956) would have understood this cosmogonic appropriation of exuvial things (Dundes 1962: 1041; cf. Douglas 1973: 101).

Fire and water are conceptual tools used to construct propositional forms in both M_{1-2} and M_3: in the former, fire has a celestial and a domestic realization, the rainbow serpent's lightning and the Wawalik sisters' domestic fire. Rather than synthesizing these positions on a vertical register (above/below; but see below a variant set of solution points that are partially formulated in terms of this dimension), a solution concept is selected by M_3, to the celestial puzzle posed by M_{1-2}, in terms of forms of periodicity. Celestial fire is associated with rains and flooding which make possible a seasonal (natural) periodicity; the cooking fire of the Wawalik sisters expresses a domestic (cultural, daily/natural, seasonal) form of periodicity. The destructive fire of M_3 and the putridity which it diffuses ("faeces smoke") very nearly destroys both forms of periodicity: it selects a solution point that defines a partial and tentative synthesis by inversion $[x^{(-1)}, y^{(-1)}]$ of the marginal positions (x, y). Celestial fire, caused by the smell of a female odor, is the overture to the rains that periodically produce a wet, fertilized world; and the stench of an old

---

[11]   We will consider Stanner's studies (1959, 1960a, 1960b, 1961a, 1961b, 1963) on Murin'bata mythology and ritual in a more extensive study of the Murngin corpus.

woman's shit—a sexually neutral bodily emission—is the means through which an earthly fire results in the nonperiodic transition to a dry and putrid world. Whereas a domestic fire (M_{1-2}) is caused by an oZ/yZ[12] cooking unsuccessfully—aborted ingestion—a destructive fire (M_3 has as its consequence a father/daughter copulating successfully: completed reproduction. In view of the widespread symbolic association between yams and penises in Australia and New Guinea, a relationship can be expressed between the beginning of M_{1-2} and the ending of M_3, the former having to do with the collection of penises by younger women, the latter with the distribution of vaginas by an older man; and if one is preceded by incest constructed on the basis of a maximal distance (clan), the other is immersed in a minimal (F/D, B/Z) distance form of incest (cf. below: the stench of incest). Slave drivers and fish diver, earth shaker and taste makers: earth diver, scatological seed of the (w)hole thing: Houyhnhnms/Yahoos matter, Tannhäuser's overture (Baudelaire 1972b: 342–343).

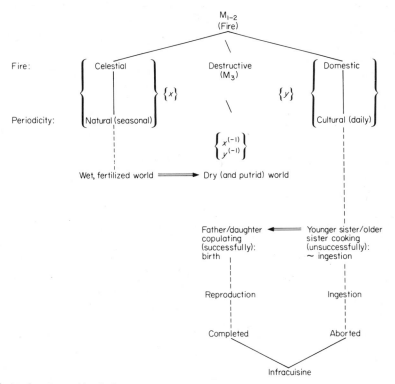

Figure 4. A putrid solution

<hr />

[12] Older sister/younger sister.

The Murngin variant of the New Guinea yam–phallus symbolism is refracted back-to-front in Warner's clan list; for the *ranga* (high) totems of the Karmalanga people include, among other things, menstrual blood, clitoris, mature woman, uncircumcized boy, and young girl: the camp name is Guruturunga, which is translated as "rotten yam" (Warner 1958: 48), naturally cooked declension of one that is hard and male rather than soft (with feeling) and female.

Thus, if

(1) defecation (+ fire) ⟶ death (almost) of humanity (culture)
and

(2) death (almost) of humanity ⟶ improper conjunctions
then,

(1.1) menstrual odor (+ water) ⟶ growth and abundance of nature

(2.1) growth and abundance of nature ⟶ (?)

We have two ordered sets of "equations" (⟨1, 2⟩, ⟨1.1, 2.1⟩) and an "unknown"—the right-hand term of 2.1—that we have to solve for, in the sense that this term is not explicitly realized in the message that the myth conveys. This parallelism, which we have euphorically referred to as "equations," expresses the interpenetration of serial constructions and paradigmatic ensembles.

We do know, from Murngin ethnography, that the serpent is the master of water and consequently the fertilizing principle in nature (Warner 1958: 387). Further:

> The rainy season forces the Murngin to disperse and take refuge in small groups in the areas which have not been submerged. Here they carry on a precarious existence, threatened by famine and inundation. A few days after the floods have receded the vegetation is lush again and animals reappear. Collective life begins once more and abundance reigns. None of this would however have been possible had the floods not swamped and fertilized the plains (Lévi-Strauss 1966: 92).

It is during this period of abundance that all the great ceremonies take place on men's ceremonial grounds: for example, the *Djungguan* (Warner 1958: 259–266), which is associated with age-grading and its spatial expression within the camp (Warner 1958: 135).

As the rains—called forth by the smell of female stench—isolate families and are the precondition of the natural abundance upon which the collective life and sacred rites of the early and middle dry season depend, fire (and "faeces smoke") isolates the shattered remnants of a family which, in turn, is the precondition for reconstructing the cycle of exchanges which makes a periodic collective life possible (cf. below, Rose 1968). The empirical and mythological situations are in a symmetrical relation.

These sacred rites involve, for young men, as a condition for the attainment of masculinity, the temporary renunciation of women and the lasting submission to the old men, the means and the masters of happiness (Lévi-Strauss 1966: 94): in order to enjoy (natural) tactile pleasure, they must allow their minds to be employed by (cultural) verbal rigors.[13] This submission is played out within a dominance structure that defines a vertical (temporal) partition of men into discrete categories in terms of their access to a body of esoteric knowledge. The right-hand term of 2.1 is therefore

(2.1) growth and abundance of nature ———→ proper distinctions between men[14]

The left-hand term (defecation) in the initial statement (1) is associated in psychoanalytical myth with a cloacal theory of birth, whereas the right-hand term in the final statement is a solution to parturition or pregnancy envy (Dundes 1962: 1038; Bettelheim 1955). As incest is the solution and the generator of improper conjunctions, the basic, derived opposition is vertical (temporal) distinctions between men/horizontal (spatial) distinctions between women. A logic and a philosophy are built upon a contrast between improper conjunctions and proper distinctions; the latter establish the legitimate class of dealers and players for the cards that are improperly dealt in the former hand: the magic isn't in the cards but between them.

Aspects of the features which underlie these relations can be expressed on a provisional basis, as shown in Figure 5 and Table 1.

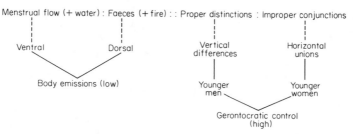

Figure 5.   Filth and grandeur

We can also interpret in these terms the logic of the elimination of the Wawalik sisters and the old woman from the scene of the action: the production of a foul smell, in both instances, exhausts their function. And as we will see, in the course of the play which constitutes the harmony of this myth, a function is baked into a meaning, and this meaning takes upon itself a rather reptilian sensibility.

---

[13]   The myth (mind)/matter (body) dualism, entailing a distinction between a systematic allocation of knowledge (*homo oeconomicus*) and an immediate play of bodies (*homo ludens*) is synthesized by the game of the old men: *homo hierarchicus*.
[14]   The proof of this derivation is provided by M₄.

The producers of intellectual constructions (the categorical base of culture) and affective destruction are, in death, memorialized (cf. Munn 1969) by an inversion of their shared function: stench. The inverse of a putrid function is a form that can only be negatively expressed in relation-ship to an olfactory code: a stone memorial; and you can't get blood from a stone, although that's what pestles and mortars are made of (Peterson 1971: 240; women, vegetable food, and stone technology).

Table 1.   The high and the low

	M_{1-2}	M_3
Olfactory code	Menstrual odor (front)	Defecatory odor (rear)
Natural elements	Water: creative, from above	Fire: destructive, from below
Sexual code	Rainbow serpent (male)	Old woman (female)
Social code	Vertical differences	Horizontal unions

The "natural elements code" suggests an initial puzzle, for destructive fire is, as we have seen, a solution point: the water/fire contrast does not interpret either of the marginal positions which define this point. We also know, from M_{1-2}, that water is an operator that diffuses putridity. These bits of information set the constraints for a synthesis of a grammar of elements composed of two categories, assessed in three dimensions. We can derive and describe a pair of solution points, one partial, the other complete, for the contrast posed by creative water/destructive fire.

The Murngin say that "When the inland lakes dry up and the small streams disappear and many of the clan water holes are empty, the thunder comes then and calls out for the rain" (Warner 1958: 382). The time of the thunder is *raer-un-daer*, the period that mediates between dry and wet seasons. Thunder comes from clouds called *kur-ka* [penis or male] *mo-la-ma* [cloud], which come from the south and east and, "a little later," copulate with, *gur-ding gur-ding* [the woman cloud] (Warner 1958: 382).

There are two kinds of lightning: ordinary heat lightning (Yiritja) and forked lightning that accompanies the roar of thunder (Dua). Thunder and lightning are closely associated; "Dua lightning is the forked tongue of the snake, and the thunder is the roar of the snake" (Warner 1958: 383).

When the lightning comes that means a light for Wongar (the totemic spirit) to see by when he makes that big noise (the thunder) and hits down at those people he fought (the Wawalik Sisters). When rainbow time comes that is the snake Wongar. He is swallowing those two women. When I see a rainbow or lightning I understand rain is coming (Warner 1958: 385).

Thunder and lightning are the heralds of the wet season, the fertilizing rains: they signal the periodic flowering of life, the transition from dry (Yiritja) to wet (Dua), from female (uninitiated) to male (initiated). This association of celestial fire and natural sound partially synthesizes the contrast between creative water and destructive fire, as shown in Figure 6. Lightning is a form of fire, although it is from above and creative, and in association with thunder, lightning is identified with the male element (penis or male) rather than with the female element, as is the case with destructive fire from below. The water that the old woman defecates in is destructive, unfit for human consumption.

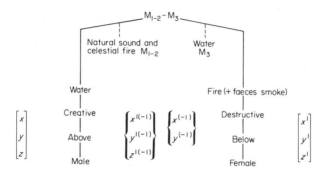

Figure 6.   Fire and water: a Murngin synthesis

At this point, we can pull together some of the elements associated with fire and water, anticipating various deductions that are modulated by subsequent variants.

Faeces, a sexually unmarked bodily emission, is metonymically associated with a part (flipper) of an animal that is a producer of bad smells, whereas menses and afterbirth, sexually marked bodily emissions, have to do with the whole (and hole) of an animal who is a good consumer of smells; and as the latter is the master of creative water, it does not seem particularly fortuitous that the former, who is cooked in his shell culturally, is associated with destructive fire and the construction of incestuous relations, whereas the rainbow serpent, who eats the Wawalik sisters naturally (raw) has to do with the destruction of incestuous siblings.

ETHNOLOGY AND MYTHOLOGY

It should not be surprising to social anthropologists that the dialectic, formulated in mythical terms, between male initiation rites and the exchange of women has been given an analytic interpretation by Rose (1968: 200–208) in support of his ideas concerning the gerontocratic base rules of Australian social, economic, and ritual organization (cf.

Rose 1960; De Josselin de Jong 1962; Lévi-Strauss 1966: 94). This is exceedingly fortunate, as it provides us with an opportunity to formulate a myth whose constituent variants have been secreted by the Murngin and social anthropology, the producers of the logic of myth on the one hand and the myth of logic on the other.

M_4 (Groote Eylandt): The Origin of Initiation Rites (from Rose)

Rose (1968: 101–102) suggests that the determination of marriage is based upon neither the "kinship system" nor the "marriage classes" but rather on the distinction that obtains between foraging and landowning groups. This distinction denotes a symmetrical relation, for the cardinal rule governing landowning group relations is that this difference is periodic, naturally induced, and transitive.

The land of one group may provide an abundance of food during the "spring," for example, while another may provide an abundance of food during the "winter." This leads to reciprocity between the land-owning groups (Rose 1968: 202).

Affinal alliances are, in Rose's view, determined by these reciprocal relations:

. . . each individual marriage is determined ultimately by the reciprocal rights and obligations existing between the actual political land-owning groups and to a less extent the reciprocal rights and obligations between members of these different land-owning groups (Rose 1968: 201).

These rights and obligations, whose contractual formations are between older men, give the exchange system a gerontocratic twist, with polygyny as a direct corollary. Polygyny is a means and an end, a possible consequence for men who have succeeded in the game of exchanging futures in woman. This well-known, Tiwi-style tendency (Hart and Pilling 1960; Goodale 1971), in which well-defined features of the political economy leave their imprint on the multidimensional space of mythologized orders, can be roughly decomposed: (1) a girl is promised to a man before or when she is born; (2) she goes to live with her initial husband when she is about nine years old; (3) older men (forty to fifty) have a monopoly on the younger women, retaining older women as "managers"; (4) older women can be the wives of men of any age; (5) during the course of their marital careers, a life-time affair for women, a woman has at least four husbands and a man at least four wives (Rose 1968: 205).

Women tend to aggregate themselves as cowives at the time of their maximum child-bearing and -raising responsibilities (approximate age: twenty-four) around men who are at the peak of their productive (political) capacities (in their early forties) (Rose 1968: 206; cf. Rose 1960). The hoarding effect that is produced by the gerontocratic operator results in (according to Rose 1968: 207) a prototypical Australian dilemma: younger women aggregated around older men/younger men's sexual drive. Rose views aspects of male initiation rites as a theoretical and pragmatic solution to this puzzle. The common features which constitute the solution go somewhat beyond the ostensible functions of instruction in ecology and the means of obtaining the wherewithal of life, and a gradual unveiling of the mysteries of ritual life: they are a lesson in the politics of patience, the virtues of deference and strategies of humiliation. "Datta, dayadhvam, damyata" (Eliot 1962: 53). *"White man got no dreaming, Him go 'nother way. White man, him go different, Him got road belong himself"* (Stanner 1965: 159): dream breakers and history makers, time-containers and -sieves: just playing for/with time. The central features are as follows: (1) the initiation spans the period from prepuberty to the middle or late twenties; (2) alliances in the political economy of connubial exchange cannot be formed until the completion of initiation; (3) during a significant segment of this period a young man is under the control and tutelage of an older man and is frequently referred to as "boy slave" or "boy wife"; (4) initiates are secluded for long periods and are obliged to travel away from areas of high temptation.

Male initiation rites mark the transition from youthful sexuality to the constraints of male political games: they are the funnel of domestication. In the language of historical materialism:

The relations of production—and essentially, as we have dealt with them here, marriage, initiation and the land-owning group relations as such—are determined by the forces of production (Rose 1968: 208).[15]

The notion of gerontocracy is not alien to Murngin thought, for

. . . the women's sociological group and women as physiological beings are [thus] subordinate to the men's group, and the Murngin age-grading system has been built on this principle. Like other Australian tribes, this peoples' "political" control might be termed a gerontocracy, but it is more than merely the rule of old men (Warner 1958: 396–397).

Of course: gerontocracy, in its contractual realization, is mythologized thought realized in practice, and it is the logic of myth which underlies thought and relates asymmetry in its gerontocratic realization to a global syntax. Only a world in which meaning had become contingent upon

[15] The notion "forces of production" "includes all the factors of production, including resources, equipment and men, which are to be found in a specific society at a specific time, and which must be combined in a specific way to produce the material goods which that society needs. The notion of relationships of production covers the functions fulfilled by individuals and groups in the process of production and in the control of the factors of production" (Godelier 1970: 341).

selection would presume to assume that gerontocracy, kinship, initiation, and exchange are discrete institutions: it provides solutions to a set of dilemmas in a mythic stratigraphy that concerns the material appropriation and allocation of nature: water, meat, women, and knowledge. These answers to mythic puzzles are related through well-defined logical procedures to seasonal periodicity, bodily emissions, and the ethnozoological base: a family of material constraints.

SEAFOOD AND CULTURAL MEAT: A METAMENU

If we may assume that ethnographic interpretations do not occupy a privileged position in relation to the mythical formations of the people whose behavior they purport to explain or account for, then it is possible to construct composite metamyths, built upon the fragments of both forms of interpretation.

The stories that are told by M_{1-2}, M_3, and M_4 all draw a distinction between an owner or holder of rights and someone (couple, one, and group, respectively) who is either given or denied access to these rights, although the content of the contrast varies from one version to the other. This variation is systematic: the story of the old woman and the turtle flipper mediates and synthesizes the contrasts formulated by the account of Rose and the story of the Wawalik sisters. This synthesis can be outlined as in Figure 7.

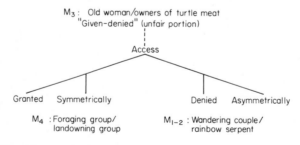

Figure 7.   The old woman's share

You should recognize the theoretical assumptions built into this possibility set, for it corresponds rather nicely with Leach's assumption (1961a: 60) that there are three possibilities where "a system of institutionalized marriage rules [Figure 8] exists in association with local descent groups, then a group B which provides wives for Group A is not compensated in kind."

1.   "That the principle of reciprocity does not apply at all and the group B obtains no compensation" (Leach 1961a: 60) says no more than

the "right-hand" position of Figure 7: rather than bestowing a mother-in-law upon his sister's sons (Shapiro 1969: 76), the rainbow serpent (their *gawel*: cf. below) ingests them.

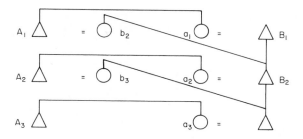

Figure 8. Patrilineal descent: marriage with mother's brother's daughter and/or own sister's daughter (after Leach 1961a: 60)

2.   The old woman's share turns the same trick as Leach's second possibility "that reciprocity is achieved by group A giving group B some form of economic or political compensation—e.g., marriage payments, work service, political fealty" (Leach 1961a: 60), while pointing, in the language of the concrete, to the problems implicit in the reciprocal exchange of commodities which are different in kind. The distributors of turtle meat who are deductible affines (cf. below) fail to find the correct distance between meat that is fatty and moist which goes to the old men (Roheim 1968: 45) and meat that is too lean and dry which goes to an old woman.

3.   The third member of Leach's set, that three or more groups, A, B, C, make mutual arrangements to "marry in a circle," are related, as consequence to cause, in Rose's variant, to the symmetric exchange of access rights by landowning and foraging groups.

The solution problem, embedded in these processes, is to select a point that is intermediate to a symmetrical exchange of rights of access (M_4) and an asymmetrical denial of such rights (M_{1-2}). The philosophical puzzle of M_3 is to determine the possibility of finding the right distance between giving everything and giving nothing at all. The solution formulated is to divide what is to be given into pieces, and this solution in turn generates a problem that is not confronted by M_{1-2} or M_4: differential valuation. The old woman rejects the point selected: she, if we may use a not-inappropriate expression, shits on the solution that is hit upon by M_3.

The failure [16] of M_3 to select a stable or nonnegotiable point produces a reshuffling of the deck in which the gerontocratic operator, in the form of

[16]   The appearance of indeterminacy is a kind of recursive function that provides a certain acceleration to the unfolding of the structure, projecting to a more inclusive group of dilemmas and synthetic operators.

men's political games, synthesizes the destructive fire (and putrid smell) of M_3 and the productive water (and celestial fire) of M_{1-2}:

$$M_3 \qquad\qquad M_{1-2}$$
destructive fire/fertilizing water
$$M_4$$
gerontocratic operator
(asymmetric distribution)

This ordering defines a right distance between an animal consumer of a malodorous thing and a human producer of a killing smell, to which fertilizing water and destructive fire stand as consequence and cause: a disjoint series of human groups who, through the introduction of time and risk, an asymmetrical exchange of rights in food and women, dialectically conjoin their differences, as producers and consumers, animals (others) and humans.

What is the difference between the intermediate point selected by M_3 and that selected by M_4? A reduction of both syntheses to the processes underlying them suggests that, despite apparently different contents, they are virtually the same, in terms of both the puzzles they construct and the solutions they propose.

The base forms from which the particular content of the dilemmas emerges are in both instances concerned with mediating a life/death contrast. The former term is realized either as fertilizing water which makes possible the periodic flowering of animal and vegetable life or as a symmetrical exchange of rights of access, indexed by the distinction foraging group/landowning group, which makes possible the periodic flowering of a collective, cultural life: both express a concern with seasonal periodicity, its natural causes, and its cultural consequences. Death is realized either as destructive fire[17] (+ putrid smell) or an asymmetrical denial of exchange: incest, a denial of the possibilities of exchange and an organized collective life, is, serially, a consequence of the former and a precondition of the latter. Conversely, both realizations of *life* affirm the

---

[17]   Fire, in Murngin mortuary rites, is believed to consume the stench of decaying flesh (smoke), as well as chasing the soul away (Warner 1958: 435, 444). And as fire and water are in complementary relationship in relation to death and life (fire : water : : death : fire [stench]), the possibility might be considered that the cycling of Murngin souls through water provides a metaphorical allusion to genetic mediums (elixir of life, mother of molecular collisions and constructions) rather than a literal ignorance of physiological paternity (Jastrow 1974: 62).

The natural medium in which the creative power of younger (menstruating) women grows, seeks its cultural counter-image in the elixir provided by the elusive essence of the layered poetics, music, dance, and art of older men. As in Joyce's *Portrait* (1964), the gestation of the soul is surrounded, at the outset (of life/in death), by matters hydrous—urine, slime, seawater, amniotic tides: embedded in the fluids of biological struggle, it emerges from water to air, from the sea of primitive sensory perceptions to soar in transcendental flight.

desirability, point to the necessity of a set of rules of exchange for the maintenance of an organized collective life; or, periodicity (natural and cultural): incest :: life (exchange of food and women): death; or see Figure 9.

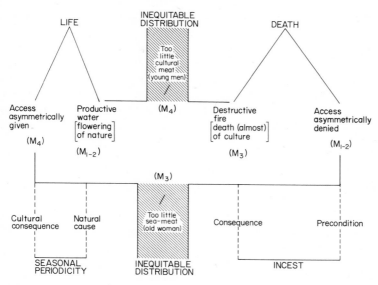

Figure 9.   Sex and seafood in savage society

AFFINES: NO JOKING MATTER

The story of the old woman and the turtle flipper does not explicitly refer to the content of the relationship between the men of the Gwiyula clan, the hunters and distributors of turtle meat, and an old woman who receives a bad (= fatless) piece. Our derivation of the nature of this relationship depends directly upon a theoretical hypothesis advanced by Lévi-Strauss in his study of "Structure and dialectics" (1963). This hypothesis is concerned with the interrelations that may obtain between myth and ritual,[18] within and between groups. In the traditional formulation of the problem, myth and ritual are viewed as mutually redundant systems: either the former is regarded as an ideological projection of the latter, or the latter is interpreted as a dramatized expression of the former. Myth formulates on the conceptual level what ritual communicates on the level of action: the correspondence between these orders is defined by a homologous relation.

[18]   Of innumerable discussions on the possible nature of this relationship, we might mention Kluckhohn (1942), Leach (1954), Stanner (1961a, 1961b), Fontenrose (1966).

The Lévi-Straussian hypothesis, demonstrated through an analysis of Pawnee myths which exemplify the pregnant-boy theme and rules for membership in shamanistic societies followed by the Mandan, Hidatsa, and Blackfoot of the American Plains, suggests a dialectical rather than a direct relationship between myth and ritual. The key to such a correspondence depends upon a series of preliminary operations (permutations and transformations) and an exploration of intercultural rather than intracultural relations.

When the Pawnee myth is correlated with the reverse of the system in Pawnee ritual, the correlation is partial and incomplete: the precipitate is a semistructure which lacks internal coherence. On the other hand, when the Pawnee pregnant-boy theme is correlated with the symmetrical and inverse ritual that prevails among certain Plains tribes, a relationship emerges which has a contrapuntal character: if the Pawnee myth is regarded as a progression, the system which prevails in Mandan, Hidatsa, and Blackfoot ritual appears as a retrogression. In more general terms, "the institutions described in the myths can be the very opposite of the real institutions" (Lévi-Strauss 1963: 229).

The Australian proof of the myth/ritual "theorem" entails the construction of a Murngin theory of joking and avoidance relations—embedded in mythical thought—whose logical complexity and tangible qualities differ from that attained by ethnological theory. This complexity is secured by an increase in elements and codes from which elements are selected: the recoding process pulls together an internally coherent piece of logic. And if the steps in the proof are regarded without reference to the labels "myth," "ritual," "normative behavior," "sacred and secular time," then it is clear that the problem of their interrelations—dialectic or direct—is an artifact of anthropological thought. They are merely elements in a derivation that is concerned not with fragments as individual content-slots, but with steps in the construction of a sensory-based theorem; the irreducible contingency of historical content, the derivable necessity of the forms of its incorporation within thought mythologized/practice ritualized (Lévi-Strauss 1973a: 474–475; Marx 1971). This approach, which may be referred to as either structuralism or deductive ethnology, as it uses mythical thought as a point of access and a medium for praxis, does not demand an absolute contrast between the Dreaming Time (Wongar) and the reality of rituals that are lived in. There is, rather, a coherence and simultaneity that obtains between the dreaming, the living, and more of the same: the intent of cold societies is to keep it together; dreaming's part of the game, you see: "Thou hast nor youth nor age but as it were an after-dinner sleep dreaming of both" (Eliot 1973).

In Daisy Bates' description (1966: 30–39) of the initiation rituals of the Koolarrabullo tribes of Broome, Western Australia, we find an account of a form of license that occurs during the beginning of the summer wet season, prior to the operation of circumcision:

At this time all licence is allowed, and the laws relating to persons who at other times are forbidden to look at each other are suspended. Mothers-in-law may even approach or address their sons-in-law, and at the supper, the *thaloo*, as the mother-in-law is called, makes the best of it. A whole year of grievances is stored up, and the son-in-law has no right of reply. She can touch him, taunt him, pull away his weapons and decorations, and make him a public mockery. Her delight is to worry and annoy, and he must keep a poker face through it all, unaware, as it were, of her presence.

Now she tempts him with a hollow scoop of vegetable food—"You hungry? Here is food. If you don't take it, I will hit you. All right, watch me eat it!"—and she snatches it away. She tears off his arm-band, head-band and other ornaments, and knocks his boomerang out of his grasp. As provider for the family, he pays the price of his betrothal in meat food, and she has much to say about this. "This meat no good!" she tells him, "why don't you bring up a tadpole?" or, "Watch me, everybody, I'm going to kill a fish," and she snatches his spear and aims it dangerously near him. The *wallang-arree* is the crowded hour of glorious life for the mother-in-law, and the whole tribe, with the exception of the son-in-law, enjoys her sallies to the full (Bates 1966: 36).

Allowable license on the level of ritualized demonstration rather than mythic formulation (M_3) is a bit more restrained, although the target of the old women's anger is more precisely defined: rather than shitting on the world, the heap is dumped directly on the young men (with words) who provide meat (food) in the normal course of events. They cannot, unfortunately, count upon either fire or water to diffuse acoustic putridity. This form of license, which is periodic, closely corresponds to Leach's idea of false noses or role reversal as sacred time in which logically appropriate ritual behavior is to play normal, secular life back-to-front (Leach 1961b: 135). This rule-governed departure from the rules of the game in secular time represents a condensation of joking relationships. The Leachian construction of the sacred/secular contrast suggests, as anthropologists have long understood (Radcliffe-Brown 1952a, 1952b), that ritually prescribed asymmetrical disrespect can only be relationally defined in terms of its logical converse, symmetrical respect or mutual avoidance. Joking, a quantitative intensification of relations, and avoidance, a qualitative impoverishment of relations, denote the extreme terms of a continuum which uses complementary message forms to express the synthetic nature of affinal relations. Exchange, the most direct synthesis of the self/other contrast, is denied on the level of social relations—messages and metamessages that are lived out rather than thought in—by being either too far (avoidance) or too close (license, joking) from that other who provides the elementary sustenance of thought mything. Now, if we transform joking and avoidance, which contrastively define the quality of relations in terms of a metaphor of quantities, then the dilemmas posed by ethnological and mythological thought are reconciled: for the former, which has to do with giving too much, takes everything by ritually denuding the other, whereas the latter, which gives too little, takes nothing at all. The right distance that is thought in by the rule "to give" is sustained by lived-out extrema that allow the self, with contrasting means to equivalent ends, to keep to itself. *Quid rides? Mutato nomine, de te fabula narratur* (Horace: *Satires* I.i.69).

The self and the polyphonic texture that it unfolds in relationship to other selves (am I/they are) suggests a neutralization of the little difference that remains between the genesis of exchange and the apotheosis of myth: sonata-allegro matters. The mythical solution, whose subject/object leitmotif is masked by a wilderness of mirrors, is: keep the right distance from each self, in order to derive, within yourself, an intelligible construction of all selves. *"Incest is fine, as long as it's kept in the family"* (Lévi-Strauss 1971b: 21; cf. 1969b: 497), *". . . a world in which one might keep to oneself"* (original emphasis).

If we examine the mother-in-law/son-in-law (*mokul/gurrong*) relationship in Murngin, we find that

The whole relationship of mokul and gurrong is one of complete mutual avoidance. He cannot speak to her; she cannot speak to him. He does not look at her; she does not look at him. They do not hand any article to each other or use each other's names. Should they meet on a path they each turn aside and walk past with their eyes averted (Warner 1958: 101–102).

As asymmetric license plays symmetric avoidance back-to-front, a dialectical relationship between myth (M_3, and ritual has been derived which is partially defined by a family of contrasts: olfactory code/acoustic code, unrestrained destruction/periodic license, diffused target/specified target. The role attributed to "shit on" in myth and ritual expresses the elementary law of mythic thought[19]: metonymical in the case of the former, as faeces and faeces smoke and the real destruction of the world which they very nearly cause are part of the mythological system; metaphorical in the case of the latter, as the notion "shit on" with words and the ritual destruction of the self which they are intended to cause is a lived-out transformation of a thought-in metonym.

That the nature of the relationship between the old woman and the men of the Gwiyula clan is affinal (mother-in-law/son-in-law) has been established by a dialectical process of deduction which requires a "lemma" entailing the convertibility of asymmetric license and symmetric avoidance, sacred and secular time. A somewhat more direct, structural proof of the affinal operator (M_3), which will allow us to unfold the relations between sexual access and edibility that we have outlined, is provided by the story of the incestuous mother-in-law (M_5): *relâche*.

---

[19]   The transformation of a metaphor is achieved in metonymy, and inversely.

M_5 *(Murngin): The Incestuous Mother-in-Law*

Three men, Daura, Burnangura, and Kalimara, who were Warumeri from Elcho Island, took a stringy-bark canoe for Wessel Island. They paddled and paddled. They were close to Wessel Island when a big wind came up. They tried to paddle against the wind, but it was too strong.

"We'll stop. The canoe will go its own way." The canoe turned north and westward. In the morning they saw land. It was an island. It was that small island north of Marung and the Crocodile Group. They went ashore. They saw a great many tracks of people who live there. The people there talk Kolpa. The three men said to themselves, "They are just the same as we are."

There was an old woman there who had three daughters. She made three camps and gave a daughter to each man. These daughters were Dua. After she had decided to give them to the men she changed her mind and decided to give only one daughter to one man and she persuaded her sisters to give a daughter to each of the other two men. When it was evening the first old woman went to sleep. When it was dark she sat with her head in her hands and thought. The husband of her daughter started fondling his new wife. The old woman sneaked up and looked. She blew on the fire in front of their hut and groaned. "I am cold," she moaned. She lied. She lay down and pretended to sleep and started snoring but she had one eye open.

The man raised up and prepared to copulate with the girl, but the old woman crawled in the hut and pushed the daughter on one side and lay down in the middle.

"I am very cold," she moaned.

In the second hut one of the other men had arisen and was preparing to have sexual intercourse with his new wife, when the second old woman crawled in between them and said, "I am cold, I want to sleep here."

In the third tent the third man was lying on top of his wife when the third old woman pushed him off and crawled in between the two. "I am cold," she said.

They stayed there all night and the husbands could do nothing. In the morning the three men talked and decided they would take the three old women in their canoes out into the middle ocean and throw them overboard. The old women said, "*Gurrong* [son-in-law], don't you take us in canoes. We're cold."

"No," protested the men, "we must go look for turtles. You must come help us."

They took their three old mothers-in-law out into the middle of the ocean and threw them in to drown. The men started paddling back to their wives, for it was miles from the land and they knew the water was very deep. The old women whined as they were thrown overboard, but when they got into the water they stretched their legs until they reached the bottom. The three men did not look back, but paddled very fast and soon were back on the shore. They walked straight to where their wives were. They looked at the breasts of their wives. Their nipples stuck out straight. They took them out to the edge of the camp under the trees. They started copulating with them and were almost to the climax when the three old women came up. The three old women once more pushed themselves in between. They said, "If you want anybody you take us. These daughters of ours are too young." They lied, because they were not too young.

The men started swearing. They said to those old women, "Why did you give those daughters of yours to us, when you act like this?"

"Oh, they are too young. We can't let them go now."

The men picked up a big log and made a club. They hit the three old women on

the head. The old women fell down and appeared to be dead. They were pretend-
ing.

"They are dead," the men said, "let us make camp."

They walked a little way into the jungle with the three girls. They made a camp
there. The three old women got up and sneaked to where they were. When the
three men were lying with their wives the three old women pushed in between
their daughters and said, "*Gurrong*, you get on me."

After this went on for a while the daughters said, "Mother, why don't you let
your *gurrong* alone? You've given us to them. Why don't you let them copulate
with us?"

The wind came from the north. The three men made a pandanus sail. "It is
better we leave these women and their daughters and go back to our own home."

The old women heard them and said, "You can take our daughters now."

"No," the men replied, "you can keep them. We'll go back and marry our own
women so we can do as we please. We won't have any fooling with our mothers-
in-law. No man likes to copulate with an old woman."

They all went back and stayed in their own country (Warner 1958: 562–564).

KEPT MEN AND LOOSE WOMEN

> From all the places where I refuse to drink,
> flights of pages, guided by his scent, come like
> magpies to suck life from the saturnine blow-
> pipe. And so that it shall not be stolen from
> them, the greybeards, organized into a
> monastery, have built upon the baron's car-
> cass a little chapel. The speckled birds have
> their dovecotes there. The people call them
> young wild duck. We pataphysicians call them
> simply and honestly shit-diggers.
>   ALFRED JARRY (1965: 201)

Although some of the Murngin "clans," such as the Warumeri, have
clan lands on Elcho Island within the general Yaernungo area, other
Warumeri are located on Warner's clan map proximate to the Gwiyula
clan (Warner 1958: 40; cf. 39, 45). Warumeri people belong to the
Yiritja moiety (the daughters are Dua) and Gwiyula to the Dua moiety,
and these affiliations are associated in Murngin logic with a set of contrasts: dry season/wet season, southeast wind/northwest wind, Wawalik
sisters/rainbow serpent, uninitiated/initiated, female/male. The reduction of M_3 (old woman/Gwiyula men) and M_5 (Old women/Warumeri
men) to their structural elements indicates that they are alternative
derivations from an invariant base.

1. The "pluralization" of old woman corresponds to a reversal of
terms and functions: an old woman is the recipient (consumer) of bad
(fatless) meat, whereas old women are the bestowers (producers) of good
cultural meat (young women: cf. D. H. Lawrence 1972: 42, "They all
looked such good meat"; Roheim 1968: 112 for central Australian
preferences).

2.   Young(er) men are either the recipients of women (M_5) or the bestowers of food (M_3).

3.   The alliance that is established by the prestation of food or women is denied by the actions of either an old woman or old women: the former, by defecating upon a system of distribution that has assigned her a bad piece; the latter, by attempting to negotiate the substitution of a bad piece for a good piece, old women for young women ("No man likes to copulate with an old woman").

4.   The old women define a disjunction between practice and theory as their words are merely playthings, a highly inflationary currency; the old woman, by choosing to play with faeces rather than with words, produces a situation in which words must be played with in order to reestablish a conjunction between theory and practice: the father reclassifies his daughter and their children to "set the exchange system straight." The inflationary escalation of old women expresses, in one sense, thru myth and practice, their spirited but doomed attempts to transpose the symmetry of the superstructure in the coin of the infrastructure, with its asymmetrical distributions (immediate/delayed exchange): pointing to the noninertness of the thing(s) given, the gift; coupled with a demand for a return in identity (kind: sexual access, immediate) rather than in contrast (food: delayed; cf. Mauss 1954: 10–11).

5.   A shared feature of M_3 and M_5 is an *overrating of relations*, realized consanguineal incest on the one hand and unrealized affinal incest on the other (cf. Lévi-Strauss 1963: 215). In Lévi-Strauss's terms:

The group controls the distribution not only of women, but of a whole collection of valuables. Food, the most easily observed of these, is more than just the most vital commodity it really is, for between it and women there is a whole system of real and symbolic relationships, whose true nature is only gradually emerging, but which, when even superficially understood, are enough to establish this connexion (Lévi-Strauss 1969b: 33; cf. Leach 1964, McKnight 1973).

There is something "childish" about all this that is signaled by petulance and a rather indiscriminate use of faeces. The old women act as if they were lustful children, mediating in Oedipal style between husband and wife. The old woman's slot is associated with childish ways in two senses, paradigmatic and developmental: the former as—like children—old women are structurally marginal, pawns in the game; the latter as, to borrow a poet's license, she prefers playing with turds to playing with words. Either preference, as we shall see, is merely a partial and incomplete expression of the association that savage thought seeks to reconstruct between stinking (bodily emissions) and thinking (male ritual language), in which the masking of the former—raw smells—is a condition for the emergence of the latter, cooked thoughts: and if one is on the tips of their tongues, the other is on the ends of our fingers. Not too great a distance. Leviathan's uses: timid arses/office of Katharsis (Joyce 1959: 151–152); ironies or polyphonies, echoes of things past, harmony in things future, the end of their end or the end of our beginning.

Why are childish manners, to play a piece of paradoxical metonymy, associated with old women? Both variants present the appearance, explicit or implicit, of relations of affinity between old women and young men which are, in both instances, naturally severed by putrid odors, or by a marked departure from normative avoidance relations, which amounts to the same thing. If we decompose the relations and transpose the elements, old/women : young/men :: old/men : young/women, we can see the essence that is both concealed and revealed by the dialectic play of the terms that, in various combinations, constitute the fundamental conditions of social life and mythical thought, old/young, male/female: the intersection of a calculus of continuous quantities and a logic of discrete qualities. A cosmological ordering is built up out of a minimal natural difference packed into a biologically continuous, culturally partitioned series. In the language of Marxist thought,

> . . . the relations that men form among themselves in order to carry out, and in the process of carrying out, the production of the material conditions of their existence determine, in the last analysis, the relations of compatibility and incompatibility *between* all levels of social life. (Godelier 1972: ix, original emphasis; cf. Rose's variant, above).

The relations on the "left side" *affectively destroy*, on the level of mythic thought, the direct inverse of relations on the "right side" that are *contractually deployed* by gerontocratic praxis. And more: this dialectic parallelism unfolds synthetic operations when the right-hand relation on each side, the element that is shit on, is transposed and interposed:

Just as young men, who naturally mediate between old/men and young/women, are kept at the right distance from both by a *deficiency of sacred knowledge*, *caused* by the systematic allocation practiced by old/men (initiation as the appropriation of knowledge: Terray 1972: 130), young women are kept at the right distance from young men by an *abundance of lustful actions*, a *consequence* of the immediate gratification desired by old/women, and whereas the former has to do with sacred combinations of words, the latter has to do with metaphors of natural smells:[20]

[20] This dialectic parallelism brings to the front a perverse tendency of ethnological thought: a mythologized distinction, based in ethno-praxis, between mythology and social

Gogolesque deliriant, odoriferous Paris, pungent sighs, great Tom nosy fellow had a good handle to his face too (Matthews 1974: 23, 32):

The sleek Brazilian jaguar
Does not in its arboreal gloom
Distil so rank a feline smell
As Grishkin in a drawing-room (T. S. Eliot, *Whispers of immortality*).

We have seen through a substitution of terms and an exploration of dialectic relations between myth and interpersonal ritual that the defecatory rejoinder of the old woman can be decoded in terms of asymmetric disrespect, what anthropologists refer to as joking relations. Affinal incest, although unrealized, is a play in excess upon a relation of contrast with the corollary of asymmetric disrespect, symmetric respect, whereas realized consanguineal incest has to do with a deficiency in the obligations entailed by symmetric respect.[21] The negotiation of rights of

---

organization, which allows the analysts of the latter to maintain a privileged position in relationship to the believers of the former. To what end: ranking differences closes a door in the face of intelligibility, ruling out the theoretical accomplishments of those others who provide raw food for our thought, while denying them the privilege of cooking the meal.

[21] Mythological thought has clearly anticipated V. W. Turner's point that "while the theory of exchange, with its ethics of giving, receiving and reciprocating, may well be one source of ritual unity, another and more important one consists in the mutual recognition of differences and failures to reciprocate" (Turner 1968: 273). The difficulty with this notion has to do with "ritual unity" and "more important," for which we would substitute "internal order" and "complementarity." In addition to the myths that we have considered, the story of Emu and Jabiru plays the same asymmetrical game with a transformation in the sexual identity of the players (Warner 1958: 543–545), still in an affinal key. Coming attraction: a real pisser. "Emu and Jabiru" suggests that a whole-step movement from solid to liquid bodily emissions is correlative with a tonal alteration from olfaction to gustation, and the external problematic of the disputation (fatty/lean) masks the sanguineous essence; both are sanguinary, a refraction within (stingray) and out, metonymical and metaphorical: pissed on, pissed, pissed off.

The contest itself is ostensibly about fatty meat, now low-lying (stingray), with a prototypical, falsely aetiological coda. Jabiru, Emu's son-in-law, consumes all the fatty meat of the ray that he has caught, leaving only lean meat for his father-in-law. On this score, a few notes are relevant.

1. Ray or skate poison is secreted by glands located from the base of the spine to its tip. This suggests several relationships between the mythology and technical activity, one of which might be mentioned: between Emu, poisoned thru the ingestion of chromatized water, and stingray, a poisoner in its natural element, the latter here a victim, the former now the victimized. As fish poison reduces the interval between nature and culture to its minimal expression (Lévi-Strauss 1969a: 279), as an intrusion of nature in culture, stingray brings about very nearly the same chromatic effect, thru an inversion of the means, now as who was mad for meat is very much like an erotesis. According to "The origin of fish poison,"

There is an Arawak myth from Guiana that provides a theme to which the story of the bird who was mad for meat is very much like a erotesis. According to "The origin of fish poison," an old man took his son with him, and wherever the boy swam, fish died. The fish resolved to defeat him, and while the lad was basking in the sun on an old log the stingray fatally stung him. He told his father that curious plants would grow wherever his blood took root, and that the roots of these plants (fish poison) would avenge his death (Lévi-Strauss 1969a: 262–263). Fish poison is produced by dirt washed off a child who was, in his own hyperbolic way, at once fish poison and a poisoner of fish, killed by a fish that poisons. Like the seducer,

sexual access described by M_5 is therefore a dialectic play on mutual avoidance, the extrema of mutual respect. Just as incest, clan (M_{1-2}), primary (M_3), or affinal (M_5), attained or attempted, is the negative inverse of exchange, joking and avoidance are the positive corollaries of the exchange of food and women: a mythologized proof of this proposition is provided by M_3 and M_5. When a bad piece is given or proposed, the analytic qualities of license and restraint are recoded in the language of sensory quantities, too much smell (olfactory code: M_3) or too much talk (acoustic code: M_5).

Let us recall, in this context, aspects of Radcliffe-Brown's final note on joking relations:

M. Marcel Mauss and I have both been seeking for many years to find a satisfactory general theory of what I have been calling relations of friendship between separate groups or persons belonging to separate groups. One part of such a theory must be a study of prestations or exchanges of goods or services. Another must be a study of "joking relationships" (Radcliffe-Brown 1952b: 113).

Jabiru poisons the social order; acting only in terms of his natural propensities, he brings together, in the manner of hypallage, what should have remained apart, disjoining what should have come together.

2. Unlike that of other fish, stingray blood has a very high content of urea; the gill tissues are not permeable to it. Although selachian tissues will not function unless the blood-urea concentration is high, there is *no urea in fat*. Providing his father-in-law with only lean meat, and keeping all the fatty meat to himself, Jabiru provides a countersubject to talk: about eating shit. The talk is now about being pissed on/off. The finality of death came into the world, according to a Dalabon myth, when the wife (black-nosed python) of Wallaby and the wife (red-bellied water snake) of Moon chose to drink the urine of Wallaby rather than of Moon (Maddock 1974: 159).

A proof that these relations are *obbligato* rather than *ad libitum* is suggested by a Ngarluma myth of urine magic and the evil (stingray) tale (Von Brandenstein 1970b: 143–146).

3. A flightless bird (Emu)—a puzzle (like childish civility) for the logic of Dalabon and Djuan ethnozoological taxonomy (Maddock 1975: 102–119; cf. Van der Leeden 1975: 87, 92–93)—brings down to earth a high-flying one (Jabiru), a matter of urinous dissonance, thru the medium of a low-lying one (stingray). Emu/Jabiru belongs to the same mythical suite as the southeast (-west) Australian Eaglehawk/Crow. Among the Djuan, Emu is identified with a gluttonous old woman (Robinson 1968: 164–169).

4. A pungent proof of the *obbligato* character of the relations whose contours we have only sketched is provided by South American ethnography:

4.1. The Desana, a subgroup of Tukano Indians, live in the equatorial rain forests of the Vaupés territory in the Colombian northwest Amazon. The *boráro*, a jaguar-like, although not quite, being, is a sometime chief of the animals, a great lover of seafood. One way of killing his victims is by urinating upon them. The urine of the *boráro* is a very strong poison, and this has a special meaning for us: ". . . a food preferred by the *boráro* is the fruit of *barbasco* (*Lonchocarpus* sp.), a powerful fish poison" (Reichel-Dolmatoff 1971: 86–88).

4.2 The Desana shaman/jaguar (*payé*) embodies a melange of power concepts. One among these has been translated as "inject, transmitted through a sting, the power of penetration" (Reichel-Dolmatoff 1971: 126). In both North and South America, the tail of the ray has come to represent an inverted, seductive penis, and is part of the same system as the vagina dentata (Lévi-Strauss 1973a: 309). Finally, in the argot of American confidence games, the step that reveals to the mark that he has been taken, the truth that reveals the lie, countersubject to the lie that concealed the truth is called the sting (Maurer 1940: 292; Goffman 1952: 451).

The discussion that follows this comment outlines the yin/yang principle and the fundamental conception of unity in duality in Dogon cosmology. Although Radcliffe-Brown never quite managed to pull these threads together in an internally coherent manner, Murngin theory—realized in a relationship between myth and ritual—that renders an interpretation of either medial to the external undecidability of the former and the internal certainty of the latter—provides a construction that satisfies an internal ordering criterion and systematically relates sensory quantities and ethnological qualities. Figure 10, a geometrical representation of the theorem whose proof we have outlined, illustrates that mythical solutions select terms and relations in order to construct a logic that needs both in order to define its fundamental concern: classes of possible relations between relations, that are destined to become relations, once again, in an exchange between empirical and transcendental deduction, an outer and an inner ecology.

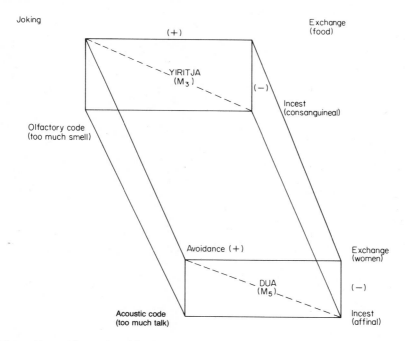

Figure 10.   Joking and avoidance: a sensory theorem

THE TABLE MANNERS OF A SNAKE

How are these bundles of bundles of relations related to our reference myth (M_{1-2}), the story of the Wawalik sisters? A reply to this query is suggested by the Wessel Island snake in his brief sermon on the table manners of a snake:

The Wessel Island snake, when he heard what Yurlunggur said, was disgusted. "You've eaten your own wakus and yeppas," he said. This was a terrible thing.

Yeppa is a term for sister (Warner 1958: 67) and, if the Wawalik sisters' sons are Yurlunggur's *wakus*, then the rainbow serpent is their *gawel* ["mother's brother," "father-in-law," "mother's brother's son's son"], as shown in Figure 11. The relations encoded by the reciprocal pair *gawel–waku* range from the consanguine mother's brother and sister's son, the latter having the former's daughter as a wife, to distant MB's and ZS's who have a trading reciprocation (Warner 1958: 93). Throughout a "waku's life he is always giving presents to gawel" (Warner 1958: 93), and

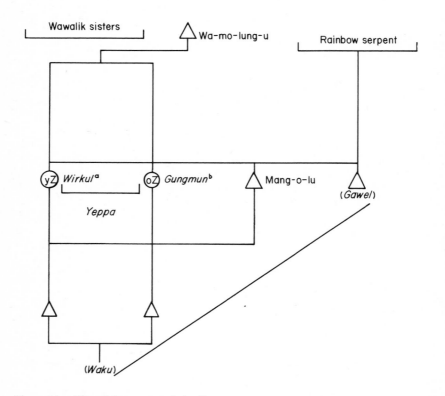

Figure 11.   The rainbow serpent's family
[a] yZ, *wirkul*: a young woman who has not had a child (pregnant).
[b] oZ, *gungmun*: a woman who has had a child: literally, "the giver." *Source*: Warner 1958: 250–251.

When it is decided that a waku is to get a gawel's daughter, the gawel shows his pleasure by giving presents to his dué, who is the boy's father, and also to yeppa, who is the boy's mother (Warner 1958: 94).

According to the all-father story (M_6: Warner 1958: 542), all black men have a great father up in the sky: his power names are Mang-o-lu, Dur-rung-na and Li-li-pi-i-na, and he is said to be the father of the children of the Wawalik sisters. The father of the Wawalik sisters, whose names are Wa-mo-lung-u [stone spear] and Bur-pa-lo-ma [stone-headed spear], lived in the Nullikin tribes' country where many flint quarries are found (Thomson 1948–1949: 65–66, 69).

Expressed in the vocabulary of a territorial code, the rainbow serpent marks a negation of exchange: an asymmetrical denial of rights of access. As an ingestor of raw meat, Yurlunggur reduplicates the same message, and the matter through which signification is organized ("genealogical specifications") provides a structural synthesis of relations between the exchange of women and edibility. The riddle is, how is it possible to translate "giving your daughters culturally" (constrained by the rules of the exchange game) into the good meat (/bad meat) language? The answer that is provided by M_{1-2} is, "eat your affines naturally" (raw). Goodale's account (1971; cf. Hart and Pilling 1960, Goodale 1962) of Tiwi marriage contracts suggests that this solution concept, which may appear to be an arbitrary derivation, is produced in the form of a symmetrical relationship between Murngin myth and Tiwi exchange rules.

The Tiwi kinship term *ambrinua*, a reciprocal term of reference [mother-in-law/son-in-law], is produced by a Type A contract which involves four principal individuals (Goodale 1971: 52), three of whom are alive when the contract is made: a mother-in-law, her father, and the man to whom futures in *alina* wives are allocated. The bestowal of futures in *alina* wives involves, in the play of the game, an exchange of futures, of Type A contracts:

The selected son-in-law is expected to provide a marriage contract for his mother-in-law's father, preferably a Type A contract. Although any two men who call each other "brother" are in the appropriate descent and generation groups to exchange correct Type A contracts, the superior value of this type of contract appears to result in its being arranged between two close kin "brothers" (Goodale 1971: 115).

A contract of this type will result in the marriage of a prepubescent girl—excluding strategic contingencies such as contractual trade-offs—to a man considerably older than herself and entails, for the son-in-law, the responsibility of "feeding" his *ambrinua* from this time (puberty rituals) until his or her death:

The obligations of coresidence and continual economic support that the ambrinua relationship demands of a son-in-law appears in an entirely new light when we see that such an exchange causes a man to assume these obligations for his close brother's daughter (Goodale 1971: 117–118).

The rainbow serpent therefore marks a direct transformation of the "economic" constraints underlying men's political games, and this transformation entails the substitution of exchange categories and food categories encoded in a genealogical idiom: (1) brothers exchange futures in women, or sisters (bestowal partners: Hiatt 1965: 41) are ingested; (2) sons-in-law feed mothers-in-law (brother's daughters: ZD in Gidjingali; Hiatt 1965: 76) or a "father-in-law" eats his sons-in-law (sister's sons) who, in Gidjingali, receive rather than become food (Hiatt 1965: 68–69).

In Wik-Mungan, one should give food indirectly to one's own father-in-law (Murngin: M_9, "Emu and Jabiru"), and it is strictly forbidden to eat one's own father-in-law's food.

We have considered aspects of transformative relations between a territorial and an edibility code, expressed through myth in an asymmetric exchange system and affinal entailments, realized in praxis, in a symmetric exchange system. What invariant features do Australian alliance systems share, symmetric or asymmetric, that provide the ethnographic basis for this dialectical parallelism? Two preliminary points. Australian alliance systems are more symmetric than asymmetric, and we have very few well-defined instances of the former (for example, Murngin, Yir-Yoront: Sharp 1934), with Karadjeri (Elkin 1932) as an intermediary form between these and prototypical Kariera systems. The second has to do with a failure to distinguish, by Warner and others (Lawrence and Murdock 1949; Radcliffe-Brown 1951), between descent lines and localized descent groups (Lévi-Strauss 1969b; Leach 1961a: 68–71) and between patrilineal descent groups and patrisequences in Australian asymmetric relationship terminologies (Shapiro 1969: 77). According to our current understanding, an intelligible construction of these asymmetric systems involves three unlike classes, or a minimum of four patri-sequences, although Murngin and Yir-Yoront have five patri-sequences (Shapiro 1969: 74).

In the traditional Murngin system the Wawalik sisters should have been initially bestowed as *mothers-in-law* by individuals of their matriline (M, MB, MM, MMB). Mythology does not fill in this line with a cast of characters, but the possibility should not be ignored that the violence that the rainbow serpent inflicts upon the Wawalik sisters has something to do with the *mirriri*, an enigmatic custom that appears to be endemic in Arnhem Land, reported from the Murngin, the Burera, and the Dalabon (Warner 1958: 66–71; Hiatt 1964, 1966; Makarius 1966; Maddock 1970c).

The *mirriri* involves "an attack by a man upon his real or classificatory sister because he had heard her sworn at by her husband" (Maddock 1970c: 166). Verbal assaults upon a wife involve a marked departure from the ritualization of daily life and a misuse of language; and if we recall that M_2 opens on an incestuous note, then the attack of the water python on his sisters falls into place, for the misuse of language and incest are closely associated in native thought. Misuses of language "are grouped together with the incest prohibition or with acts evocative of incest. What does this mean, except that women themselves are treated as signs, which are *misused* when not put to the use reserved to signs, which is to be communicated" (Lévi-Strauss 1969b: 495–496).

This mutual convertibility of the use and misuse of words and women *as signs* is realized, once again, in a dialectical relationship between myth and praxis: in the former, the exchange of sexual and reproductive (bestowal) rights in women is misused, for the Wawalik sisters engage in incestuous relations with avoidance partners (not maritally permitted males: cf. Maddock 1970c: 173) whereas in praxis a husband verbally

prohibited males : prescribed males : : incest : verbal abuse

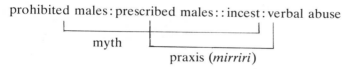

assaults his wife, and if one has as its consequence a spear in the ear (for a sister) the other presents us with sisters in the stomach.

Ethnography provides us with an olfactory variation on verbal abuse, up and over an inch or so from his mouth to her nose, from a consanguine (brother) to an affine (husband), for Winnebago husbands traditionally punished unfaithful wives by cutting or biting off their noses (Lurie 1961: 129–130, n. 14; cf. Radin 1920: 429, n. 116; Raffolovich n.d.: 6). And if you remove the self (I) from abusive noise—which in Ambrose Bierce's (great Mugwump) lexicography is a stench in the ear, undomesticated music, the primary product and authenticating sign of civilization (Bierce 1958: 91)—it's as clear as the nose on your face; for the adultress makes the cock-old the victim but never the beneficiary of mythical thought, so to nonose at all. In return for that gift he emits stench in the tone of sound or prevents her from receiving stench in the tone of smell; some act like men, others be them: ethnography, holy discipline of shit-eaters, the gift of pity for the other.

The Wawalik sisters' sons are in the "sister's sons" category in relation to the rainbow serpent, and they should therefore have an exclusive claim to his daughters (water lubras, flying foxes, and so on), whom we have not considered in this essay, as a consequence of mother-in-law bestowal (Shapiro 1969: 76). And it is these jural arrangements, which make the mother-in-law the primary object of bestowal (cf. Thomson 1948–1949: 42–45, 50–51, on food and affines), that group Australian exchange systems, symmetric and asymmetric, and differentiates them from South-east Asian ones such as the Kachin (Shapiro 1969: 77, 79; e.g. Leach 1954, 1961a).

Another Murngin myth explores the convertibility of food categories and sexual access in the opposite direction: speaking of oedibility, it comes and goes.

M_7 (Murngin): Mother and Son

In the time of Wongar a Gwiyamil boy was groaning in the camp of his mother. His mother asked him what was the matter but he did not answer and kept on groaning. "Shall I give you honey?" she asked. "No," he groaned. "Do you want some kangaroo?" "No," he groaned. "Would you like some turtle eggs?" "No," he groaned. "Or porpoise?" "No," he groaned. The mother named all the good things to eat and drink and all the other good things in the world, but the boy only groaned in reply. Then she said, "Would you like my vagina?" "Yes," he cried, "that is what I want" (Warner 1958: 561–562).

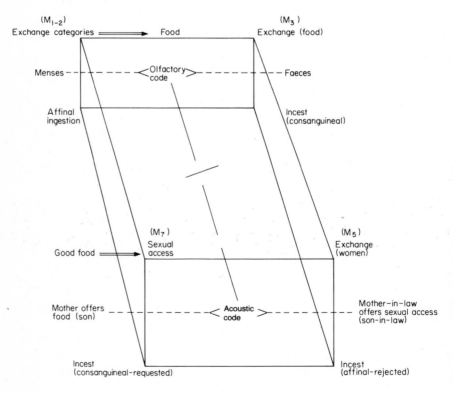

Figure 12.   A good recipe for incest

In the story of the Wawalik sisters and the rainbow serpent, exchange categories are converted into food ("affinal cannibalism"), whereas M_7 translates good food into the language of sexual access: the former is linked to M_3 through an olfactory code (faeces/menses: cf. above), sons-in-law produce a bad piece of meat for their mother-in-law/sons-in-law become a good piece of meat for their father-in-law. In the case of the latter, there is a well-defined contrast with M_5 that is generated by the deletion (or addition) of an affinal transformation: a mother offers her son good natural food/mothers-in-law offer their sons-in-law bad (old, rather than fatless) cultural food (sexual access): like the old woman (M_3), the son and sons-in-law reject the point selected, the former by requesting "consanguineal incest," the latter by rejecting "affinal incest." Talk: about Oedipal dreams and earthy schemes, now using the offer of good foods rather than the gift of young women (M_5), by a relatively younger male consanguine rather than relatively older female affines, as a point of access. The extremes are explored in myth, rejected in practice: mutually lamentable truth-values of being between and being; ruled out and bought in. If we delete joking and avoidance from the sensory theorem and fold the sensory codes onto the vertical planes, then these metarelations can be graphically constructed as in Figure 12.

A GLUTTONOUS FUGUE

> Myth and music thus appear as conductors of an orchestra of which the listeners are the silent performers.
>
> CLAUDE LÉVI-STRAUSS

We have previously noted a metonymized relationship between turtles and faeces within a text and the uses of shit as a metaphorical operator between texts and within gerontocratic praxis: shit is mythically bad to smell and good to think. In American English, shit points, among other things, to good thinking, as contrast and identity, as in "that's a bunch of shit," which in the same code provides an inversion of the opposite pole, the logical procedure known as "getting your shit together": fecal metaphors either mark a departure from dressed-up thoughts or provide the costumes for a fancy-dress party. In "it's all about who gets to do the shit jobs," stench implies an evaluative ranking of productive activities: as it trickles down from the top, shit hits the bottom. And this intersection of directional and olfactory differences is encoded in tactile imagery: a "shit job," which is at the bottom, is a hard lot, whereas a good job, which is higher up, has to do with the soft life: some are made out to have a touch of class/others make themselves a bit of an ass. This manner of speaking is metonymically transposed in practice, conjoining either end of the alimentary canal: in the Manchester of which Engels wrote in 1844, still the sewers back up into the kitchens, the others live in shit, our other side of the coin (Kermode 1974: 6, 8, 12; Gould 1969): *ecclesia super cloacam* (Burke 1957: 413).

That a contiguous relation between turtles, particular hawk-bills, and faeces is not merely a contingent formation within a particular text (M_3) but rather a metaphorical necessity between texts is one of the things that the story of "Ure and the bush fire" (M_8) points to: and the path that faeces opens leads us to a reptilian polyphony.

Ure is an alternative name for Bamapama, the Murngin trickster hero who is a central figure in a cycle of trickster myths (Warner 1958: 545–561; cf. Bamapama *garma* ceremony from Marunga Island, Warner 1958: 564–565). Bamapama is associated with a wide variety of asocial acts, many of them incestuous, and is characterized as a rather gay, stupid fellow, filled with inordinate lust, an undisciplined breaker of tribal laws, a crazy man. Further, all Murngin possess two souls, the *warro*, the soul from the heart, which is from the totem well, and a *mokoi* (trickster), an evil shadow soul which, after death, is driven into the jungle (Warner 1958: 413, 416, 445–446). Ure is a *mokoi*.

Although partial and incomplete, a provisional synthesis of the selections developed through aspects of the trickster cycle with other texts within the Murngin corpus suggests that decompositions of the trickster figure across mythological universes (Kerényi 1969: 171–191; Jung 1969: 193–211) should be viewed as complementary to recompositions within them.

M_8 (Murngin): Ure and the Bush Fire

One of the Groote Eylandt men went out to look for turtle. He said, "Come on, older brother, we'll go harpoon some turtle."
The other brother said, "Yes, we will."
They took a canoe and a turtle-harpooning outfit and paddled out to the ocean. They harpooned two hawksbill turtles.
"Where will we cook it, older brother?"
"Let us cook it on that sandbank over on the mainland."
They paddled then to the mainland.
Ure and his Udal people—they are like *mokoi* and murdering people—had a camp in the bush. They could smell the turtle cooking. When they smelled this, Ure said, "All of you people stay here and I'll go down to the beach and find out what this is."
He put boomerangs all around his belt and his two hands. [To the minds of the Murngin this identifies him as a tribesman from the more remote south.] He put feathers all over his body the way we do in the *Djungguan* ceremony. He painted himself as we do the *mokoi* in this ceremony.
The two Groote Eylandt men had cooked their turtle and were eating the liver. They heard Ure crying out, "*Lak!! Lak!! Lak!!*" This was to make a big wind. Ure

had on a *Guna* headdress. It had feathers on top of it. [This also identifies Ure as a man from the southern tribes, since the northern clans of the Murngin do not possess the *Guna* ceremony, or have only recently acquired it.] The Groote Eylandt men saw Ure. They were afraid. They said nothing, but they picked up their turtle and gave it to him. They put all the turtle in his huge mouth on the top of his head. He swallowed the bones, the shell, and the meat in one huge gulp. The men said, "What will we do now? He has eaten all our turtle in one swallow."

Ure said, "*Wakus*, we will sleep here, all of us, all three of us, and I will let you go tomorrow."

"All right," they said.

"You two *waku* listen to me," said Ure, "and I'll give you a song for the dead." He was lying to them and making fools out of them.

When they made camp the two men took care of the fire and Ure went down to the beach and ate the turtle's excrement. He also ate the leaves on which the meat had been placed, the stones for roasting the turtle, and the ashes from the fire. He came back to the camp. When the two men were in a dead sleep Ure took his big singing stick and hit them on the back of the neck and killed them. He picked up the first man and swallowed him whole. He picked up the older brother and swallowed him too. Ure went back to his camp and went down to the hole.

"Father," said his children, "what have you eaten?"

"Only a little piece of meat," he said.

"Why didn't you bring us some?"

"There was too little to bring," he said.

"But, father, your stomach is full. You must have eaten something more than that."

"Oh, only two men," he said, "they were very small." The men he had eaten were very large.

The Groote Eylandt tribe waited and waited for the return of the turtle hunters but they did not come back. They waited and waited and still the men did not return. After four or five days they heard a roar. It was Ure. He was a long way off on the mainland. They said, "Oh, that is Ure. He has eaten those men. He is now defecating them out."

The Groote Eylandt men took a large number of canoes to the mainland. There they found the canoe of the two Groote Eylandters, which Ure had neglected to eat. Soon they heard Ure. The noise was louder and louder as they got nearer. The men, before they left, had collected bundle after bundle of hooked spears. When they came near Ure's camp they whispered among themselves to decide what they were to do. It was agreed they would send four men here and there until they completely surrounded the Udal, then they would set fire to the spear grass and burn them to death.

Ure heard them. He raised his buttocks and put his hands on his knees and looked back. He defecated as though he were throwing spears at them, for he was trying to put the fire out. He turned his anus around and around, firing at them to prevent the fire from getting to him, but it was no use. He could not. Even though he made a wall of defecation about him, higher and higher, it was no use. The fire came on and on. Ure ran this way and that but every way he ran it burned him. His skin came off. His children were dead. His wives were burned and died choking with the smoke. Finally the fire reached the Udal men and all of them were killed. When they were burned to death the skin broke open in the center of their chests and abdomens. Underneath Ure's insides they found the two Groote Eylandt men. They were carried out by their Groote Eylandt tribesmen and taken to the salt water. They were washed in the salt water and put in the canoes to be returned to Groote Eylandt, where they were buried, for a man's bones are always carried back to his own country for their last burial (Warner 1958: 557–559).

The exchange axis of M_3 is a deducible relationship between a mother-in-law who is given too little food (turtle) by her sons-in-law; M_8 tells us about an explicit relationship between a father-in-law who takes too much food from his sons-in-law, and whereas the former shits offensively (eats shit metaphorically) to redress her raw deal, the latter shits defensively (eats shit metonymically) as a consequence of his good meal. Flatulence, the overture to defecation, as offense and defense, is played out syntagmatically in M_8. For you will recall that Ure produces a big wind as a means for securing food and, in the end, farts up a noxious storm to defend himself against the consequences of his gluttonous display.[22]

The function of fire and water, like the consumption and production of faeces, speaking literally and playing figuratively, is inflexively synthesized. For if fire is used offensively by a mother-in-law who has been given too little (good) meat (M_3), fire can also be played against a father-in-law who has taken too much meat, and if fresh water is made putrid to destroy those who have taken too much, then salt water is used to reach him who has given nothing at all: M_5 tells us that salt water can be used to leave them (singular masculine/plural feminine) who have given something and received nothing in return.

Tricky Ure turns up on the other side of the gluttonous operator in the story of "Ure and frilled-neck lizard" (M_9). This lizard (*Chlamydosaurus kingii* Gray) is a member of the Agamidae family (dragons), which also includes monitors. Frilled-neck is the most spectacular Australian lizard: growing to a length of two and a half feet, the frill of adult males, in the Northern Territory, is splotched with pink, black, brown, and white. The chest and throat are black. During mating displays and when excited by intruders, the frill is erected, spanning a foot across, and the lizard stands on its hindlegs, with its pink mouth opened widely, slowly rocking from side to side and hissing. Frilled-neck is a tree-climber, an occupant of rough-barked trees, descending to the ground after rainstorms to feed on small mammals, ants, and other insects and spiders. According to Worrell (1966: 72), "Western Arnhem Land blacks associate this lizard, 'Bemmung, the Blanket Lizard,' with circumcisional rites, associating the spectacular frill with the human prepuce."

---

[22]   Our modern societies need no longer concern themselves with the stench of methane for, thanks to the U. S. Department of Agriculture, a farewell to flatulence is at last at hand (*Newsweek* 1973: 69).

M₉ *(Murngin): Ure and Frilled-Neck Lizard*

Ure, that man with the hole in the top of his head and no mouth, was chopping down a hollow tree with a stone axe because it had a honeybees' nest in it. He was then in the Merango country.

Far off at the other side of the Merango country the big-eared lizard (frilled-neck lizard) heard the man cutting down the tree. Big Ear was a man in those days. He raised himself up and listened. "Ah," he said, "that *mari* of mine is cutting down a honeybees' nest. I think I'll go visit him." He started running, and as he went he named the *garma* places in the Merango country. He would run a short distance and then become confused because he could not hear the sound of the chopping. Whenever this happened he would run up a tree and listen to locate it again, just as Big Ear does today. He did this a number of times on the way over to where Ure was and named the localities as he did so. Soon he was close to where Ure was cutting. He hid behind a tree and watched until Ure had cut the tree down and had split the hollow log and found the hive. When all the work had been completed Big Ear came out. "Oh, *kutara*," he said. "I have come to visit you."

Big Ear was very greedy and he rushed over and hid the honey with both hands. He was so greedy that he swallowed wax and bees and other refuse that was in the honey. He swallowed it as fast as he could. In his greediness he took a particularly big mouthful with something hard which caught in his throat. It was one of the long spires of wood which is left by the white ants when they hollow out a tree. (This spire of wood is a high totemic emblem today for many of the Murngin clans.) Big Ear started coughing and as he coughed the stick pushed back and forth in his throat. He coughed and coughed. He cried, "*Mari*, pull this stick out of my throat."

Old Ure tried to extract the eucalyptus spire from the mouth of Big Ear, but by this time Big Ear was so excited he was running around and around in circles. It was no use. He started changing. His legs pulled up and went inside him and his hands changed and became legs. He was no longer a man. He ran up a tree and became a true big-eared lizard exactly the same as he is today. When he had got very high up in the tree he called down to Ure. "I'll be a lizard from now on," he said. "This stick will no longer be a stick. It's now my tongue and always will be. In all the days to come I'll run up trees and hold on to each side of the trunk with my feet and hide behind it when man comes near, and you will always look for honeybees' nests and I'll come around when you are looking for them." (Warner 1958: 556–557).

Fresh honey enclosed within the interior of a tree has to do with natural cooking (cf. Thomson 1948–1949: 30), like menstrual blood (M_{1-2}), an elaborated substance (Lévi-Strauss 1973a: 255), whereas turtle cooking has to do with culture, as, according to Murngin culinary practice, the head and neck of a turtle are cut off, the anus and neck stuffed with leaves, and the turtle turned on his back for cooking (Warner 1958: 142). The turtle's shell is made into a steam oven, a container for cooking the turtle's body, whereas honey is naturally contained and eaten raw from its surroundings (M_8, M_9).

If fire was used to smoke out or drive away bees, to separate food which can be eaten raw from its natural producers, then there would be a straightforward set of contrasts with turtle-cooking: naturally con-tained/cultural container, raw/cooked, smoked out/smoked in. But the gathering of honey is not literally associated with the use of fire and techniques of smoking (Warner 1958: 144): the bees are stingless, although the honey is separated from its cultural producer by the invoca-tion of kinship obligations, a kind of smokescreen for frilled-neck's gluttony (on *mari–kutara*, cf. Thomson 1935, 1948–1949: 54–55). Honey and turtle—rather than honey and tobacco—correspond, in the logic of myth, to contrasts internal to the category of noise.

Frilled-neck hears the percussive chopping of a hollow tree which has to do with culture, and Ure cries *"Lak!! Lak!! Lak!!"* to simulate the nonpercussive sound of a big wind. The producer of a raw, natural food which he will not consume is associated with a discontinuous sound, whereas the consumer of a cooked cultural food which he did not produce is associated with continuous sound; and while in the case of the former, the consumer ("Big Ear") suffers from a deficiency in the reception of sound, in the case of the latter, the consumer is noted for a proficiency in the production of smell. The *waku/gawel* and *mari/kutara* reciprocals mark a doubly stressed contradiction: in the case of the former, food is taken rather than women being given, whereas in the latter, a gluttonous transition to nature departs from an expected transition to adult culture: *mari* should teach *kutara* good manners.

Another of Ure's adventures develops the relationship between frilled-neck lizard and the Udal people's big man and between the latter and M_{1-2}.

M_{10} *(Murngin): Ure (Bamapama) Spears the Sun*

Far away in the bush country, very deep inside, the men have no mouths in the proper place, but it is found on top of their heads. The sun does not go down there but stays in one place all the time. One of the men there went to look for a honeybees' nest. He found a hive and filled a basket with honey. He put the basket over his head and made a small hole in the bottom of it and let the liquid honey leak into his stomach. Everybody in that country is like that. We call these people Udal. This hole opens like a door and is covered over with skin. The top of the head around the hole is bald. The skin is kept in place with wax. The children and women of these people are just the same. They put all their food into their bodies in that way. The women have milk in that country in their breasts just as they have here, but babies must drink it through the top of their heads. When a baby cries there it is like someone talking when his mouth is closed.

Ure is a big man among these people. He lives underneath the ground. He can come outside because there is a hole there for him to come through. When they kill any kind of game they cook it near this hole before they go down inside. The place underneath the ground is just the same as this country except there is no shade and no trees, but there is grass everywhere. There are both Dua and Yiritja moiety people there. The hole they go down is somewhere in the Nulliken or

Rainbarngo country (the direction, incidentally, where all unknown things are placed, except the Island of the Dead).

Ure was sitting down. This Ure was a bushman. He was a robber man and just like old Wongar men. He is no good and is a friend of those two Wawalik women. He comes from the Dur-i-li people, He is all the same as Bamapama. He got up and walked a little way and sat down again. He was thinking. He said, "I think I'll go up above and hunt some kangaroo."

When he got up above he saw our sun. He saw a big Yiritja kangaroo, too. He sneaked up. He took a stone spear. The sun was that kangaroo. That kangaroo ran toward the west a long, long way. Ure went after him. That man-sun went down quicker and quicker. Ure was still after the kangaroo. The sun went down; it was dark. Ure did not understand this. "Why is it dark?" he said. He continued chasing the kangaroo and came nearer to it. The kangaroo was a spear's distance away when it stopped and sat up. Ure sneaked up, but he looked about and it was gone and it was dark completely. Ure was afraid and started crying out in fear. He climbed a tree to see if it would be lighter, but it was still dark. He came down. He lay down and went to sleep. He put his hands over his eyes. He cried all night. Finally he went to sleep.

In the morning he got up. He saw the sun. "Ah, it is daylight," he said; "it is a good thing the way they do things up here on top of the ground. They sleep and get up in the morning time. That's a very good thing. I'll go tell all my people."

He went home and told them. He brought his people up from out of the earth. "See, here I killed this big kangaroo. I made a camp here and after I killed him it was dark."

"Why didn't you come home?" they asked.

"It was too dark. The sun is different here. We must sleep here at night. This is a very good way." He talked to them in the late afternoon. "You all camp here and watch me, because I understand this thing."

When it became dark some of his people were very frightened. The headman said. "Don't be afraid of this dark because we are to sleep now until the sun comes up."

But when it became completely dark all of them were so afraid that the men, women, and children climbed up in trees. He got them out of the trees and persuaded them to go to sleep.

In the morning the sun came out. "Oh," they said, "this is good. This is better than down below, for it is too hot there. It is better that we stay up here. There is plenty of wood and bark to make fires with when it gets cold and there is nothing to make fire with down underneath the ground."

All these people now live on top of the ground in this country. They are south of the Nullikens. (Warner 1958: 554–556).

Both Ure and frilled-neck lizard climb up and down trees, one to hear a seductive sound, the other out of fear of a repulsive absence of light: for frilled-neck lizard, treetops are a means for finding the right direction, whereas for Ure they serve as an end, a secure form of protection. Ure and the Udal people, unaccustomed to darkness, live in a light, dry hole beneath the surface of the earth and are associated with a daily (day/ night) periodicity which has to do with an unsuccessful quest for death (hunting); the rainbow serpent inhabits a dark, wet hole and is associated with a seasonal periodicity (wet/dry) that has to do with the successful production of life (birth and female stench). Both are consumers of producers and their products (M_{1-2}, M_8), one good to eat (turtle), the other good to think (ritual knowledge).

On the assumption of intradomain exclusivism ("monosemy"), the interrelations of the reptilian deductions enclosed in M_{1-2}, M_3, and M_9 remain hidden behind the stench of mystification: bringing a member of the ethnosociological chorus (old/women) to the front of the stage clears the air, defining the intersection of two axes played by an unlikely quartet.

We already know that a water python (the rainbow serpent) is a good consumer of smells and a hawksbill turtle is a producer of bad smells: the same combination is played by M_5 and M_9 with a modulation in the sensory key, now concerned with the production and consumption of culturalized sounds rather than naturalized smells. A lizard (frilled-neck, "Big-Ear"!) suffers from a deficiency in the reception of sound, whereas old women have to do, as we have seen, with a certain promiscuity in the production of sound: the former climbs high to find the right direction, whereas the latter are willing to sink pretty low in order to transmit their true intentions.

There is a further exquisite poetic of the concrete that unfolds when we play the eater and the eaten back to front within M_9 rather than between M_9 and some other variation. Big Ear, who is, mythically speaking, a bit hard of hearing, is naturally acting a masterful recipient of auditory signals, according to comparative measurements of cochlear potentials and histological inventories of hair cells, with auditory acuity in lizards ranging from a maximum in the nocturnal geckos to a minimum in the autarchoglossids, who depend primarily upon chemical signs (Blair 1968: 303).

In terms of the communicative use of possible sensory channels for emission and reception, there appears to be an array of continua that are marked, on either end, by the taxa categories ascalabotids and autarchoglossids: the latter, of minimal limbs and snake-like elongation, rely, like their true-snake kin, heavily on chemical signals, whereas the former, with true limbs and not too much stretching of the center, rely primarily upon visual signals. The gecko neutralizes these sensory differences: good enough at chemical, visual, and auditory signals; words out one end or the other, in both, or not just a matter of holes, the whole's a sign, that's possible too: look at frilled-neck.

Like other lizards, Big Ear has femoral glands, physiologically coupled with the genitals, which serve as sexual attractants, suggesting an identity (sexual signals) and contrast between the consumer and the producer of the consumed: 2-decenoic acid serves both as the signal through which virgin honeybee queens inhibit worker ovarian development and the rearing of new queens and as the olfactory sexual attractant of the nest queen (as well as a food trail—not so with the *Meliponini*, Frisch 1967:

307; cf. below): a single compound synthesizes primer (endocrine-mediated) and releaser (immediate-behavioral) effects (Wilson 1968: 76).

More to this point, as it helps us to understand the (mythical) auditory problems encountered by Big Ear and the solutions that it arrives at, is the ability of bees to orient by osmotropotaxis (Wilson 1968: 81). And if you can see that M_9 appropriates trees as metaphorical antennae to augment frilled-neck's mythical auditory deficiencies—no service here: whole rather than holes (some defense/giving offense)—then we should know that the olfactory proficiency of the eaten's producers, rather than the auditory deficiency of the eater's production, is metonymically localized in the real workers rather than in the mythical exploiter's antennae (animal/vegetable), which allow them to scan the air (be in the air) for odoriferous (/acoustic) gradients (on the relationship between odor groups and natural properties of odoriferous molecules, Wright 1966). Bee olfactory acuity, aside from its use in the dark beehive, coupled with the bee's genius for qualitative discrimination, is of sensory significance in localizing (workers from foragers) nearby (rather then far-away: Big Ear), specific floral scents, which to bees are signs of odor categories rather than specific odors (Frisch 1967: 507–508). Both the time of emission of floral odors and the quality of the essence is coordinated with the visitation of bees (consumer and consumed, animal with vegetable in their morphological symmetry: Oldroyd 1970: 188), as well as carrion-loving (carrion-like floral scents) flies (blow-flies, in Murngin, are metonymically linked to adultery and putrescence: Warner 1958: 80) and beetles: little things mean a lot, "the holiness of minute particulars" (Blake 1971).

The producers of a natural commodity that is culturally raw and naturally cooked use (real) animal antennae to localize, by natural smells, nearby raw materials for an interiorized cooking and secretion of their honey (by olfactory invitation of the materials), whereas a mythical consumer uses vegetable antennae to localize, by culturalized sounds, synthetic each to each other, the finished product.

Mythical poetics conducts a synthesis of the horizontal and the vertical, reduplicating metonymically, within M_9, between a producer and a consumer, what it seeks to express metaphorically between M_8 and M_9, in the relationship between the consumer in one and the consumed in the other, homophony merged with polyphony: between rather than being.

There is yet more to the dialectical affinities that are deducible between lizards and bees than their conjoined willingness to be seduced and seducers, to and through things mellifluous, and the sensory and directional symbolism that this taste evokes in mythical thought transposed to a disjoint disputation played in the key of gluttony: something to fight about, not just anything will do. Ure (the trickster) is tricked by passively assuming the kinship constraint that Big Ear imposes upon him. Thought he had the battle won: tricked trickster.

And what is hard and easy to come by pulls it a bit closer together between M_9, M_{10}, and M_{1-2}, the celestial compass for these diurnal beings, the sun and the polarized light of the sky (Frisch 1967: 444; 448–449): across variations rather than within one; something to gain, nothing to lose, something old, nothing new (Goodwin, n.d.).

Easy matters first. Frilled-neck gives place names to the *garma* (lower-totemic) localities in the Merango country (sacred name: hear; country: tree with wild beehive, southwestern Arnhem Bay; Warner 1958: 44), on his way to eat honey (M_9), a metaculinary secretion, found in the interior of trees (vegetable), on the *hither* side of cooking (Lévi-Strauss 1973a: 17–19), whereas the Wawalik women (M_2) give place names to all the clan territories and localities on their way to be eaten as a consequence of their secretion (interiorized, animal) of a substance on the hither side of honey (Lévi-Strauss 1973a: 361), which functions as fish poison, the active ingredients of which are related by botanical identities and molecular affinities to tobacco. The consumers and masters of earthly fire (cf. M_{12}, below) and celestial water, a mythical auditory deficiency and a real olfactory proficiency; the producers (Ure, the Wawalik sisters) are associated with the emission of faeces and menses, sexually complementary modalities in mythical thought (Lévi-Strauss 1973a: 209). The proof of this complementarity is provided in a characteristically topsy-turvy style: only women who are relatively older, marked by an extrusion from menstrual things, are associated, on a physical or psychological level, with a capacity for giving, when they have not been given enough, large quantities of fecal matter. This disjunction between production and consumption is a holey matter: for one producer has a hole on the top (Ure) into which too little honey goes, and the other (M_{1-2}) has a hole on the bottom from which a bit too much menses comes (honey/menses: cf. Lévi-Strauss 1973a: 255; and honey, menses, faeces), and as the former is physically identified with the production of large (physical) quantities of excrement (M_8), so to the metaphorical inverses of the latter (M_5), psychologically playing rather than literally speaking.

A link between M_9 and the tale of "Emu and Jabiru" (Warner 1958: 543–545) can be stated, although not adequately refracted: despite a minor modulation in the dialect of affinal relationship, in both a stick of eucalyptus, either a natural spire (*guiparu*: Warner 1958: 45) or a cultural spear (Warner 1958: 485) is transformed into a culturalized glutton's naturalized weapon for securing food, in the air (frilled-neck lizard) or the water (Jabiru): the senior affine in one is paradoxically passive (trickster); in the other hyperactive (Emu).

Moving over one trickster variant, we can decode, on a provisional basis, a marsupial identity, wet-nurse answer in need of a question: "The sun was that kangaroo" (M$_{10}$: myth is never irresponsible (Graves 1973: viii).

This quest for a question or a circle of premises from which a query might be adduced draws us through the logic of totemic affinities to the nomenclature of sections and subsections rather than the other way round, which is more frequently the case, and we now list them in their male speaking variants: the female subsection lexicon is formed by suffixing *djint*" or "*-tjint*" to the root (Warner 1958: 118, 116–123); see Table 2.

Table 2. Murngin subsections by moiety

Dua	Yiritja
Buralung	*Narit*
Ballung	*Burlain*
Wamut	*Kaidjawk*
Kamerdung	*Bangardi*

The base of the Kariera four-section system, refracting inward and pointing out to fragments of astronomical (sun/moon), seasonal (dry, cold/moist, heat: drought/fire), and hydrous (gentle and sea water; exuding moisture, dew and moist heat, [nature]/[culture] saliva, sweat, vomiting, mucus) ethno-bases, is an aboriginal physiognomical typology: the couples which compose the relations between the relations can be provisionally translated by strings, the initial elements of which are sanguinary followed by a partition of goannas (*Varanus*, elsewhere monitors, iguanas, Iguanidae) and kangaroos (Von Brandenstein 1970a: 42, 46–47), bloody good beasts to self-and-other reflect upon:

Pannaga: cold-blooded, savage goanna, fast, busy, stretched, lean, wiry, muscular, hard, dry.

Purungu: cold-blooded, lazy goanna, slow, lazy, massive, fat, plump, glandular, flabby, liquid.

And in the wet-nurse argot of marsupials (cf. Lévi-Strauss 1973a: 289, 294, on the transformational relationship of an opossum between cleanliness and carrion-rotten and her milk to bees and their honey, between wax and rottenness; as well as tortoise affinities):

Karimarra: warm-blooded, plains kangaroo, sharp-maker, hot fellow.

Palt'arri: warm-blooded, hill kangaroo, pliable, gentle.

The couples are disjoined through the sanguinary contrast (cold/warm) and conjoined by the active/passive distinction.

What the sections cannot confess, in their fearful symmetry, is the possibility of an asymmetry (time and risk: delayed/immediate) in the play of the pieces out of which they are constructed: a combinatorial out-of-jointness with itself in the psychological and morphological codes:

cool water on the outside, savage fire on the inside. Considered solely and arbitrarily in terms of the affinities that they propose for exchange and the contrasts that they require in descent—as denuded propositions in the superstructure—they give off the appearance of operations in a manner similar to that of styles in systems which have been called complex. And it is in this restricted sense that the point of mystification is embedded between the appearance of the format for exchange in the superstructure, which expresses an unwavering symmetry, and the operation of exchange value in practice, which is either asymmetrical *de jure* (Murngin), in which case it must be harmonized through biological periodicity (generation alternation) with the subsections, so that they can preserve a solid front, or asymmetrical *de facto*: different names for the same game: poker or chess. The marginalist rationale aside, women are values as well as signs, persons even in a man's world, and generators of signs (Lévi-Strauss 1969b: 496): by their nature and through culture they enter into multi-dimensional ensembles of relationships with other sensory signs, and as persons there are limitations on the quantity of investment, despite the quality of individual play and the contingencies which arise in the course of it. Surplus value composes itself as an irreducible image of ritualized distances within rather than between generations, where (Melanesia) the signs exchanged are disjoined rather than conjoined from the values which they inflect in a more inclusive semiological web: sea (shells) shit rather than she-shit.

In the western and northern Aranda realizations, the "head, skin or hair" of the physiognomical typology is combined with four other terms in their eight-subsection system, not too different from the Murngin arrangement (cf. Von Brandenstein 1970a: 39, 43). Pannanga: Purula; Kaamarra: Paltarra. We can see an echo of the Kaamarra (Aranda) form in the Murngin term Kamerdung, and Karimmara (Kariera) Kangaroo is associated with the sun, fierce, hot fire, which as a (plain) kangaroo belongs to the Yiritja moiety (Warner 1958: 555), setting this marsupial in a contrastive relationship with frilled-neck lizard (M_9), who is in the country of Dua (Marango: classification/territorial localization), and on several other levels as well, which conjoin lizards (goanna and frilled-neck transformations: shows colors after/before, offensive/defensive displays; Bertin 1973b: 305) and bees, disjoining them from kangaroos, like them and their opossum wet-nurse kin (Tembrock 1968: 343–344), masters of chemical as well as acoustic (optical as well in kangaroos, bees, and lizards) signaling.

Bees do not go flying out at night. But at times there is dancing at night in the hive by "marathon dancers" (*Dauertänzerinnen*), and then one sees that they indicate the direction of the goal to which they flew during the day—as in a dream, one might say—in accordance with the nocturnal azimuth of the sun, concerning which they have no knowledge from experience (Frisch 1967: 351).

They "calculate" the course of the sun's movement, from the west across the north to the east (Frisch 1967: 449).

This talent for nocturnal, celestial navigation is shared with, among others, lizards, of course. But these bees are stingless (*Melipona*), transmitting information by the flower's odor, which clings to the forager, and by unoriented vibratory movements of the body, rather than by a dance with rhythmic figures (Frisch 1967: 307; cf. Sebeok n.d.: 44, on iconical rhythm in indexical display). The relationship is between cold-blooded (frilled-neck rather than goanna) and warm-blooded (kangaroo), as is the case with the Kariera, Aranda, Aljawarra, Pulanja, Kukatja, Lardil (on Mornington Island), Kabi, and numerous other groups, refracting, in and out, to directional, astronomical, culinary, and hydrous symbolism.

A kangaroo that is mythically identified with celestial fire (the sun and dry heat) moves during the day, while being pursued in the hunt (the hunted), to the west; real lizards (earthly fire), hunters of bees' honey, calculate and orient to the sun's unseen movement from west to east; whereas two women, hunted by the master of celestial and earthly water, on the condition of an odoriferous (menstrual) secretion, come from the west (M_1) to? And we can see a further relationship between the hunted and the hunter in M_9 and the hunter in M_{10}: the former puts the light into the nighttime (nocturnal orientation to the sun), whereas the latter, in emerging from the infinitely light, subterranean hole where he lives (with his people), and in which he cooks, paints the daytime black: diurnal/nocturnal shadows.

As lizards are roasted on coals on the surface of the earth and identified with night light (the moon, coolness), kangaroos (plains, herbivorous, Great Grey Kangaroo?) are baked—like turtles and emus—in an earth oven (well-done/relatively rare: Gould 1969: 35; cf. 17: the hindquarters, as in our classification, provide the choice cuts) and are identified with daylight (the sun, heat, fierce fire: kangaroo: rainbow serpent :: daily celestial fire : annual celestial fire) and drought. Their images have mythical affinities with salt water, exuding moisture from the vegetable and animal kingdoms (glandular, lazy, fat goanna: wet-nurse reptilian refraction of a dreaming python) and gentle water (gentle hill kangaroo; Von Brandenstein 1970a: 42, 46).

The Wawalik sisters (M_{1-2}) and the old woman (M_3) are metonymically on the side of the hawksbill as producers of stench: the selection of alternative realizations within the category of the rotten puts them metaphorically on the side of the lizard and the old women, respectively. The latter has been established on the basis of a symmetrical decomposition of M_3 and M_5: the former has to do with a transcultural, mythologized affinity of honey and menstrual blood, both naturally cooked and interiorized, elaborated substances (cf. Lévi-Strauss 1973a).

This relationship between meta- and infraculinary secretions has an unassessed association with sexual and other criteria in Arnhem Land. In Wik-Mungan, different kinds of honey-bag are differentiated by dimensions such as the amount of honey, the formation of wax, the size and habits of the bees. The dominant feature, according to McKnight (1973: 201), is the size and shape of the entrance to the hive, which generates five composite lexemes, ordered on a linear scale. The extreme terms are *mai kuyan*, the male sugar bag with a protruding *kunch* (also the word for penis) which may reach three inches; on the other side of convexness is *mai atta*, a longitudinal opening concave with the tree, which is female, as it lacks a *kunch* and contains the most honey, although the *mai kuyan* is more important, for it is enshrined in mythology, plays a part in initiation, and is associated with a story place.

This dialectic that knows what it is doing in the poetic world of men is refracted with an accretion rather than an inflexion in the selection of artistic themes where, in x-ray representations, there and here, like upper paleolithic cave sanctuary art (Kanowski 1973: 98–99), there is an emphasis on animals (hunting: men) rather than on vegetables and fruits (gathering: women), although the bulk of the daily food is vegetable and provided by women (Warner 1958: 140; Thomson 1948–1949; fleshy/nonfleshy: Gould 1969: 18–19): Isolde to Mélisande?

The relationship that obtains between M_{1-2} and M_9 depends, in part, upon a consideration of their aetological functions: in the former, the seasonal transition from dry to wet has to do with the periodic crystallization of cultural forms, whereas M_9 is concerned with the episodic development of natural differences. The cycle of variations played by this unlikely quartet comes full circle toward harmony in and through the relations that obtain between the rainbow serpent and the old women (M_5). For the former is successfully seduced from his resting-place by menstrual blood, which functions as a transformation of fish poison[23] (Lévi-Strauss 1973a: 254, 286; cf. Lévi-Strauss 1969a: 268, 276), an intrusion of nature in culture, whereas the latter, as unsuccessful seducers, formulate a related point of entry, now on the level of discourse rather than in the language of stench (Wiener 1966; Wilson 1968).

The mythologized series of affinities that we have sketched—between the collection of honey and the cooking of turtle; honey and menstrual blood; menstrual blood and fish poison; fish poison and seduction—can be traced around to a derived association between fish poison and tobacco which, as we will show elsewhere, narrows the distance between Australians and their South American cousins. The intervening step that starts to pull it together is the emu-man, who, in mythological accounts, is

---

[23]   Female filth differs from fish poison through certain special features: "it is animal in origin (rather than vegetable), for it comes from the human body; and at the same time its cause is cultural, since the filth in question is acquired by a woman through her function as cook" (Lévi-Strauss 1969a: 268; cf. McKnight 1973, on yam pulp).

associated with the rainbow serpent (Oenpelli: Mountford 1956: 212–214; cf. McConnel 1930b: 202, on emus and waterholes): this relationship is between the accidental, mythologized (with menses: M_{1-2}) pollution of the rainbow serpent's waterhole and actual hunting techniques employed against the emu.

In certain areas of central Australia, the pituri plant is used to stun the emu, who is apparently not only highly inquisitive but given to gazing about in a somewhat aimless manner (Spencer and Gillen 1968: 20–21, 182–183). References discussing the uses of pituri for emu-hunting in central Australia antedate Spencer and Gillen, whose work was originally published in 1899, and have been usefully summarized by a zoologist and a pathologist (Johnston and Cleland 1933). Pituri (*Duboisia* Hopwood) denotes emu or camel poison (cf. Thomson 1948–1949: 19 on *Tephrosia leptoclada*). In his diary of 1873, when he was on the Marryat Creek, to the east of the Musgrave Ranges, Gosse wrote

. . . found plenty of water by digging where the natives had made drinking places for the emu . . . people would be wise to avoid using water from these drinking places, or any small hole of surface water, as the blacks often put in some preparation to stupefy the emu (in Johnston and Cleland 1933: 205).

Shortly thereafter, Bancroft (1879: 10 in Johnston and Cleland 1933: 209) pointed out that

All evidence, practical and theoretical, goes to prove the identity of the two alkaloids, pituri and nicotine; and it is a marvelous circumstance that the black man of Central Australia should have dropped upon the same narcotic principle as the red man in America in a plant differing so remarkably in external aspect.

A naturally elaborated substance (menses), secreted by the founders of culture, and a cultural solution procured from a natural narcotic (pituri) produce, as consequence and cause, either the arousal of a water python or the stupefication of the emu.

An alternative realization in practice, which seeks to attain the same results while deforming the grid of means (Thompson 1961: 299) is evoked when the signifier thru the ensemble of elements is, as a systematist, turned back to front in the signified: the hunters become rather than produce poison, in a dry rather than a wet hole (circular brush blind, bush screen, or the interior of a tree: Gould 1969: 9; Warner 1958: 141–142), metonymizing a (natural) metaphorical proficiency in the consumption and production of smell, in terms of a culturally induced deficiency in the communication of chemical signs, hunter to hunted (bush screens: wind direction and the odor of sweat).

Murngin emu-hunters transform themselves into metaphorical opossums, secluded in the interior of trees by waterholes, with double-pronged spears (cf. below: the oppossum's forked penis), stepping on the dead bird's abdomen in the hope of an abundant outpouring of excrement, which to them is a sign for good (fatty) meat, dining initially upon the food/fecal-matter converter (intestines; Warner 1958: 141–142); a mythical libertine stalks a real eponym of conjugal constraint (monogamous emu): another fart or a change of heart.

Emus, in real contrast to the founding mothers (the Wawalik sisters), with whom they are mythically disjoined and conjoined, as consumers and producers of chromatic matter (Lévi-Strauss 1969a: 265–266, 269–270), both the hunted rather than the hunters, eponyms of atonality in the tone of sexuality (incestuous sisters) or of conjugal constraint (monogamous beings) and paternal responsibility (/maternal irresponsibility) in nest construction, hatching, and caring for the brood (Bertin 1973a: 358).

That same alkaloid that brings the emus down lifts them up high, for, according to Roheim (1968: 47), they all love to chew the leaves and stalks of the *pitjeri*: that bird's poison is their stone.

This achievement, more probably based on careful observation, classification, analysis, and experimentation, provides a proof, in concrete data, for the circle of symbolic associations whose contours have been outlined, and which underlie the (Murngin) mythologized equations that we now consider in their syntagmatic rather than paradigmatic expression.

The symbolic association of fish poison and seduction, well-developed in South Amerindian mythology, is documented in a Murngin myth that we are unable to consider extensively at this point: "The adultery of a Wangurri woman and Kalpu man" (M_{11}: Warner 1958: 531–532). The introduction and social identification of the seducer, who will copulate with a Wangurri woman in a real and then in a magically induced sleep (while his opossums are cooking) before receiving her assent on the condition that she will first eat charcoal, makes the point, while delicately covering it with a bit of social classification. "A Kalpu clansman from Blue Mud Bay by the name of Ka-pi went out in the bush to look for opossums" (Warner 1958: 531), the story begins. The Murngin (1) regard the opossum, like the seducer, as a libidinous fellow (forked penis, wet-nurse icon of gluttony and re-surrection: Lévi-Strauss 1969a: 173), and in Warner's clan list, (2) "Kalpu" is an alternative designation for the Kapin people; (3) "Kapin" refers to a grass used to poison fish; and (4) "Wangurri" refers to freshwater (Warner 1958: 41–42): (3) and (4) are related as a disruptive substance and the medium in which it acts, in the same manner as a seducer and the seduced. Principles of seriality appear to take hold (M_{11}), as rape shades into conditional seduction.[24]

[24] "For the most part the word, seduction, indicates effort of a persevering, thoughtful sort. When it is successful we naturally look about for a lack of resolution and resistance in the object; guile and insistence are clever at uncovering pockets of complicity. A seduction is the very opposite of the abrupt, which is, of course, rape" (Hardwick 1973: 3).

The set of perception verbs is filled out when we consider the relationship between the old women and the rainbow serpent in terms of the complementary sensory modalities which they employ: the old women create a malodorous situation because they can see what they are missing, whereas the rainbow serpent destroys the producers of a fetid substance because he cannot hear the rituals which are intended to protect them from him: water pythons feel vibrations rather than hear sounds, unfolding the double convertibility of an overt, negative auditory (positive tactile)/positive visual (negative tactile) distinction and a covert synthesis of the master of olfaction and the mistresses of loquaciousness.

This mythologically based ordering is relevant to Hale's discussion (1972: 478–479) of Walbiri verbs of perception which, on semantic, syntactic, and morphological grounds, are said to belong to a special lexical subset: *nja-* [to see]; *puda-nja* [to hear, feel]; *panti-nja* [to smell]. According to Hale:

An important aspect of the internal structure of this lexical subset can be revealed, in standard Walbiri usage, only by recourse to a syntactic device, i.e., negation. The abstract semantic structure of the subset must provide that each of the three perception verbs be paired by an antonym—it is relatively apparent that the three verbs cannot themselves be contrasted with one another in any way which is obviously consistent with the principle of minimal opposition (Hale 1972: 478–479).

This linguistic assumption of a special lexical subset has as its consequence the conclusion that the domain (perception) is lexically defective; the converse assumption that there are neither deficient domains nor privileged lexical subsets within a mythologized discourse between things finds that they have no difficulty at all in satisfying our principle of minimal opposition.

The contrast is obtained through a lotus-eater's algorithm: (1) the formulation of intersecting axes which provide mythically realized, prefixed contrasts within sensory keys; (2) a demonstration of the transformative relationship of adjacent positions, rather than a synthesis of the initial set of contextual contrasts; (3) the derivation of inter- rather than intrasensory contrasts, unrealized, although implicitly given by (1); see Figure 13.

Frilled-neck lizard is also associated with the passage of fire into culture, and this transition is organized and expressed through the *gawel/waku* relationship: lizard's interlocutor in this dialogue is crocodile.

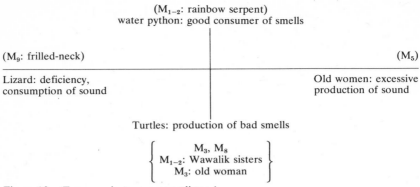

Figure 13.   Economy in two senses: glissando

M₁₂ (Murngin): The Bringing of Fire

Crocodile, in the days of Wongar, took a fire stick and rubbed it between his fingers, but he was very clumsy and broke it. He tried again and again to whirl it between his fingers so that he could make fire, for there was no fire in the world then, but every time he tried he broke the drill.

There were broken fire sticks lying all about where he had used them. He piled them all up into a big heap.

Baltjurda, the frilled-neck lizard Wongar, came along. He sat down and continued working on a small basket that he had started. Crocodile said to him, "You come try these fire sticks. My hands are all cut and bleeding from trying to make fire."

Frilled-neck had some fire sticks of his own. He took them out of his basket. He said to Crocodile, "You don't hold the stick properly. You squeeze it too hard. That's what hurts your hands. You should press it with the bottoms of the palms of your hands."

Lizard then did as he told Crocodile to do and he made fire immediately. Crocodile said, "*Waku* of mine, it is a good thing you are my relative and it is a good thing that you made fire for us, for all people." He took some grass and rubbed it in his palms and put the new fire in it. He then made a huge fire. Crocodile was a Komait and spoke the Koparpingu language. Baltjurda was a Merango and he spoke Djambarpingu. Baltjurda belongs to all Dua, and Crocodile belongs to all Yiritja, in the eastern part of Arnhem Land among those clans who are near the Gulf of Carpentaria.

Black men today make fire the way those two made the first fire. They know the proper tree to make their fire sticks from because of those two (Warner 1958: 519–520).

A likely candidate for the recipient of fire is the estuarine crocodile (*Crocodylus porosus* Schneider), a resident of the mangrove-fringed mudbanks of the rivers and estuaries of the far north of Australia. The preferences of crocodiles on the raw/cooked axis have given rise to tales suggesting a taste for the putrid: crocodiles, so the story goes, anchor newly killed food with a stone, returning somewhat later to ingest the putrid flesh. There appears to be no evidence to support this, although crocodiles have been frequently observed eating the decaying flesh of other crocodiles a fortnight dead (Worrell 1966: 2). Their principal food in salt water is fish and crabs and crayfish, fish and water rats in fresh water. It is perhaps not wholly fortuitous that a creature with a reputed taste for the putrid is the instrument through which firesticks came into the possession of men.[25] The casting principle reproduces that used for ritual language: given by women (the Wawalik sisters) and henceforth denied to them, the producers (women) and consumers (crocodile) of rotten smells, in which a *gawel* eats his *waku* naturally (raw) or a *waku* gives his *gawel* fire, making it possible for men to eat their food culturally (cooked).

A Dalabon myth, collected on the Beswick Reserve in the far north of the Northern Territory (Arnhem Land), provides a tentative synthesis of the Murngin accounts of the bringing of fire and the master of water (Maddock 1970b: 175–176):

M_{13} (Dalabon): The Origin of Fire

Originally the crocodile was the boss over fire and, in spite of repeated requests, would not share his fire sticks with the rainbow bird who had neither light nor a campfire to provide warmth and who ate his food raw. Finally, the rainbow bird snatched the crocodile's fire sticks and put fire in every kind of tree (except the pandanus) in every country, made light, and cooked crocodile and tortoise. "I'll be a bird. I'll go into dry places," the rainbow bird called out; "you can go down into the water. If you go in dry places you might die. I'll stay on top." The rainbow bird gave fire to men and put the fire sticks in his behind. They are the long feathers which protrude from the *wiridwirid*'s ["tail-tail" in Djauan] tail.

Maddock discusses some of the contradictions which the myth evokes for him:

The myth purports to explain a feature of the real world: the possession of fire by men generally, and by men alone. It does this by positing an initial situation which is in some sense the opposite of the real situation. In reality fire is readily and generally available to all members of one species, the human, and humans alone cook their food. Fire is shared and is symbolic of sociality. Yet according to the myth, fire is possessed successively by two species, both animal, who cook their food by it, while men eat raw. Fire is denied to him who wants it, and is a thing competed for. Together with the contrast between the real situation and the imagined situation is a double, but inversed, progression: from a natural to a cultural condition for men (by the events narrated in the myth they will acquire food and eat cooked); from a cultural to a natural condition for the animals (they lose or renounce fire and will eat raw or rotten or both). The other "contradiction" expressed in the myth arises out of the general world view of the aborigines.

[25] In the eastern Yiritja sea-tide *garma* cycle of songs, the crocodile is associated with celestial fire and fatty food (stingray) that is good to eat (Warner 1958: 419).

There is among them what can only be described as a profound resistance to crediting themselves with their own cultural achievements. All that they will claim credit for is fidelity to tradition or, as they put it, for "following up the dreaming," the cultural features of human societies having been established entirely by the acts of mythical beings who, demiurges or animals-to-be, are alone conceived of as active and creative, men being passive beneficiaries of unmotivated generosity (Maddock 1970b: 177–178).

Our immediate concern is restricted to the selection of animal characters and their distribution, relations, and metarelations in Dalabon and Murngin. Why are the rainbow bird and the crocodile played against one another in relation to fire in Dalabon, whereas the rainbow serpent and the crocodile play against other protagonists in relation to fire and water in Murngin? The two sides of the question, when transposed, interpret each other.

The rainbow bird is classified by ornithologists as Meropidae (*Merops ornatus* Latham) and is consequently referred to in the ornithological literature as a bee eater. As subterranean nesters, the bee eaters cannot raise their young in coastal areas during torrential downpours: they move from the more arid interior to the sea during the dry season and withdraw at the breaking of the rainy season. As bee eaters spend a great proportion of their time in intense sunlight, they are unusually liable to decolorization (Deignan 1964: 393).

The casting of the central characters is inextricably tied up, in mythical thought, with the antinomy between the continuous and the discontinuous, humanity in the world and humanity set apart and above the world, the modesty and the arrogance of men. Rather than using a chronological code, distinctively defined by the relationship between *before* and *after* (Lévi-Strauss 1966: 258–260), the logic of the concrete deploys a code that is based upon multidimensional assessments, logical complexity, and internal coherence. This logical hoarding rather than small-change spending (Lévi-Strauss 1966: 267) of pieces of thought, ordered in terms of principles of simultaneity rather than of sequentiality, in which the principal agents are animal rather than cultural actors, suggests the possibility that Arnhem Land casting rules constitute a group (cf. above/below).

The rainbow bird, who flies high in the sky and is associated with dry, subterranean places, comes down to earth in order to steal fire for men; the rainbow snake, who lives in the subterranean waters of his sacred well, goes high in the sky to water the world. A chthonian being effects the natural seasonal transition from dry to wet, which benefits all forms of life, whereas a uranian bird—a dweller of the sky world and a nester in the earth (like turtles)—fixes the cultural transition from raw to cooked, which benefits humanity alone. The former shows his polychromatic scales, the latter risks the decolorization of his tails (*wiridwirid*). Crocodile (Murngin) is given fire and unselfishly gives it to men, whereas the Dalabon crocodile selfishly retains fire and it passes to humanity only on the condition that it is stolen from him.

The empirical deductions formulated by the Dalabon and Murngin myths are closely related to the objective properties of estuarine communities: the brackish zone in which river and sea waters meet are defined by marked fluctuations in salinity. The resident animals have to adapt themselves to variable osmotic pressures and to changes in buoyancy, current, and temperature. In using residents of estuarine communities to think with, we are confronted with a paradoxical situation. On the right side, they are protected from aquatic predators unable to adapt to constantly changing conditions; on the left, as estuarine waters are invariably shallow, their occupants are liable to attack from the air by birds (Dowdeswell 1961: 135, 130–136; cf. White 1971: 143, 144).

The theft (M_{13}) and the gift (M_{12}) of the means to cook food culturally are realized through animals who, in ornithological and mythical accounts, are the consumers of the producers (frilled-neck lizard) and commodity (rainbow bird) of food cooked in nature (bees and their honey):[26] put in naturally, taken out culturally. Both variants obliquely encode ecological properties of estuarine environments, the relationships between members of these communities and sky-dwelling or quasi-uranian creatures with an in-stink for subterranean nesting: mythologized relations between two sets rather than the distinctive properties of one or the other.

The hole in the puzzle that, once solved, will allow the pieces to fit themselves together, is that colorful lover and protective landlord, frilled-neck lizard. Big Ear plays a role in the Ulmark ceremony which is performed in the dry season and—like the *Djungguan* and the *Gunabibi*—is associated with age-grading. The dance of the frilled-neck lizard is enacted by two men who "climb up a tree and hold on with their knees while waving their arms. A fire is lit beneath them. The two lizards jump into the fire and then run away" (Warner 1958: 324). The "native interpretation" provided by Warner identifies the escape of the lizards from the fire with the escape of the reptiles from the Wawalik sisters' cooking fire into Mirrirmina, from the women's impurity to the rainbow serpent's sacred waterhole (Warner 1958: 324, 375).

In ritual and myth, Big Ear synthesizes the directional and sensory symbolism of the rainbow bird and the rainbow snake: the three principals

---

[26]   The Murngin regard the opossum as a libidinous fellow (cf. above) who is to be found, like honey (interiorized animal: interiorized secretion :: rape (seduction : abrupt/continuous) : gluttony), whose erotic overtones and undernotes are widely noted in mythology (cf. Lévi-Strauss 1973a: 52), in the interior of hollow trees. There are some kinds of honey that are, like pituri, alkaline in composition and that have a laxative effect. This is the honey of some species of Meliponidae who, as we have already seen, transmit navigational information through both odoriferous and vibratory means. We would be lax if we did not point out that, on a chemical level, alkalis bring chromatic effects: colorimetric transformations.

are polychromatic in nature. The uranian bird sees fire and goes down unselfishly to procure it for men, so that they will no longer have to eat animal meat naturally, whereas a chthonic snake smells blood and goes up to provide water for all forms of life, while eating cultural meat naturally: the former insures that people will eat other animals culturally, the latter eats people naturally. A lizard who is tellurian, although he dwells in-between (in hollow trees), hears a chopping sound and goes up and down to track it to its source, in order to consume with consummate gluttony a natural food that has been culturally procured (with a stone axe).

The fertilization of the world (rainbow snake) or the reproduction of self (rainbow bird) involves a doubly inverted, symmetrical transformation: from resting (chthonic ⟶ uranian) to nesting (uranian ⟶ chthonic), and whereas the former has to do with the gift of water, the latter is associated with the theft of fire and its passage into culture. They induce forms of periodicity, seasonal (water: dry to wet) or daily (fire: raw to cooked), the natural and cultural (domestication of fire) conditions of sociality: between them are disjoint realizations of incest (the inverse of exchange), expressed not in terms of sexuality but through an edibility code, negatively played (gluttony: Ure [M_8, M_9] and frilled-neck lizard [M_9] or the retention of fire: crocodile [M_{12}]), either an excess of the consequences of cooking (cf. "Emu and Jabiru," Warner 1958: 543–544) or a deficiency in the means of cooking. But frilled-neck lizard and crocodile occupy a paradoxical position in the semigroup: for if separately (M_9, M_{13}) they are on the side of a denial of exchange, which allows us to see the inverse relationship of the sharing of food and fire to an incestuous operator (grouping the exchange of the means and consequences of cooking, language, and sexuality), together (M_{12}) they cooperate to domesticate the uses of fire. Two reptilian presences: one as food provides the meat cooked best in culture (roasted, well-done: larger baked animals run to rare and bloody); the other as feeder is reputed to enjoy meat cooked well in nature (putrid and decaying): culturalized imputrescible, naturalized putrefaction. We have already noted that three of the terms are polychromatic entities; four terms are variant expressions of interiorization: beneath the surface of the earth (M_{1-2}: dark, wet; M_{10}: light, dry; M_{13}: dark, dry) or in the interior of trees (frilled-neck; dark, dry; the animal consumer of an interiorized commodity): about inanition, confessions, declensions, or cloacal obsessions: rejoyce.

How do mothers-in-law and their ordure, metonymically given or metaphorically derived, relate to this reptilian harmony: as successful producers of consanguinal incest and unsuccessful consumers of affinal incest (conversely, young men [sons-in-law] as unreliable debtors: M_3, M_5); in their relations, direct and dialectic, with joking and avoidance, these affines are victims of a negative sociality (M_3) and victimizers of positive gluttony (M_5), the former played in an edibility code, the latter in the vocabulary of sexual access. We can see that the words embracing categories of affines, although translatable in a syntax of genealogical specifications, are operators between things in a mythologized discourse where they contextually point to many things, exterior to kinship and interior to a more inclusive semiology of exchange, as shown in Figure 14.

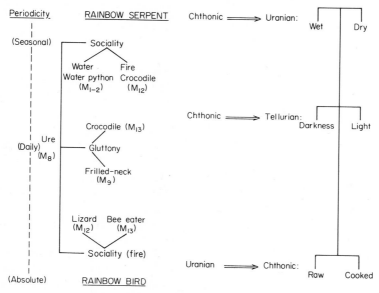

Figure 14.   A gluttonous exchange

Such a semiology of exchange, in reply to its inflexive spirit, will question answers rather than answer questions, using everything that is possible rather than only what is necessary, presuming neither the absolute reality of the disjuncture between nature and culture nor the privileged character of human language within a multiplicity of sensory channels for emission and transmission (Sebeok 1968), striving for difference rather than replicability, neither for nor agin history, but, for better or worse, in it to *speak silently*. Complicity with all/duplicity with none: we lie between.

The inclusion of contextual necessity and referential ambiguity provides a solution to the puzzle posed by these relations: why are these old women, who are in culture, paradigmatically on the side of beings in nature? The solution, from South America (Lévi-Strauss 1969a, 1971b, 1973a) to Arnhem Land, from East Africa (Edgerton and Conant 1964) to the distribution of fruit-flavored vaginal deodorants in Western marketing (Ephron 1973, Greer 1971), puts women, as producers of the fetid, on the side of the rotten, which has to do with things cooked in nature: a metonymized paradox built in and pointing out from the category of the feminine.[27] Ethno-bases, elementary deductions of mythical practice, the attainments of women on the peripheries, transposed to the ritualized mystifications of men in the center, a culture in a dialectic itself against itself: resurrected in myth, buried under practice, oral politicians and moral physicians, eponymous of madness or sadness.

THE PAWNS IN THE GAME

A puzzle of M_{1-2}, M_3, and M_4 is concerned with defining a reasonable distance between the (symmetric) affirmation and the (asymmetric) denial of exchange, between the flowering of nature and the death of humanity, between a world that is too wet and one that is too dry and foul-smelling (rotten). Once again, an invariant base form produces surface realizations that, although seemingly disparate, hit upon related solutions: they are transformations of one another.

The base form may be labeled either inequitable distribution or politicized exchange, that is (1) a categorical decomposition of the exchanged commodities, (2) the masters and (3) the benefactors of the game, and (4) a mapping from (2) to (3) (rules of distribution). In effect, a multidimensional synthesis is obtained by the perception that the right distance between giving everything and giving nothing at all is marked by a politically based distribution rather than by an equalitarian model of exchange, by asymmetric rather than symmetric exchange. The selection of the right distance, the choice—in the vocabulary of social anthropology—between restricted and generalized exchange, is generated by the combinatorial possibilities of the marginal positions. Of these possibilities, only asymmetric exchange provides a positive synthesis of the contrast access symmetrically granted/access asymmetrically denied, for the negative synthesis—symmetrically denied—would be like constructing a system of exchange solely on the basis of avoidance relations: no-thing funny about that.

This relationship between a symmetrical set of classes and an asymmetrical operation, the former encoding a totemized conception of order (Von Brandenstein 1970a), the latter encoded within a mythologized ordering, is replayed in that other crystallization of symmetrical exchange: among speakers of the Dravidian languages of southern India

---

[27]   A recognition of the problems encoded in this mythical solution, when it is played out by men on the level of discourse, has been provided by a ruling of a Cameroon Magistrate's Court: "It is unlawful to insult the lower part of women" (Bonjongo Civil Cause Book 2/1956:135/56, cited in Ardener 1973: 425)

as well as Tamil and Sinhalese speakers of Sri Lanka (Ceylon). Given the conjunction of a preference for cross-cousin marriage and a gerontocratic constraint on its realization (that the husband be older than the wife), Reid (1974) has shown that (in the Telaga-Kapu caste of coastal Andhra Pradesh) there are twice as many matrilateral as patrilateral cross-cousins in the appropriate relative-age category. The magnitude of the theoretical ratio, on the level of actualized selections, reduplicates this result while expanding the differences: it can be defined only in terms of the interpenetration of overt demographic constraints and latent differential preferences for the matrilateral solution. What, we wonder, are the mythical constraints through which this latent solution is expressed?

The point selected by M_3 gives "too little sea-meat" to an old woman; the point selected by M_4 gives "too little cultural meat" to (old women) young men. The old woman is not excluded from the process of exchange, she is rather given a piece that is relatively tasteless and meatless: $M_{4, 5}$ pulls off the same trick by leaving, at best, some old women for the younger men. Neither are completely out of the game: their position within it, however, is made perfectly clear.

The operators that resolve the dilemmas posed by the myths do so by defining relations between edibility and sexual access: the young men and the old woman are at the margins of the system of distribution, having a bit too much to give in return or a bit too little. Men in their productive years are in the very center: they receive what is denied to both, young women and good meat (cf. Thomson 1948–1949: 39 ff.).

The distances defined, in the metamenu, by the dimensions sexual access and edibility are domesticated in the course of play (gerontocracy) by a sort of multiplier function: multiple alliances————→distribution of food. By insuring that the former will operate as a condition of the latter, the game effectively politicizes the base dimensions.

That the distances defined by M_3 and M_4 are not stable solutions may be illustrated by contrasting the puzzles and solution methods which they generate; see Figure 15. The old woman's revenge is to burn the world and make it putrid by depositing her faeces on the fire. When we recall that the rainbow serpent ate the Wawalik sisters (and their children) "raw and bloody," it is apparent that the coupling of sexual access and edibility expresses, on another level, a dilemma that is concerned with the selection of a distance intermediate to

1. M_3: old woman overcooks the world; and
2. M_{1-2}: rainbow serpent undercooks the Wawalik sisters (and their children).

M_4 furnishes a solution by selecting this point. Rather than acting with feeling and anger (M_{1-2}, M_3), the mature, productive men formulate a rational, rule-governed (cultural) solution: initiation rites cook young men ("just right") culturally, in order to provide domesticated players for

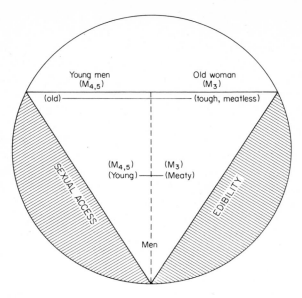

Figure 15.   The allocation of good meat

the game whose deal they will ultimately control. The old woman burns and makes the world putrid naturally, making it necessary to reconstitute a system of exchange by denying at the outset the constraints upon which such a system is based.

M_4: well-cooked (initiation rites)

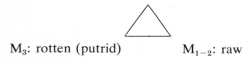

M_3: rotten (putrid) M_{1-2}: raw

THE STENCH OF INCEST

> These with a thousand small deliberations
> Protract the profit of their chilled delirium,
> Excite the membrane, when the sense has cooled,
> With pungent sauces, multiply variety
> In a wilderness of mirrors. What will the spider do,
> Suspend its operations, will the weevil
> delay?
>
> T. S. ELIOT, *Gerontion*

The gerontocratic operator described by M_4 provides an empirical interpretation of relative-age incest (older men married to young girls, young men married to older women): incest is played out in terms of age categories and is masked by categories of relationship. Conversely, the mythological interpretation (M_3, M_7) describes a situation of real incest (father/daughter, mother/son), and if M_3 and M_4 point to actual solutions (real or relative), M_5 and M_7 refer to requested constructions, either by relatively older female affines or by an absolutely younger male consanguine: clan incest (M_{1-2}) synthesizes these positions.

The incest tangle is interpretable as a triangular order, a branch with three twigs and a set of possible misuses of the edibility code rising up to meet it. Real (absolute) incest, actualized or requested, between a father and his daughter (as well as B/Z), or a mother and her son, is associated, within a text (M_3, M_7), with food that is either withheld in an affinal key (by a son-in-law) or rejected in a consanguineal key (by a son). A shift to relative-age incest, consumed or presumed, between older men/younger women or older women/younger men, between (rather than within) texts ($M_4 : M_9 :: M_5 : M_8$), has to do with gluttony, too much (rather than too little) food that is taken by either a junior or a senior affine, from a senior and a junior affine, metonymically associated with a continuous (wind) or discontinuous (chopping) sound. Clan incest, as we have seen, has as its mythical consequence the ingestion of consanguines and affines who are taken as sustenance rather than given for venery.

Incest and adultery are complementary axes of a warped space in a code for communicating signs between groups of men in a mythologized dialogue: a tentative Murngin proof is enclosed in aspects of a myth (M_{11}) of ravishment and cuckoldry that we have briefly considered and to which we tentatively return.

After a Wangurri woman copulates in a normal and then in a magically induced sleep, she and her Kalpu seducer proceed to wash in a stream. The Wangurri woman refrains from speech, until Kapin throws a green ants' nest in her eyes. The Kalpu man then offers her all the good food possible, but she selects a piece of charcoal and then gives herself to Kapin.

The Murngin use an infusion of the acid from green ants as a treatment for vomiting and stomachache (Warner 1958: 220), which has to do with an aborted digestive process, whereas the Wangurri woman chooses to eat the means for cooking (burnt and vegetable) rather than the consequence of cooking (cooked and animal). A skewed sexual code, as is the case with incest (absolute rather than normative), is metonymically refracted in a misused or aborted edibility code. This refraction is reduplicated by M_1 with an invariant in the tone of (anti-) edibility code and a minor modulation in the tonality of sexual access, now concerned with clan incest rather than adultery, rape, and seduction. For when the Yurlunggur totemic trumpet, after emerging from the well, blew over the two women and their sons, "They were lying there like they had fainted. Some green ants came out then and bit the women and children. They jumped."

(Warner 1958). Talk: about too much to eat; gluttony as one possible difference from the rules of distribution of good meat, mythically inflecting incest (clan, primary, not relative-age) and adultery (yes, relative-age): try an antacid.

An atonality that is distinctively on the side of nature harmonizes the contrapuntal devices that have been ordered in terms of the misuse of a sexuality (adultery, incest: clan, relative-age, absolute) or an edibility code (gluttony, food withheld or rejected, the ingestion of kin or charcoal): they share a refusal to commit themselves to a privileged key. The laws of counterpoint harmonize subjects selected from the logic of the concrete and of the abstract.

$$\left\{\begin{array}{l} \text{seduction} \\ \text{honey} \end{array}\right. \quad \begin{array}{c} . \\ . \end{array} \quad \left.\begin{array}{l} \text{pituri} \\ \text{menses} \end{array}\right\} \quad \begin{array}{c} . \quad . \\ . \quad . \end{array} \quad \left\{\begin{array}{l} \text{incest} \\ \text{adultery} \end{array}\right. \quad \begin{array}{c} . \\ . \end{array} \quad \left.\begin{array}{l} \text{gluttony} \\ \text{charcoal} \end{array}\right\}$$

The parallel operation of a misappropriated sexuality and edibility code, realized in the conjunction of elements derived from myth (M_3: faeces and incest that is too close) and praxis (the *mirriri*) allows us to decode a Mnong Gar usage reported by Condominas (1973: 210, 218, 220–221) and provides a proof of the symbolic associations that have been outlined (faeces, incest, edibility); see Figure 16. According to Condominas's account, the (close) elder brother of a woman who was found lying with a distant brother collects and "feeds" to the offending couple a mixture of the excrement of pig and dog. Talk about eating shit.

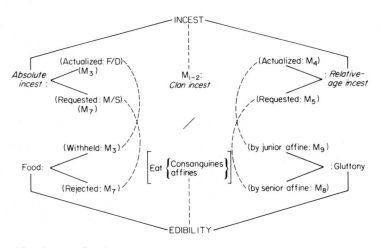

Figure 16.   A warped code

By the way, the Murngin use the yellow pollen found in a honey-bees' nest, eaten dry, to relieve constipation (Warner 1958: 221; cf. Lévi-

Strauss 1973a: 55), and we know that the Wik-Mungan associate morphological variations in the passage to honey with male and female sexual
organs (McKnight 1973). But that is another story, that is the same story,
that is . . .

To step a bit off the straight and narrow for a moment, perhaps it is not
holey fortuitous that, on the one side, incest and its atonal compatriot
within the heartland of its image and enemy, adultery, metonymically
refract a matter of faeces, and, on the back side, the acquisition of wings in
cloud-cuckoo-land provides the back-to-back avian solution to "a sudden
need to crap" and an adulterous quicky while the cock-old's gone in
Aristophanes' "The Birds" (Arrowsmith 1969: 55–57), while birds and
other high climbers (frilled-neck lizard who signifies distress like a stingless bee signifies floral matter—stingless to stinging—". . . was learning,
and on several levels at once. But it was to take years of patient practice
before his protective camouflage fitted him without a wrinkle, like a
second skin": Matthews 1974: 35–36; cf. Lévi-Strauss 1966: 26–27,
plate facing p. 148, on Clouet's frill) secure fire, which is on the side of the
culturalization of nature rather than of the naturalization of culture (cf.
above/below). A quick and easy derivation from all this can be expressed:
when the object of exchange is a pure sign, disassociated from the subject
as a value (Lévi-Strauss 1969b: 496), then the fecal refraction may well
be "centered" from the margins—shell-money: sea-shells (gathered in
nature)/sea-shit (shit of the sea: surplus value in culture): no values no
more, a wilderness of signs signifying—nothing.

In the case of M_{1-2} and M_3, relations are described which are encoded
as incest. But incest is also an analytic category whose meaning is deriva-
tive from its position within the language of anthropology: as the negative
inverse of exchange. The category incest is, in the lexicon of ethnoscience,
a head-term, and the notions of "real incest" and "clan incest" are
realizations of this term played out in stories that the myths tell. In the
case of M_4, we have observations of marrying behavior that are assigned
an ethnographic interpretation: gerontocracy. This politicized encoding
of the formation of alliances is recoded in the metamyth as relative-age
incest. The solution is, however, untenable, as real incest and clan incest
denote a discontinuity in a sequence of alliances, defined biologically
(naturally) or culturally: clan incest is a marginal position. How can we
order the positions that we have in terms of the relational features which
define them and the tangible qualities through which they are expressed?

The mythological unfolding of the incest tangle bears a close relation to
the European custom of charivari (or horning, Legman 1968: 478, 480),
a well-known example of a noise-making ritual in the Western popular
tradition that has been decomposed by Lévi-Strauss in association
with the widespread custom of producing a din during the period of an
eclipse (Lévi-Strauss 1969a: 286–289, 329–330). What is at issue is not

simply a reprehensible juxtaposition of two terms in a syntagmatic sequence, but rather a breaking of the sequence, a distortion in which a "foreign element" appropriates one term. "Charivari," according to the *Encyclopédie* complied by Diderot and d'Alembert, is defined as follows:

The word . . . means and conveys the derisive noise made at night with pans, cauldrons, basins, etc., in front of the houses of people who are marrying for the second or third time or are marrying someone of a very different age from themselves (Lévi-Strauss 1969a: 286).

The issue at issue is a question of distance—alliances which are too far from suitable correspondences in matters such as wealth, age, and civil status call forth a use of the sound (rather than edibility) continuum which departs, in one form or another, from ordinary, secular uses of language: a joking/avoidance operator realized in terms of an inappropriate use of culinary implements. The distance marked by derisive noise swallows language—while retaining its denotative power—as the sociological monster swallows his prey (by appropriating an appropriate position), or the cosmological monster swallows the sun or the moon during the period of an eclipse. The key to a solution derives from the perception of a homology between a cosmological and a sociological code. There is a right distance between the sun and the earth, between the wet and the dry season, the day and the night, feeling and reason (for, as we have seen, feeling shows its reasons and reason hides its feelings, for reasons and with feeling), that is reduplicated in the syntax of an appropriate distance between social categories in a syntagmatic chain that is defined by the rules of the game of matrimonial alliances. Mythic thought seeks a relational harmony between all material manifestations that allows it to define itself as itself, a thing among things.

Real incest is too close, clan incest is too foreign, relative-age incest, a contractually stable process of alliance formation, is just the right distance. Real incest is a solution to a rotten (and putrid) world, and if we substitute the contrasting analytic category and tangible quality for these terms we derive clan incest (cultural rather than biological) and a flooded world (too wet rather than too dry and putrid). The solution to relative-age incest, according to M_3 (male initiation rites), occurs between the wet and dry seasons, when the world is neither parched by the sun nor flooded by the rainbow serpent. The augmented intervals are the extrema of natural periodicity: the right distance between these extrema generates the elementary terms and ordering rules of a language of cultural periodicity: trust that that isn't too cut and dry. There is a correlative series of discontinuities, now interiorized rather than exteriorized (wet/dry), concerned with a natural rather than a cultural periodicity, a monthly rather than an annual disjunction, a failure to conceive human life rather than the resurrection of all life, the lunar menstrual cycle, from dry to wet with a heavy discharge of excrement not infrequently marking the boundary, faeces between in practice, ruling the margins in myth: the natural respiration and cultural pulsation of the music of mythical poetics (Stravinsky and Craft 1960: 113).

Jest a little bite more (on the doubly contradictory determination of the relationship of laughter to nature and through culture: Baudelaire 1972a: 148). Relative-age incest, conjoining differences between old men and young women (employ/enjoy), is tonally antiodoriferous, a domesticated concave/convex duet: but it is surrounded on all sides by a matter of faeces which disjoins holey differences and conjoins others. Incest and exchange, which appear in practice as marked discontinuities (contrasts), are revealed in myth as a continuum of identities, empathetic similarities, variant combinatorial realizations, whether incest is constructed naturally (primary) or culturally (by clan or section) a step *a-head* and a step *be-hind* their times (cosmopolite and provincial, appeal and repulsion, one's kicks, the other's easy tricks), ruled-out and looking-in at angles, scenes of slow death in the provinces, dreams of fast life in the center: surrealist bluff (Sontag 1974: 23), savage poetics, the labyrinth of Daedalus, nihilist satire, *somayajna* (Hubert and Mauss 1964: 15–16, 110), *siddhi*, Ubu sounds, *fleurs du mal*, Euterpe's pheromes, the worm Shamir, Sisiutl's fugue, Rhenish night, or primitive magic? Swiftian epitaph: *ABI VIATOR ET IMITARE SI POTERIS*

OEDIBILITY: FREE FANTASIA

The incest tangle provides a possible solution to the "functionalist question" posed by Boon (1972: 97) in his commentary upon Lévi-Strauss's "scandalous assertion" (1969a: 12) that myths think themselves out in men without their knowing it:

Lévi-Strauss suggests the parallel case of a grammar which in no way purports to reveal how men consciously think during speech acts. The difficulty with this parallel is that a grammar necessarily generates *all* articulate native thought (or at least, any thought that can be linguistically communicated to us for study), while myth is a particular variety of expression which (for analytic purposes) must temporarily be separated from other varieties. Again one confronts that functionalist question of how unconscious resolution in myth can be instrumental in justifying behavior in other realms.

It is not that unconscious resolution in and between myth(s) justifies behavior in other realms, but that behavior in other realms unconsciously resolves (M_4) contradictions posed by mythic thought (relative-age incest), or provides marginal positions that allow myths to find their own resolution (landowning/foraging group). The functionalist dilemma stems from a mythologized belief: in terms, taken literally, rather than in relations, given metaphorically. Bearing in myth the neutralization of these contrasts, it becomes clear that myths provide answers to questions as well as questions to answers formulated by practice: and the other way round.

The derivation that we have outlined suggests that the incest tangle is amenable to a charivari-type solution. The solution, as we have seen, requires a smelly lemma that insures the mutual convertibility of an auditory code and a succulence/desiccation contrast, complex and elementary structures. Alternatively, the former may be expressed by translating two stressed sensory codes: auditory (sounds too loud: charivari) and olfactory (smells too strong [faeces smoke/menses]: the incest tangle). The problems posed by mapping elementary structures into complex structures, which are the extreme terms of a series, a group which can take intermediary values such as Crow-Omaha, are not likely to be solved by a direct, formal approach, for the unfolding of the group is constrained and defined, we would suggest, by the crystalline growth of groups embedded in the logics of myth: ours and theirs.

Whether the intermediate values, in their mythic expression, display a concern with principles of seriality or play the diachronic construction of exchange in relationship to paradigmatic ensembles, we have nothing to lose: mythical thought can only enrich our impoverished intelligibility (cf. Boon 1970).

A tiny paradox: how can you say he's wrong when he's saying everyone's right, right or wrong: hypercritical or hypocrite, buying in or selling out, ethnology caught in a double bind itself with itself (Bateson et al. 1956; Bateson 1960: 96–98), proving in negation what it seeks to disprove thru hesitation, global polyphonies, elementary harmonies, all—each to each other—natives in the world.

In the case of M_3, a rotten world creates discontinuities in the game of exchange that is resolved by real incest; the relative-age incest of M_4 (M_5) provides a skewed distribution of the younger women that is resolved by cooking the young men just right ritually: they are, like the victims of M_3 (M_8), shit upon, culturally speaking rather than naturally smelling. So we have Figure 17.

Figure 17.   A fecal stew

The interpretation yields a candidate formula: edibility:sexuality:: smell:noise. The sensory quantities on the right-hand side of this proposition are both *emphatically stated*: ritual language and putrid smell. The analytic qualities on the other side are *weakly stated*: they are defined by an absence of young women and good meat.

This analogical formula, derived from dialectical relationships that obtain between Murngin myth, performance, and ethnological interpretation, is ethnographically confirmed by the path to sacred knowledge that turns boys into men: the *Djungguan* and the *Gunabibi*. The *Djungguan*, which is ostensibly concerned with circumcision and the ritual re-creation of the story of Yurlunggur and the Wawalik sisters, begins with the separation of boys from their mothers and ends with food restrictions and the ritual cooking (steaming) of circumcised youths (Warner 1958: 260–262, 287, 288). The *Gunabibi*, which begins with the making of the *mandelprindi* [bull-roarer], the sacred noise of Yurlunggur (Muit), ends on an atonal note: with the ceremonial exchange of wives (Warner 1958: 290, 292, 293, 296, 306–308). The abstention from certain foods, imposed upon younger women in the *Gunabibi*, is metonymically associated with ritual cleanliness, an absence of female stench (Warner 1958: 298–299). For younger men: fasting, silence, and subservience; dialectic declensions of initiates and initiators (Durkheim 1957: 310).

We have considered some of the relations that obtain between edibility and sexuality, the production and consumption of acoustic and olfactory signals, between sexuality, smell, and noise: an ethnohydrological study of Von Brandenstein (1972), suggests a further association between edibility and noise through water. According to this study, the longitudinal zigzag design, incised on weapons such as spear-throwers, shields, and swords, as well as bull-roarers (the producers, with old men, of sacralized noise), symbolize rivers, or water in general, and are stylized maps of watercourses, encoding information on the genesis of river systems, insights into geological formations, and assessments of the physical processes involved, with well-established correspondences between riverine directional changes and horizontal design cuts (Von Brandenstein 1972: 227, 228, 230–231; cf. Davidson 1937; McCarthy, 1958). Further, our old friend, the rainbow serpent (mirror to Eve's face: Leach 1969: 15), has to do with the concentric (counter-current zigzag) transformation of the longitudinal zigzag design.

McCarthy's (1958) concentric diamond design, which I prefer to call counter-current zigzag, most likely symbolizes the tidal moves of seawater observable along the coast or in estuaries.

The concentric ring design, by implication, means waterhole. A serpent, the creator of all water sources, can appear together with, or without, the just mentioned water symbols to indicate the same element (Von Brandenstein 1972: 238).

We have come round full circle and can smell out a bit of harmony: for if noise has pointed, among other things, to a sacralized or profane discourse, produced by (old) men/women, then the sound of the bull-roarer (*mandelprindi*: Warner 1958: 290, 292, 293), as instrument rather than map, creates in the *Gunabibi* a duet between a musical noise on the one side and the voices of men *and* women on the other. And the bull-roarer, as artifact and map, couples edibility and sacralized noise as the two primary poles of sustenance: good (cooked) meat and water, a mythologized consequence and cause. All that is missing is the means to transform a natural cause (fertilizing water: our male-mother) into a cultural consequence (men's: good meat), and that path between is traveled through noise to fire by percussion, the means for making a natural thing into the fat that glues together allocation criteria in exchange relationships. The distribution of this procedure for procuring fire extends from South Australia as far as northeastern New South Wales and southeastern Queensland (Mountford and Berndt 1941) and has recently been ethnographically established for Tasmania (Völger 1973): do we hear an echoecho in Arnhem Land or a declension in our mind?

The mythical disjunction of an irregular supply of meat, provided by men, rather than a steady supply of roots, fruits, and vegetables (hunting/gathering), given by women, makes possible the conjunction of high beings (for protection, to escape detection, to find the right direction) who come low to secure fire and a low being who flies high to provide water, like Don Ramón's Quetzalcoatl of the Morning Star, Eagle and Snake (Scorpio's choice), earth (water) and air (fire): Lord of the Two Ways (D. H. Lawrence 1959: 373–374), shedder of skins, dry to wet passage on the outside, nasal to cloacal voyage on the inside: incalculable, inescapable, undefinable object, inner and outer, your admiration for their accomplishment: crucible of being.

Although it is just one among many things, this rainbow serpent is positioned as, to borrow a musical item, a chromatic piece, between polychromatics and monochromatics, deified in its mythical appearance, mask and penumbra to its sensory essence, synthesizer of ontological and psychological time, similarity and contrast, counterpoint between: the interiorized musical experiencing of time (*chronos*) and the exteriorized passage of time which, in itself, seeks to deny itself a point of access to itself (cf. Stravinsky 1970: 30–31). This God is a crystalline piece, a piece in which the movement from tone to tone (as in incest to gluttony) is "colored," rather than diatonic, by half—or whole—step alterations of frequent accidentals from tone to tone. An operation of the interval of the fifth, music's magical number, to the order of accidentals for *any key*, yields a symmetrical inversion of the complete order of seven accidentals, expressing the chromatic essence of the Two-Directional Lord: from right to left, the order of flats, from left to right, the order of sharps (Newman 1967: 72, 90–91): Pope of the One and Many, mutually refracted problematic of musical and mythical thought (Stravinsky 1970: 30–33).

FALSE CODA

There is really no defensible way to tidy up all of this in order to produce a nice clean ending[28] for such a smelly myth, and, as we all know, myths are in-terminable. *"Le style est l'homme même"* (Buffon or buffoon). So, like the Perils of Pauline, to be continued by some-thing,[29] and the next-to-last word belongs to Lenny Bruce (1966: 155), who appropriately disowns it:

If sometimes I take poetic license with you and you are offended—now this is just semantics, dirty words. Believe me, I'm not profound, this is something that I assume someone must have laid on me, because I do not have an original thought. I am screwed—I speak English—that's it. I was not born in a vacuum. Every thought I have belongs to somebody else.

The final word belongs to Miss McKintosh,[30] my elderly first-form etiquette instructress at the Horace Mann School, who always reminded us that before going out to face our myth each morning, we should make sure that we clean the dirt from under our fingernails (must we shine our shoes today, the other she sez they care about that: two). After all, it's only good manners; don't swallow that story: no-thingz sacred, every-thing is sacred: God nose.

---

[28] Old men ought to be explorers.
And the end of all our exploring
Will be to arrive where we started
And know the place for the first time (T. S. Eliot, *Little Gidding*).
[29] Not just anything will do.
"And Polo said: 'The inferno of the living is not something that will be; if there is one, it is what is already here, the inferno where we live every day, that we form by being together. There are two ways to escape suffering it. The first is easy for many: accept the inferno and become such a part of it that you can no longer see it. The second is risky and demands constant vigilance and apprehension; seek and learn to recognize who and what, in the midst of the inferno, are not inferno, then make them endure, give them space' " (Vidal 1974: 21).
[30] On the relationship between commitment, passion, authenticity, and a complete identi-fication with the object: Barrett 1957: 392–395. We might recall that, in Joyce's *Finnegan's Wake*, "the universal human symbol of the writer has now become the infant Earwicker twin (refraction of the image of Everymanthewriter) scrawling with his own excrement on the floor!" (Barrett 1957: 391).

APPENDIX: LIST OF MYTHS

M$_1$ (Yirrkalla):   *"The story of the Wawalik sisters."*
M$_2$ (Murngin):   *"The Wawalik women."*
M$_3$ (Murngin):   *"The old woman and the turtle flipper."*
M$_4$ (Groote Eylandt): *"The origin of initiation rites"* (from Rose).
M$_5$ (Murngin):   *"The incestuous mother-in-law."*
M$_6$ (Murngin):   *"The all-father story."*
M$_7$ (Murngin):   *"Mother and son."*
M$_8$ (Murngin):   *"Ure and the bush fire."*
M$_9$ (Murngin):   *"Ure and frilled-neck lizard."*
M$_{10}$ (Murngin):   *"Ure (Bamapama) spears the sun."*
M$_{11}$ (Murngin):   *"The adultery of a Wangurri woman and a Kalpu man."*
M$_{12}$ (Murngin):   *"The bringing of fire."*
M$_{13}$ (Dalabon):   *"The origin of fire."*

REFERENCES

ALTHUSSER, LOUIS
   1970   *For Marx*. New York: Vintage.
ALTHUSSER, L., ETIENNE BALIBAR
   1970   *Reading capital*. London: New Left Books.
ARDENER, SHIRLEY G.
   1973   Sexual insult and female militancy. *Man*, n.s. 8 (3): 422–440.
ARNDT, W.
   1965   The dreaming of Kunukban. *Oceania* 35 (4): 241–259.
ARROWSMITH, WILLIAM, *editor*
   1969   "The birds" (translated by W. Arrowsmith), in *Aristophanes three comedies*. Ann Arbor: University of Michigan Press.
ASHLEY MONTAGU, M. F.
   1937   *Coming into being among the Australian aborigines*. London.
BARNES, J. A.
   1965   "Forward," in *Kinship and conflict, a study of an aboriginal community in northern Arnhem Land*. Lester R. Hiatt. Canberra: Australian National University.
   1967   *Inquest on the Murngin*. Royal Anthropological Institute of Great Britain and Ireland, Occasional Paper 26. London.
BARRETT, WILLIAM
   1957   "Writers and madness," in *Art and psychoanalysis*. Edited by William Phillips. New York: Criterion.
BARTHES, ROLAND
   1972a   *Mythologies*. New York: Hill and Wang.
   1972b   "To write: an intransitive verb," in *The structuralist controversy*. Edited by Richard A. Macksey and Eugenio Donato. Baltimore: Johns Hopkins University Press.
BATES, DAISY
   1966   *The passing of the aborigines; a lifetime spent among the natives of Australia*. New York: Praeger.
BATESON, G.
   1960   "The group dynamics of schizophrenia," in *Chronic schizophrenia*.

Edited by L. Appleby, J. M. Scher, and J. Cumming. Glencoe, Ill.: Free Press.

BATESON, G., D. D. JACKSON, J. HALEY, J. H. WEAKLAND
1956   Towards a theory of schizophrenia. *Behavioral Science* 1: 251–264.

BAUDELAIRE, CHARLES-PIERRE
1972a   "Of the essence of laughter, and generally of the comic in the plastic arts," in *Baudelaire: selected writings on art and artists.* Translated by P. E. Charvet. Harmondsworth: Penguin.
1972b   "Richard Wagner and Tannhäuser in Paris," in *Baudelaire: selected writings on art and artists*. Translated by P. E. Charvet. Harmondsworth: Penguin.

BECKETT, SAMUEL
1965   "The unnamable," in *Three novels by Samuel Beckett*. New York: Grove.

BERNDT, R. M.
1951   *Kunapipi*. Melbourne: F. W. Cheshire.

BERTIN, LÉON
1973a   "Birds (class Aves)," in *Larousse encyclopedia of animal life*. Revised and adapted by Maurice Burton. London: Hamlyn.
1973b   "Reptiles (class Reptilia)," in *Larousse encyclopedia of animal life*. London: Hamlyn.

BETTELHEIM, BRUNO
1955   *Symbolic wounds*. London: Thames and Hudson.

BIERCE, AMBROSE
1958   *The devil's dictionary*. New York: Dover.

BLAIR, W. FRANK
1968   "Amphibians and reptiles," in *Animal communication*. Edited by Thomas A. Sebeok. Bloomington: Indiana University Press.

BLAKE, WILLIAM
1971   *William Blake. A selection of poems and letters*. Edited by J. Bronowski. London: Penguin.

BOON, JAMES A.
1970   Lévi-Strauss and narrative. *Man* 5 (4): 702–703.
1972   *From symbolism to structuralism. Lévi-Strauss in a literary tradition*. Oxford: Basil Blackwell.

BRUCE, LENNY
1966   *How to talk dirty and influence people*. Chicago: Playboy Press.

BURKE, KENNETH
1957   "Freud—and the analysis of poetry," in *Art and psychoanalysis*. Edited by William Phillips. New York: Criterion.

BURRIDGE, KENELM
1973   *Encountering aborigines; a case study: anthropology and the Australian aboriginal*. New York: Pergamon.

CASTANEDA, C.
1977   *The second ring of power*. New York: Simon and Schuster.

CONDOMINAS, GEORGES
1973   "The primitive life of Vietnam's mountain people," in *Man's many ways*. Edited by Richard A. Gould. New York: Harper and Row.

DAVIDSON, DANIEL S.
1937   A preliminary consideration of aboriginal Australian decorative art. *Memoirs of the American Philosophical Society* 9 (Philadelphia).

DEIGNAN, HERBERT G.
  1964   "Birds of the Arnhem Land expedition," in *Records of the American-Australian scientific expedition to Arnhem Land*, volume four: *Zoology*. Edited by R. L. Specht and C. P. Mountford. Melbourne: Melbourne University Press.

DE JOSSELIN DE JONG, P.
  1962   A new approach to kinship studies. *Bijdragen tot de Taal-, Land- en Volkenkunde* 118: 42–67.

DOUGLAS, MARY
  1973   *Natural symbols: explorations in cosmology*. New York: Random House.

DOWDESWELL, W. H.
  1961   *Animal ecology*. New York: Harper.

DUMONT, LOUIS
  1966   Descent or intermarriage? a relational view of Australian descent systems. *Southwestern Journal of Anthropology* 22: 231–250.

DUNDES, ALAN
  1962   Earth-diver: creation of the mythopoeic male. *American Anthropologist* 64: 1032–1051.

DURKHEIM, ÉMILE
  1957   *The elementary forms of the religious life*. London: George Allen and Unwin.

DURKHEIM, ÉMILE, M. MAUSS
  1963   *Primitive classification*. Translated, edited, and introduced by R. Needham. Chicago: University of Chicago Press.

EDGERTON, R. B., F. P. CONANT
  1964   *Kilipat*: the shaming party among the Pokot of East Africa. *Southwestern Journal of Anthropology* 20: 404–418.

ELIADE, M.
  1973   *Australian religions: an introduction*. Ithaca, N.Y.: Cornell University Press.

ELIOT, T. S.
  1962   *The waste land and other poems*. New York: Harcourt, Brace and World
  1973   *Four quartets*. New York: Viking.

ELKIN, A. P.
  1930   The rainbow-serpent myth in north-west Australia. *Oceania* 1: 349–352.
  1932   Social organization in the Kimberly Division, north-western Australia. *Oceania* 2: 296–333.
  1932–1933   Marriage and descent in east Arnhem Land. *Oceania* 3: 412–416.
  1969   Elements of Australian aboriginal philosophy. *Oceania* 40: 85–98.

EPHRON, NORA
  1973   Dealing with the, uh, problem. *Esquire* 79 (3).

FALKENBERG, JOHANNES
  1962   *Kin and totem: group relations of Australian aborigines in the Port Keats District*. Oslo: Oslo University Press.

FERENCZI, SANDOR
  1956   *Sex in psycho-analysis*. New York: Dover.

FONTENROSE, JOSEPH
  1966   The ritual theory of myth. *Folklore Studies* 18. Berkeley: University of California Press.

FREUD, S.
   1908   *Character and anal eroticism* (standard edition 9). London: Hogarth.
   1917   *On transformations of instinct as anal eroticism* (standard edition 17). London: Hogarth.
FRISCH, K. V.
   1967   *The dance language and orientation of bees*. Cambridge: Belknap Press of Harvard University Press.
GEERTZ, CLIFFORD
   1966   Person, time and conduct in Bali. *Cultural Report Series* 14, Yale University Southeast Asia Studies.
   1973   "Deep play: notes on the Balinese cockfight," in *Myth, symbol, and culture*. Edited by Clifford Geertz. New York: W. W. Norton.
GEERTZ, H. and C. GEERTZ
   1975   Kinship in Bali. Chicago: University of Chicago Press.
GERAS, NORMAN
   1972   Althusser's Marxism: an account and assessment. *New Left Review* 71: 57–86.
GODELIER, MAURICE
   1970   "System, structure and contradiction in *Das Kapital*," in *Structuralism: a reader*. Edited by Michael Lane. London: Cape.
   1971   Myth and history. *New Left Review* 69: 93–112.
   1972   *Rationality and irrationality in economics*. London: New Left Books.
GOFFMAN, E.
   1952   On cooling the mark out. Some aspects of adaptation to failure. *Psychiatry* 15: 451–463.
GOODALE, JANE C.
   1962   Marriage contracts among the Tiwi. *Ethnology* 1: 452–466.
   1971   *Tiwi women*. Seattle: University of Washington Press.
GOODENOUGH, WARD H.
   1970   *Description and comparison in cultural anthropology*. Chicago: Aldine.
GOODWIN, DANIEL
   n.d.   "Something old, nothing new." Unpublished manuscript, University of Texas, Austin.
GOULD, RICHARD A.
   1969   *Yiwara: foragers of the Australian desert*. New York: Charles Scribner's Sons.
GRAVES, ROBERT
   1973   "Introduction," in *New Larousse encyclopedia of mythology*. London: Prometheus.
GREER, GERMAINE
   1971   "The smell sell." *Sunday Times*. July 25, 28.
HALE, KENNETH
   1972   "A note on a Walbiri tradition of antonymy," in *Semantics: an interdisciplinary reader in philosophy, linguistics and psychology*. Edited by D. D. Steinberg and L. A. Jacobvits. Cambridge: Cambridge University Press.
HARDWICK, ELIZABETH
   1973   Seduction and betrayal: I. *The New York Review of Books* 20 (9): 3–6.
   1974   *Seduction and betrayal. Women and literature*. New York: Random House.

HART, C. W. M.
1970   Some factors affecting residence among the Tiwi. *Oceania* 40 (4): 296–303.
HART, C. W. M., A. R. PILLING
1960   *The Tiwi of north Australia*. New York: Holt, Rinehart and Winston.
HIATT, L. R.
1964   Incest in Arnhem Land. *Oceania* 35: 124–128.
1965   *Kinship and conflict: a study of an aboriginal community in northern Arnhem Land*. Canberra: Australian National University.
1966   A spear in the ear. *Oceania* 37: 153–154.
HUBERT, HENRI, MARCEL MAUSS
1964   *Sacrifice: its nature and function*. Chicago: University of Chicago Press.
JAKOBSON, R.
1962   *Selected writings, I. Phonological studies*. The Hague: Mouton.
JARRY, ALFRED
1965   *Selected works of Alfred Jarry*. Edited by R. Shattuck and S. W. Taylor. New York: Grove.
JASTROW, ROBERT
1974   Are we alone in the cosmos? *Natural History* 83 (6): 62–65.
JOHNSTON, T. H., J. B. CLELAND
1933   The history of the aboriginal narcotic, pituri. *Oceania* 4: 201–223.
JOYCE, JAMES
1959   "The holy office," in *The critical writings of James Joyce*. Edited by E. Mason and R. Ellmann. New York: Viking.
1964   *A portrait of the artist as a young man*. New York: Viking.
JUNG, C. G.
1969   "On the psychology of the trickster," in *The trickster, a study in American Indian mythology*. Edited by Paul Radin. New York: Greenwood.
KANOWSKI, M. G.
1973   Towards an understanding of the x-ray technique in art: clues from other art traditions. *Oceania* 44: 96–100.
KERÉNYI, KARL
1969   "The trickster in relation to Greek mythology," in *The trickster, a study in American Indian mythology*. Edited by Paul Radin. New York: Greenwood.
KERMODE, FRANK
1974   Grandeur and filth. *The New York Review of Books* 21 (9): 6–12.
KLUCKHOHN, CLYDE
1942   Myths and rituals: a general theory. *Harvard Theological Review* 35: 45–79.
KROEBER, A. L.
1952   "Causes in culture," in *The nature of culture*. Chicago: University of Chicago Press.
LA BARRE, WESTON
1968   *The human animal*. Chicago: University of Chicago Press.
LA FONTAINE, J. S., *editor*
1971   *The interpretation of ritual*. London: Tavistock.
LAWRENCE, D. H.
1959   *The plumed serpent*. New York: Vintage.
1972   *Aaron's rod*. New York: Viking. (Tenth printing.)
LAWRENCE, ROBERT
n.d.   "From exchange to exchange value." Unpublished manuscript, University of Texas, Austin.

LAWRENCE, W. E., G. P. MURDOCK.
1949 Murngin social organization. *American Anthropologist* 51: 58–65.
LAYTON, R.
1970 Myth as language in aboriginal Arnhem Land. *Man*, n.s. 5 (3): 483–497.
LEACH, EDMUND R.
1954 *Political systems of highland Burma: a study of Kachin social structure*. Boston: Beacon.
1961a "The structural implications of matrilateral cross-cousin marriage," in *Rethinking anthropology*. London: Athlone.
1961b "Time and false noses," in *Rethinking anthropology*. London: Athlone.
1964 "Anthropological aspects of language: animal categories and verbal abuse," in *New directions in the study of language*. Edited by Eric H. Lenneberg. Cambridge: Massachusetts Institute of Technology Press.
1967 "The language of Kachin kinship: reflections on a Tikopia model," in *Social organization*. Edited by M. Freedman. London: Cass.
1969 *Genesis as myth and other essays*. London: Jonathan Cape.
LEGMAN, G.
1968 *Rationale of the dirty joke. An analysis of sexual humor*. First Series. New York: Castle.
LÉVI-STRAUSS, C.
1955 "The structural study of myth," in *Myth: a symposium*. Edited by T. A. Sebeok. Bloomington: Indiana University Press.
1963 "Structure and dialectics," in *Structural anthropology*. New York: Basic Books.
1964 *Le cru et le cuit*. Paris: Plon.
1965 The future of kinship studies. *Proceedings of the Royal Anthropological Institute for 1965*. London.
1966 *The savage mind*. Chicago: University of Chicago Press.
1968 "The concept of primitiveness," in *Man the hunter*. Edited by Richard B. Lee and Irven DeVore. Chicago: Aldine.
1969a *The raw and the cooked*. New York: Harper and Row.
1969b *The elementary structures of kinship*. Boston: Beacon.
1971a "The deduction of the crane," in *Structural analyis of oral traditions*. Edited by E. Maranda and P. Maranda. Philadelphia: University of Pennsylvania Press.
1971b *L'homme nu*. Paris: Plon.
1973a *From honey to ashes*. New York: Harper and Row.
1973b Structuralism and ecology. *Social Science Information* 12 (1): 7–23.
LOWENSTEIN, J.
1961 Rainbow and serpent. *Anthropos* 56: 31–40.
LURIE, NANCY O.
1961 *Mountain wolf woman*. Ann Arbor: University of Michigan Press.
MADDOCK, KENNETH
1970a Rethinking the Murngin problem: a review article. *Oceania* 41: 77–89.
1970b "Myths of the acquisition of fire in northern and eastern Australia," in *Australian aboriginal anthropology; modern studies in the social anthropology of the Australian aborigines*. Edited by Roland M. Berndt. Nedlands: University of Western Australia Press.
1970c A structural interpretation of the *mirriri*. *Oceania* 40: 165–176.
1974 *The Australian aborigines. A portrait of their society*. Victoria: Penguin.

1975   "The emu anomaly," in *Australian aboriginal mythology. Essays in honour of W. E. H. Stanner*. Edited by L. R. Hiatt. Australian Aboriginal Studies 50. Canberra: Australian Institute of Aboriginal Studies.

MAKARIUS, R.
1966   Incest and redemption in Arnhem Land. *Oceania* 37: 148–152.

MARX, KARL
1971   *Grundrisse*. Edited by D. McLellan. New York: Harper and Row.

MATHEWS, ROBERT H.
1899   *Folklore of the Australian aborigines*. Sydney: Hennessey Harper.

MATTHEWS, T. S.
1974   *Great Tom, notes towards the definition of T. S. Eliot*. New York: Harper and Row.

MAURER, D. W.
1940   *The big con*. New York: Bobbs-Merrill.

MAUSS, MARCEL
1954   *The gift. Forms and functions of exchange in archaic societies*. Translated by I. Cunnison. London: Cohen and West.

McCARTHY, FREDERICK D.
1958   *Australian aboriginal decorative art*. Sydney.
1960   "The string figures of Yirrkalla," in *Records of the American-Australian scientific expedition to Arnhem Land*, volume two: *Anthropology and nutrition*. Edited by C. P. Mountford. Melbourne: Melbourne University Press.

McCONNEL, URSULA
1930a   The rainbow serpent in north Queensland. *Oceania* 1: 347–349.
1930b   The Wik-Munkan tribes. Part II. Totemism. *Oceania* 1 (2): 181–205.
1931–1932   A moon legend from the Bloomfield River, north Queensland. *Oceania* 2: 9–25.

McKNIGHT, DAVID
1973   Sexual symbolism of food among the Wik-Mungkan. *Man*, n.s. 8 (2): 194–209.

MEAD, MARGARET
1934   The Marsalai cult among the Arapesh with special reference to the rainbow serpent beliefs of the Australian aborigines. *Oceania* 4: 37–53.

MERLEAU-PONTY, MAURICE
1964   "The Yalta papers," in *Signs*. Translated by Richard C. McCleary. Evanston, Ill.: Northwestern University Press.

MÉTRAUX, ALFRED
1972   *Voodoo in Haiti*. New York: Schocken.

MOUNTFORD, C. P.
1956   "Aboriginal art of Australia," in *Records of the American-Australian scientific expedition to Arnhem Land*, volume one: *Art, myth, and symbolism*. Edited by C. P. Mountford. Melbourne: Melbourne University Press.
1972   "Introduction," in *The first sunrise, Australian aboriginal myths*. Paintings by Ainslie Roberts. New York: Taplinger.

MOUNTFORD, C. P., *editor*
1960   *Records of the American-Australian scientific expedition to Arnhem Land*, volume two: *Anthropology and nutrition*. Melbourne: Melbourne University Press.

MOUNTFORD, C. P., R. M. BERNDT
1941   Fire-making in Australia. *Oceania* 11: 342–344.

MUNN, NANCY
1969 "The effectiveness of symbols in Murngin rite and myth," in *Forms of symbolic action: Proceedings of the 1969 Annual Spring Meeting of the American Ethnological Society*. Edited by Robert F. Spencer. Seattle: University of Washington Press.

NEWMAN, WILLIAM S.
1967 *Understanding music*. New York: Harper and Row.

Newsweek
1973 "A farewell to flatulence." *Newsweek*, July 9: 69.

NUTTALL, ZELIA
1901 "Fundamental principles of Old and New World civilization," in *Archaeological and ethnological papers of the Peabody Museum*, volume two. Cambridge.

OLDROYD, HAROLD
1970 *Elements of entomology*. New York: Universe.

PANOFF, F.
1970 Food and faeces: a Melanesian rite. *Man*, n.s. 5 (2): 237–252.

PARKER, K. LANGLOH
1905 *The Evahlayi tribe*. London: Constable.

PIDDINGTON, R.
1930 The water-serpent in Karadjeri mythology. *Oceania* 1: 352–354.

PETERSON, NICOLAS
1971 "Open sites and the ethnographic approach to the archaeology of hunter-gatherers," in *Aboriginal man and environment in Australia*. Edited by D. J. Mulvaney and J. Golson. Canberra: Australian National University Press.

RADCLIFFE-BROWN, A. R.
1926 The rainbow-serpent myth of Australia. *Journal of the Royal Anthropological Institute* 56: 19–25.
1930 The rainbow-serpent myth in south-east Australia. *Oceania* 1: 342–347.
1951 Murngin social organization. *American Anthropologist* 53: 37–55.
1952a "On joking relationships," in *Structure and function in primitive societies*. Glencoe, Ill.: Free Press.
1952b "A further note on joking relationships," in *Structure and function in primitive societies*. Glencoe, Ill.: Free Press.

RADIN, PAUL
1920 "The autobiography of a Winnebago Indian," in *University of California publications in American archaeology and ethnology*, volume sixteen: 381–473.

RAFFOLOVICH, DANIEL
n.d. "Mother's brother in Wisconsin: a structural study of the Winnebago hare cycle." Unpublished manuscript, University of Texas, Austin.

REICHEL-DOLMATOFF, G.
1971 *Amazonian cosmos. The sexual and religious symbolism of the Tukano Indians*. Chicago: University of Chicago Press.

REID, RUSSELL M.
1974 "Relative age and asymmetrical cross-cousin marriage in a south Indian caste." Unpublished manuscript, University of Texas, Austin.

ROBINSON, ROLAND
1956 *The feathered serpent*. Sydney: Edwards and Shaw.
1968 *Aboriginal myths and legends*. Melbourne: Sun.

ROHEIM, GEZA
  1968   "The psychology of Australian culture," in *Psychoanalysis and anthropology; culture, personality and the unconscious*. New York: International Universities Press.
ROSE, FREDERICK G. G.
  1960   *Classification of kin, age structure and marriage amongst the Groote Eylandt aborigines, a study in method and a theory of Australian kinship*. Berlin: Akademie.
  1968   "Australian marriage, land-owning groups, and initiations," in *Man the hunter*. Edited by Richard B. Lee and Irven DeVore. Chicago: Aldine.
SCHEFFLER, HAROLD W.
  1972   "Afterword," in *Kinship and behaviour in North Queensland. A preliminary account of kinship and social organization on Cape York Peninsula*. By D. F. Thomson. Australian Aboriginal Studies 51. Canberra: Australian Institute of Aboriginal Studies.
SCHEFFLER, HAROLD W., F. G. LOUNSBURY
  1971   *A study in structural semantics: the Sirionó kinship system*. Englewood Cliffs, N.J.: Prentice-Hall.
SEBEOK, THOMAS, A.
  n.d.   "Zoo-semiotics" (appendix), in *Six species of signs: some propositions and strictures*. Preprint, Department of Linguistics, Catholic University of Leuven.
SEBEOK, THOMAS A., *editor*
  1968   *Animal communication*. Bloomington: Indiana University Press.
SHAPIRO, WARREN
  1969   Asymmetric marriage in Australia and Southeast Asia. *Bijdragen tot de Taal-, Land- en Volkenkunde, Anthropologica* 11 (125): 71–79.
SHARP, LAURISTON
  1934   The social organization of the Yir-Yoront tribe, Cape York Peninsula. *Oceania* 4: 404–431.
SMITH, WATSON
  1952   "Kiva mural decorations at Awatovi and Kawaika-a: with a survey of other wall paintings in the Pueblo Southwest," in *Papers of the Peabody Museum of American Archaeology and Ethnology*, volume thirty-seven. Harvard University, Cambridge, Mass.
SONTAG, SUSAN
  1974   Shooting America. *New York Review of Books* 21 (6): 17–24.
SPENCER, BALDWIN, F. J. GILLEN
  1968   *The native tribes of central Australia*. New York: Dover.
STANNER, W. E. H.
  1959   On aboriginal religion I. The lineaments of sacrifice. *Oceania* 30: 108–127.
  1960a On aboriginal religion II. Sacramentalism, rite and myth. *Oceania* 30: 245–278.
  1960b On aboriginal religion III. Symbolism in the higher rites. *Oceania* 30: 100–120.
  1961a On aboriginal religion IV. The design-plan of a riteless myth. *Oceania* 31: 233–258.
  1961b On aboriginal religion V. The design-plans of mythless rites. *Oceania* 32: 79–108.
  1963   On aboriginal religion VI. Cosmos and society made correlative. *Oceania* 33: 239–273.

1965   "The dreaming," in *Reader in comparative religion*. Edited by W. A. Lessa and E. Z. Vogt. New York: Harper and Row.

STEVENSON, MATILDA C.
1887   The religious life of the Zuni child. *Bureau of American Ethnology Fifth Annual Report*: 533–555.

STOW, CATHERINE S.
1953   *Australian legendary tales*. Collected by K. Langloh Parker. London.

STRAVINSKY, IGOR
1970   *Poetics of music*. Cambridge: Harvard University Press.

STRAVINSKY, IGOR, ROBERT CRAFT
1960   *Memoirs and commentaries*. London: Faber and Faber.

TEMBROCK, GÜNTER
1968   "Land mammals," in *Animal communication*. Edited by T. A. Sebeok. Bloomington: Indiana University Press.

TERRAY, EMMANUEL
1972   *Marxism and "primitive" societies*. New York and London: Monthly Review Press.

THOMPSON, D'ARCY W.
1961   *On growth and form*. Cambridge: Cambridge University Press.

THOMSON, DONALD F.
1935   The joking relationship and organized obscenity in north Queensland. *American Anthropologist* 37: 460–490.
1948–1949   Explorations among an unknown people (Arnhem Land). *Geographical Journal* 112, 113, 114.
1949   *Economic structure and the ceremonial exchange cycle in Arnhem Land*. Melbourne: Macmillan.

Times Literary Supplement
1974   "The anti-structuralists," a review of *Structuralisme ou ethnologie*, by Raoul and Laura Makarius (Paris: Anthropos). *Times Literary Supplement*, January 18 (3): 750.

TURNER, TERENCE
1973   Piaget's structuralism (review article: *Genetic epistemology* and *Le structuralisme*, by Jean Piaget). *American Anthropologist* 75 (2): 351–373.

TURNER, VICTOR W.
1968   *The drums of affliction: a study of religious processes among the Ndembu of Zambia*. Oxford: Clarendon.

VAILLANT, GEORGE C.
1962   *Aztecs of Mexico. Origin, rise and fall of the Aztec nation*. Garden City, N.Y.: Doubleday.

VAN DER LEEDEN, A. C.
1975   "Thundering gecko and emu: mythological structuring of Nunggubuyu patrimoieties," in *Australian aboriginal mythology. Essays in honour of W. E. H. Stanner*. Edited by L. R. Hiatt. Australian Aboriginal Studies 50. Canberra: Australian Institute of Aboriginal Studies.

VIDAL, GORE
1974   Fabulous Calvino (review article: *Invisible cities*, by Italo Calvino). *New York Review of Books* 21 (9): 13–21.

VÖLGER, GISELA
1973   Making fire by percussion in Tasmania. *Oceania* 44: 58–63.

VON BRANDENSTEIN, C. G.
1970a   The meaning of section and section names. *Oceania* 41: 39–49.

1970b   *Narratives from the north-west of western Australia in the Nagarluma and Jindjiparndi languages*, volume one. Australian Aboriginal Studies 35. Canberra: Australian Institute of Aboriginal Studies.
1972   The symbolism of the north-western Australian zigzag design. *Oceania* 42 (3): 223–238.

WARNER, W. L.
1958   *A black civilization* (revised edition). New York: Harper.

WHITE, CARMEL
1971   "Man and environment in northwest Arnhem Land," in *Aboriginal man and environment in Australia*. Edited by D. J. Mulvaney and J. Golson. Canberra: Australian National University Press.

WIENER, HARRY
1966   External chemical messengers I. Emission and reception in man. *New York State Journal of Medicine*, December 15: 3153–3170.

WILDEN, A.
1972   *System and structure*. London: Tavistock.

WILSON, E. O.
1968   "Chemical systems," in *Animal communication*. Edited by Thomas A. Sebeok. Bloomington: Indiana University Press.

WORRELL, ERIC
1966   *Reptiles of Australia*. Sydney: Angus and Robertson.

WRIGHT, R. H.
1966   Why is an odour? *Nature* 209: 551–554.

Biographical Notes

IRA BUCHLER (1938–   ) was born in New York City. He received his B.A. degree from Washington Square College, New York University and his Ph.D. in social anthropology from the University of Pittsburgh. He has taught at Boston University, Williams College, The University of Chicago, and is currently Professor of Anthropology at The University of Texas. He has been a Special Fellow of the National Institute of Mental Health, and a Research Fellow at the Laboratoire d'Anthropologie Social, Collège de France (Paris). His publications and edited volumes include *Kinship and social organization* (1968, Macmillan), *Game theory in the behavioral sciences* (1969, University of Pittsburgh), *A formal study of myth* (1969, University of Texas), as well as forthcoming volumes on *Savage kinship* (Holt, Rinehart and Winston, 1979) and *Mathematical anthropology*.

KENNETH MADDOCK (1937–   ) was born in Hastings, New Zealand, and educated at Auckland Grammar School and the University of Auckland, where he took a law degree. He was admitted as a barrister and solicitor of the Supreme Court. He later completed a degree in anthropology, and between 1964 and 1970 he carried out extensive fieldwork in southern Arnhem Land for the Australian Institute of Aboriginal Studies. As a result of this work he was awarded a Ph.D by the University of Sydney. Dr. Maddock is presently Senior Lecturer in Anthropology at Macquarie University in New South Wales. He spent the year 1972–1973 in Wassenaar, The Netherlands, where he was awarded a one-year fellowship by the Netherlands Institute for Advanced Study in the Humanities and Social Sciences. His special interests lie in the study of the religion, social organization, and customary law of the Australian aborigines and other peoples who have traditionally not led a settled life.

He has about twenty publications on aboriginal kinship, ritual, myth-ology, and law, including *The Australian aborigines: a portrait of their society*. He spent 1976 at the University of Nijmegen, The Nether-lands, where he studied Dutch-language studies of Indonesian *adat* law. He is spending the first half of 1978 in the Northern Territory, Australia, where he will be studying aboriginal customary law.

CHARLES PERCY MOUNTFORD (1890–1977) was born at Hallett, South Australia, where he attended the local primary state school. An early contact with the Australian aborigines developed into an active lifelong interest in their culture, especially in their art and myths.

Mountford received his M.A. (1963) and D.Litt. (1975) from the University of Adelaide, South Australia and his Dip.Anthrop. from Cambridge, England (1959). He was a Nuffield Research Scholar in England (1957–1959).

He led many expeditions to central and northern Australia, among them being the Australian Commonwealth National Geographic Society of America Expedition (1948) to Arnhem Land, northern Australia, and the National Geographic Society Expedition to Melville Island, northern Australia (1954). He also received many honors including the O.B.E.; Hon. D.Litt., The Melbourne University, Melbourne, Victoria; Hon. Life Fellow, and the Franklin Burr Award, both from the National Geographic Society of America; John Lewis Gold Medal, Royal Society, South Australia; Founders Gold Medal, Royal Geographic Society of Australia (Queensland Branch); National History Medallion of Australia (1949), and the Sir John Verco Medal, Royal Society of South Australia (1961). Mountford was the author of 15 books, and over 80 scientific papers.

Index of Names

Index of Subjects

Aboriginal art. *See* Cave paintings
Aborigines: belief in mythical creatures, 23–25; metaphysics of mythical view of the world, 99–117; mythological terms, etymology of, 99–103; Myths, *see* Myths; ritual, *see* Ceremonies; Rituals
Adnyamatana tribe, 27
Adultery, 193–195
Affiliations in Murngin logic (dry/wet, male/female, etc.), 156–161
Akaru, rainbow serpent of Adnyamatana tribe, 27, 28, 29; myths, *see* Myths
Akurula Creek, 29
Aljawarra tribe, 179
All-Fathers, 4n, 104, 163
Alligator River, 78
All-Mother, symbolizing the Uterus, 2, 11, 12, 17, 103–105, 111, 115–116
Amata, 54
Ambiguities in aboriginal depictions of rainbow serpent, 5–10, 19
Andrenjinja, rainbow serpent of Pennefather River tribes, 62
Andului totem, 88
Aneri Spring, 46, 51–52
Angoroko River, 86
Animal characterization by Murngin and Dalabon tribes, 186–190
Anna Springs, 25, 34
Aranda tribe, 38, 130, 179; subsection system, 178
Arnhem Land, 8, 11, 12, 25, 26, 65–66, 69, 76, 78, 80, 90, 94
Art of the wandjina, The (Crawford), 84
Atain-tijina, rain-man of Aranda tribe, 38–39
Atila Spring, 45–50, 52

Australian Institute of Aboriginal Studies, 4, 99n
Awanyu, serpent east Pueblos, 126n
Axes, stone, 26; associated with lightning-man and lightning-woman, 91, 92; mythical origin, 90; as thunderbolts, 90
Ayers Rock, 27, 40–41

Bād tribe, 7, 8n; version of rainbow-serpent myth, 8n, 11, 13
Bakanji tribe, 64
Bamapama, character in Murngin trickster myths, 168, 172
Banar, cultural hero of Unambal, 17; mythical bird, 15
Bandicoot, 133
Barron River, 63
Barwon River, 59
Bathurst Island, 26, 80; mythical lizards (*maratji*), 88–90
Bee-eaters. *See* Rainbow bird
Bees: olfactory acuity, 175; orienting by osmotropotaxis, 175; symbolical, 171–172, 174–175, 178–180, 187
Beswick Creek Settlement, 99, 108, 185
Billabongs, 101
Bilumbira, rainbow serpent of Cape Arnhem, 65–66
Birds in aboriginal mythology, 9, 47, 104, 104n, 105, 110, 125. *See also* Eaglehawk; Emu
Bisexuality of rainbow serpent, 6
Bloomfield River, 61
Bodily emissions metaphysically categorized, 139–145
Body odors. *See* Odors
Body-painting, 59